A CULTURAL HISTORY OF CHILDHOOD AND FAMILY

VOLUME 6

A Cultural History of Childhood and Family
General Editors: Elizabeth Foyster and James Marten

Volume 1
A Cultural History of Childhood and Family in Antiquity
Edited by Mary Harlow and Ray Laurence

Volume 2
A Cultural History of Childhood and Family in the Middle Ages
Edited by Louise J. Wilkinson

Volume 3
A Cultural History of Childhood and Family in the Early Modern Age
Edited by Sandra Cavallo and Silvia Evangelisti

Volume 4
A Cultural History of Childhood and Family in the Age of Enlightenment
Edited by Elizabeth Foyster and James Marten

Volume 5
A Cultural History of Childhood and Family in the Age of Empire
Edited by Colin Heywood

Volume 6
A Cultural History of Childhood and Family in the Modern Age
Edited by Joseph M. Hawes and N. Ray Hiner

A CULTURAL HISTORY OF
CHILDHOOD AND FAMILY

IN THE
MODERN AGE

Edited by Joseph M. Hawes and N. Ray Hiner

Oxford • New York

KH

English edition
First published in 2010 by
Berg

Editorial offices:
First Floor, Angel Court, 81 St Clements Street, Oxford OX4 1AW, UK
175 Fifth Avenue, New York, NY 10010, USA

Berg is the imprint of Oxford International Publishers Ltd.

Library of Congress Cataloging-in-Publication Data

A catalogue record for this book is available from the Library of Congress.

British Library Cataloguing-in-Publication Data

A catalogue record for this book is available from the British Library.

ISBN 978-1-84788-799-3 (volume 6)
       978-1-84520-826-4 (set)

Typeset by Apex CoVantage, LLC, Madison, WI, USA

Printed in the UK by the MPG Books Group

www.bergpublishers.com

9/2/11

CONTENTS

ILLUSTRATIONS

INTRODUCTION

CHAPTER 1

CHAPTER 2

CHAPTER 3

CHAPTER 4

CHAPTER 5

CHAPTER 6

CHAPTER 7

GENERAL EDITORS' PREFACE

The literature on the histories of children and the family has reached a critical mass. The proliferation of encyclopedia, conferences, and professional associations reflects the vitality of these closely related but independent fields. The two subjects are naturally linked; Western conceptions of the family have virtually always included children, and children and youth are irrevocably shaped by their time growing up in families.

A Cultural History of Childhood and Family aims to bring order to these sometimes disparate histories and historiographical traditions with original material written especially for these volumes. More than six dozen editors and authors from five continents and thirteen countries were commissioned to take a comprehensive look at the subject from a Western perspective with more than casual glances at the world beyond. Based on deep readings of the secondary literature and on representative primary sources, each of the chapters is an original work of synthesis and interpretation.

It is our hope that imposing a standard table of contents on a project covering literally thousands of years and hundreds of ethnicities, religious faiths, and communities will help us find otherwise hidden patterns and rich contrasts in the experiences of children and families and in humankind's attitudes about them. There is inevitably a bit of overlap; issues related to children and the family do not form and develop according to convenient beginning and ending dates. But there is also a variety of viewpoints, even on similar topics. Indeed, as general editors we embrace the divergence of interpretations, emphases, and even writing and organizational styles that emerge from these five dozen chapters. Some of the diversity follows naturally from the vastly different conditions facing children and their families in different eras, while in other cases it is inspired by the authors' expertise and personal approaches to the field.

There have always been many childhoods and many families in the West. The purpose of these volumes is not only to look at the constructions of childhood and the family, particularly as they reflect evolving ethnic, gender, religious, national, and class assumptions, but also the lived experiences of children and of the families in which they spend so much of their lives. The symbiotic relationship between child and parent, between brother and sister, and between the individual and the family to which he or she belongs is reflected in the intertwined historical literature on children and families. By studying both, we can learn more about each.

Elizabeth Foyster
Clare College, University of Cambridge

James Marten
Marquette University

Introduction

JOSEPH M. HAWES AND N. RAY HINER

Few persons living in 1900 could have imagined what life would be like for children and families in 2000. The twentieth century brought improved nutrition, widespread immunization, lower mortality rates, greater access to schooling, more opportunities for communication and learning, and better legal protection for children, including female children, minority children, and children with disabilities. However, the importance of these achievements should be balanced by a recognition of tragic failures in the twentieth century to protect and promote the best interests of the child and the family. Wars, economic depression, exploitation, commodification, abuse, and ethnic, racial, gender, and class discrimination all damaged the lives children and families in the twentieth century. Thus, a very mixed and complex picture emerges that deserves more precise description and analysis.

CHILDREN AND FAMILIES IN 1900

At the beginning of the twentieth century children constituted about half the populations of industrialized countries and an even higher proportion in the less developed parts of the world. But this pattern was already beginning to change. Families were becoming smaller. That is, the birth rate was declining, and other factors combined with that to reduce the average number of children per family across the industrialized world. This decline was not evenly distributed. Urban middle-class families showed the greatest decline, while the families of the urban

FIGURE 0.1: *At the Foot of the Cliff, 1886.*
William-Adolphe Bouguereau, artist. Courtesy
of Memphis Brooks Museum of Art.

working classes (many of whom had only recently come to the cities) continued
to have more children than the middle classes. Rural families and the peoples
of the nonindustrialized world continued to experience a high birth rate. The
demographic transition, which had begun in the eighteenth century, had not
come to affect all people even at the dawn of the twentieth century.

DECLINE IN BIRTH RATE AND WOMEN'S STATUS

How and why the birth rate declined is a complex and still debated issue.
One of the more important factors in the decline was the changing roles and
status of women in industrial societies. Women in those societies claimed more
autonomy and were in the process of becoming full individual members of
society, a long-term process just emerging at the beginning of the twentieth

century. Another factor in the declining birth rate was the wider availability of birth control methods and information. Women married later and did take steps—with the cooperation of husbands—to limit their fertility. But this information was not available equally. For example, there were laws in the United States against the distribution of birth control information, and efforts such as those of Margaret Sanger to make this information more widely available there were thwarted by arrests and prosecutions.

A rising interest in women's needs and social roles—the new forms of feminism—sought to combat the sexual double standard of the nineteenth century (and the threat of venereal disease) in several ways. Sex education was promoted as a way to combat both venereal disease and prostitution. Moralists such as Anthony Comstock in the United States sought to eliminate all public references to sexuality. Women campaigning for suffrage indicated that they would try to bring moral improvement to public life, and indeed they campaigned for laws that made prostitution a criminal act, and in the United States they lobbied for and won legislation that made the production or sale of alcoholic beverages illegal. And during World War I, the well-known brothels of most major American cities, such as Storeyville in New Orleans, were shut down. Other campaigners sought to aid women in their efforts to control their own bodies. Although the enfranchisement of women and the availability of divorce did not spread across the developed world quickly or smoothly, these emerging patterns marked the beginnings of a major change in the roles and status of women in industrialized societies.[1]

Yet another factor in the decline of family size was the persistence of high rates of infant mortality—even among the more affluent members of society. This can be confusing, because the rate of infant mortality was declining across the industrialized world in 1901, but the rate at that time was so much higher than it would be in 2001 that it seems unimaginable looking back. Beyond infant mortality, child mortality was itself also quite high, as children became victims of industrialization themselves. As child laborers, they worked in difficult and dangerous situations, and they suffered death and injury from unregulated and hazardous factories, mines, shops, and the streets. So widespread and appalling were the numbers of child deaths that the entire structure of insurance and child value to families had to be recast.[2]

RURAL AND URBAN DISTINCTIONS

At the end of the nineteenth century, most children still lived on farms in the rural countryside. Some of them had access to schools, and in the industrial countries the majority of children were probably literate, but only the fundamentals of elementary education were available. Children whose families had migrated to the towns and cities may have been closer to schools, but often they were working rather than going to school. Except among middle-class and elite families children had always worked. They added to the pool of labor in rural households and were expected to do their share from about age six upward. The kind of work that they did on the streets of the cities and in the mines and factories was far more danger-ous and much harsher than chores on a farm. This employment of children as street hustlers—as vividly portrayed by Charles Dickens in *Oliver Twist*—was common in cities as the nineteenth century ended. Before school attendance be-came compulsory, only families who could spare the labor of their children sent them to school. School attendance marked both the rising status of families who could afford to forego the labor of their children and a way to escape the rigors and limitations of child labor whether in factories or in the street trades.

EXPANSION OF SCHOOLS

By the end of the nineteenth century the structure and design of school systems whose expansion characterized the twentieth century were emerging. Age-graded systems were becoming more common, and high schools were beginning to replace the preparatory departments at colleges and universities. School atten-dance beyond learning some basic skills was not a common experience for most children, but it was becoming the experience of increasing numbers of children. And when school attendance became compulsory, it became the common experience of almost all children.

ATTITUDES TOWARD CHILDREN

As the nineteenth century ended, attitudes about children—most children and not just those of the middle classes—began to shift. If children had been regarded as economic assets before—as cheap labor or as social security for their parents in old age—they now came to be valued for themselves. That is, children became more valuable emotionally as they lost value economically. When children gained in sentimental value they also gained in social support. Efforts to improve child health and the lives of children generally began in the nineteenth century and achieved remarkable results in the twentieth century. Milk stations where parents could obtain pasteurized milk were set up as a way of combating the ravages of tuberculosis and its impact on children's mortality. The medical specialty of pediatrics was developed to try to improve the health of children in the developed world. But it was during the twentieth century that ways were found to combat the childhood diseases that caused much of the child mortality in the nineteenth century.

INFANT AND CHILD MORTALITY

From the vantage point of the twenty-first century, it is difficult to imagine the frightful rates of infant and child mortality in the developed world, let alone the rates in the less developed parts of the globe. At the turn of the century in the United States, for example the mortality rate for children under five was twenty-five percent (i.e., one in four children died before reaching the age of five). Diseases of all sorts—pneumonia, influenza, scarlet fever, measles, whooping cough, and diphtheria—accounted for many of the deaths, but what made the ravages of disease so much greater among the lower classes was poverty itself. Poor people often lacked the means to seek medical attention, and the state of medical practice was such that little could be done. Another factor that contributed to a high infant and child mortality rate was the lack of pure water (and pure food).

CHANGES IN FAMILIES

Even as so many children were dying, a new conception of children and childhood stressing the emotional significance of children was emerging in the Western world. This in turn led to a shift in the internal dynamics of families. Over the nineteenth century, the patriarchal family of the preindustrial world had given way to a more democratic order in which the members had more influence on the functions of the family. At the same time, the family saw many of its functions shifted to the public sector. Education became a public responsibility, as did welfare and corrections. Families were bound more by emotional ties than by economic necessity or tradition. As the family became less dependent on the labor of its members, family members gained more control over their lives, which in turn led to greater independence and autonomy. And the divorce rate began to increase. This latter change shocked society, and efforts to make divorce more difficult became nearly universal. It should be noted that these trends did not take place uniformly.[3]

Middle-class families were more likely to be bound by emotional ties than were lower-class families, and rural families ordered themselves in more traditional ways than did city dwellers. Recent migrants to cities clung to their traditional ways until they had gained an economic foothold, but ethnic communities in the cities preserved some of the old ways while at the same time allowing some aspects of the modern middle-class democratic family to flourish. These changes did not come about easily or quickly, and generational conflicts were widespread among new migrants to the city. Still, trends toward greater individual autonomy even within families were visible at the beginning of the twentieth century.

MIGRATIONS BETWEEN COUNTRIES AND FROM RURAL TO URBAN ENVIRONMENTS

The great migration of peoples from the rural countryside to cities and to the western hemisphere began in the nineteenth century and reached its zenith in the early decades of the twentieth century. The migration resulted from a host of factors—notably, a shortage of tillable land and a rising population pushed people to migrate. The attractions of city life included a chance to earn money, the possibilities of a new life, and greater personal freedom. But the change in residence helped create new patterns of life: smaller families (ultimately), more individual autonomy within families (though not without conflict), and higher divorce rates.

REFORMS AFFECTING FAMILIES AND CHILDREN

The great influx of people into cities made the lower classes more visible. Reformers, threatened both politically and personally by the number of migrants from different regions and cultures across the globe, sought to remake the city in the images of nineteenth-century middle-class respectability. Or, failing that, they tried to control the masses in such a way that the status of the urban middle classes was not itself in any danger. In pursuit of these aims, a host of reforms appeared: campaigns against child labor, broadening access to schools, efforts to combat juvenile delinquency and to control the leisure time of children now found in great numbers on city streets. The reformers sponsored legislation, formed clubs and other institutions designed to shape children's behavior and supplement the family life of the new migrants. Notable among these organizations were the Ys—the YMCA for young men and the YWCA for young women—the Boy Scouts and the Girl Scouts, and a host of similar organizations across the industrialized world.

As reformers puzzled over the rising tide or urban problems in the late nineteenth century, some concluded that the city itself was responsible for many of the ills, both social and physical. Believing that the situation could be remedied, some reformers (notably Great Britain's Dr. Thomas Barnardo) concluded that children should be removed from the evil cities and transported to such places as Canada and Australia where the rural environment and fresh air would reinvigorate them. Barnardo's efforts reminded people of the Children's Aid Society of New York, which during the late nineteenth century had shipped hundreds of city children to the rural parts of the United States.[4]

Even as these organizations sought to address urban problems and to buttress and instruct migrant families, families began to come apart in the urban environment. The stresses of urban life and the uncertainty of continuous employment made urban life more precarious, and city dwellers often lacked the resources of kin networks in the rural countryside. Families were thus less stable, and, at the same time, they were becoming smaller, although at a slow and uneven pace. Married women were emerging from the status of being dead before the law, although some would argue that even at the beginning of the twenty-first century there are still many factors that keep women subordinate and dependent. As the economic ties between family members weakened, the emotional ties became more important. These ties were for men far less binding than economic dependence had been.

DIVORCE

Through most of the nineteenth century divorce remained rare (or often non-existent), but late in the century the rate began to climb. Most divorces (where they could be obtained) were sought by women. Women sought to escape domestic violence, the ravages of alcoholism, or the stigma of venereal disease, and they filed for divorce because they believed that they had an option to support themselves in an expanding world economy. As the rate of divorce rose, social leaders and moralists, thinking to preserve the family as a conservative institution, condemned the rising practice and worked to pass new laws severely restricting access to divorce. Among the lower classes, formal divorce was less common than separation—what was referred to as the poor man's divorce. As a consequence, families entered the twentieth century with changed internal dynamics and the increasing possibility that a marriage could end before the death of one of the partners.

LIFE CYCLE: THE INVENTION OF ADOLESCENCE

The dawn of the twentieth century intensified a long-developing trend, the social construction of adolescence. Biological maturation, also called adolescence, was certainly not new, but the idea of choosing a path or goal in life had emerged for young men as modernization (the broad expansion of industry, cities, and education) made more choices possible. By the end of the nineteenth century, more choices had appeared for young women too. Adult single women could now support themselves (although for many this was a difficult proposition) and thus become independent from their family of origin. As if to acknowledge this, young women began to attend school in increasing numbers. And they stayed in school longer than their brothers did. Schools expanded too, as jobs created by industrial development required greater literacy and increased skills. Young people who remained in school expected to make a living by using their skills and knowledge instead of through their labor alone.[5]

As the family gave up its many supportive functions such as education and welfare, social institutions arose to meet these needs. Likewise as children became more valued for their emotional appeal, a range of social institutions and services arose to address these new social needs. As the twentieth century opened, schools were expanding in both actual numbers and also in the number of years of instruction offered. Schools also became more specialized as they imparted both vocational skills to their students and prepared some of them for college and other advanced study.

SOCIAL WORK AND REFORM

But the expansion of schools did not draw all the school-aged children, and somewhat to the dismay of the promoters of urban and industrial expansion not all the new residents prospered. As migration to cities increased, so did urban poverty. Philanthropists and city promoters had struggled with the existence of poverty throughout the nineteenth century. By the end of the century, social work had become a recognized profession. New social institutions appeared, including schools, the juvenile court, and new approaches to juvenile correction. Some also sought to find ways to support single mothers, of whom many had been deserted by their husbands, but because some single mothers had been sexually active outside marriage it was difficult to find widespread social support for all single mothers (and their children).

Reformers worried about both the high rate of infant mortality and the high birth rate. They worried that unsupervised children would grow up to be adult criminals and that chaotic families among the lower classes and recent migrants constituted a serious social problem that in turn required vigorous efforts based on serious scientific study of individual and social problems. They wondered if the city were a healthy environment for young people, and some came to believe in the restorative qualities of fresh rural air. As a consequence, the beginning of the twentieth century saw the emergence of a wide array of social reform (and perhaps also social control) efforts throughout the developed world.

To respond to the newly perceived urban problems, new ways of studying society emerged and became professionalized in the late nineteenth century—sociology, anthropology, and psychology, among others. These social sciences sought the technical expertise needed to address and eliminate the social problems associated with the emerging world of the twentieth century. At the turn of the century, there was high hope that technical expertise, or social engineering, would solve the most pressing of social problems and create a better world—the century of child among other things.

It should be remembered, however, that almost all of the changes in family life underway in 1900 only affected those societies that had an industrial economy and where most people lived in urban environments. For most of humanity in 1900, traditional patterns and ways characterized life. Thus, large rural families working close to the earth or other primary activities coexisted with the emerging middle-class family. Those families that migrated from the rural countryside to the cities were both part of the modernizing trends of the early twentieth century and also profoundly affected by them.

CHILDREN AND FAMILIES IN 2000

By 2000, the forces of change had transformed the lives of children and families, especially those in the West and other developed countries. Incredible achievements and tragic failures were evident as the twentieth century ended and the twenty-first century began. On the positive side, evidence of progress for children and families was widespread and undeniable, even in developing nations. Nutritional levels had improved greatly, hundreds of millions of children were immunized, and infant and child mortality rates had dropped to historic lows. Schooling was available to unprecedented numbers of children and youth, especially in the West, and literacy rates rose accordingly. In 2000 opportunities for electronic communication and learning were expanding at an exponential rate. Finally, the human rights of children, including female children, minority children, and children with disabilities, were recognized in international law.

The importance of these achievements should not be underestimated, but it should be balanced by recognition of very real failures to consider fully and adequately protect what the United Nations' *Convention on the Rights of the Child* identified as "the best interests of the child."[6] Even in some of the world's wealthiest nations, poverty continued in 2000 to exact its toll on many children and families. For example, slightly more than twenty-two percent of children in the United States and slightly less than twenty percent of children in the United Kingdom lived in poverty.[7] Furthermore, between 1992 and 2003, approximately twenty-one percent of the world's almost six billion people lived on less than one dollar per day. In the world's poorest, least developed countries, as much as thirty-nine percent of the population, including a large proportion of children, were forced to live on that amount.[8]

This widespread poverty had very detrimental consequences for children and families caught in its grasp. Malnutrition and poverty were closely linked. More than 209 million children, or almost forty percent of children under the age of five in the developing world, were stunted because of persistent malnutrition.[9] Poverty also prevented many children in poor countries from receiving adequate health care, including the critical immunizations that were available as a matter of course to most children in the West. In 2000 HIV/AIDS claimed the lives 800,000 to 900,000 children, mostly in sub-Saharan Africa.[10] Thus, mortality rates for children in poor countries remained extremely high by modern standards. In addition, children living in poor countries often had very limited access to education, which resulted in high rates of illiteracy, increased vulnerability to exploitation and abuse, and wasted potential. Child labor was widespread in many poor countries, and child pornography and the sex trade were thriving industries in many areas.[11] In addition, many children in poor countries were tragically caught up in the numerous major armed conflicts that occurred between 1990 and 2003.[12]

This brief synopsis of the situation for children and families in 2000 makes it clear that although great progress was made over the course of the twentieth century, it was not spread evenly around the world or even within the West. A very mixed picture emerges that deserves more precise description and analysis. Moreover, there were significant developments affecting children and families in 2000 that do not fit easily into the achievement/failure model but that also deserve attention.

DEMOGRAPHIC CONVERGENCE

The remarkable improvement in mortality rates for children that occurred in most of the world during the last half of the twentieth century was accompanied by steep fertility declines and birth rates below the 2.0 replacement level in most industrialized countries.[13] This fertility decline was so widespread by

2000 that almost half of the world's population lived in countries with fertility rates below replacement level.[14] Even in poor countries the fertility rates were trending down and were lower than ever before. In 2000 the average fertility rate for industrialized countries was 1.7. In developing countries the rate was 2.9, whereas in the least developed countries it was 5.1. To put these numbers in perspective, the world's fertility rate in 2000 was 2.7 compared to 5.2 in 1900.[15]

Many demographers believe that this second demographic revolution and associated birth deficit will produce world population stabilization by 2050 and an actual decline in the world's population by the end of the twenty-first century.[16] According to the demographer Chris Wilson, "the overwhelming trend is for low fertility to become a general feature of poor and rich countries alike."[17] This worldwide convergence toward lower fertility was a truly revolutionary development with far-reaching implications for children and families. For example, children in 2000 had on the average fewer siblings, smaller extended families, relatively older parents, and experienced more childcare outside the home than did children in 1900.

How can this striking decline in fertility be explained? Why did parents in the West and elsewhere in 2000 choose to have fewer children? Several interrelated factors contributed to this decline, although they obviously differed among societies and regions. First, as mortality rates improved during the twentieth century and fewer children died before adulthood, they did not have to be replaced, as had been the case in many traditional, rural societies where children contributed significantly to the family economy. In the urbanized, industrialized West, children were much less likely to work and therefore became more expensive in part because they brought higher opportunity costs—that is, resources devoted to the care and nurture of children were obviously not available for other uses.[18] Furthermore, in most countries in the West, public and/or private pension plans were in place, which made children less necessary as insurance for their parents' old age. Reflecting on this phenomenon, Philip Morgan and Rosalind King conclude, "the economic rationale for children has become anachronistic."[19] Nancy Folbre makes a similar point that "parenthood seems to promise moral and cultural rewards but no economic rewards."[20] As the economic value of children diminished in rapidly urbanizing developing countries, the cost of rearing them increased, and many parents in these countries, like their counterparts in developed countries had been doing for some time, chose to have fewer children.

Increasing literacy, especially among girls and women, also contributed significantly to fertility decline. It is well known among social researchers that "the more education women have, the later they tend to marry and the fewer children they tend to have" and "the more likely" they are "to have opportunities and life choices and avoid being oppressed and exploited."[21] By 2000, female literacy was virtually universal in industrialized countries and was expanding in all but the poorest countries.[22] Moreover, as women became more educated, they were more likely to enter the work force, thus further increasing the opportunity costs of staying at home and having more children.

Another factor contributing to the rising opportunity cost of children in the West and elsewhere was the growing consumerism that strongly encouraged short-term satisfaction over long-term commitment.[23] In this context, young couples could see the opportunity cost of having children in very explicit, consumer-goods terms. To have children could require postponing or foregoing the purchase of a new car, a home entertainment center, a vacation, or any other of the almost limitless numbers of goods and services provided by the consumer economy. It should not be surprising, then, that for many couples in 2000, postponing children was an attractive option, which as demographers know, puts downward pressure on fertility rates.

Postponing children was technically much easier for most couples in 2000 than it had been during much the twentieth century. The appearance of the birth control pill and the intrauterine device (IUD) had an especially powerful effect on decisions about whether and when to have children. This new birth control technology meshed nicely with the culture of individualism and autonomy that was emerging in most developed countries. Personal happiness and self-fulfillment had become powerful goals for many people, and children could be seen implicitly or explicitly as interfering with the attainment of these goals. Birth control provided a convenient means of avoiding or postponing this conflict.[24]

Given the powerful factors encouraging lower fertility (rising costs, greater female literacy, pervasive consumerism, and convenient birth control technology), why did millions of parents in the West still choose to have children? Certainly this was an authentic question for potential parents in 2000. An increasing number of adults chose to have fewer children, postpone them, or not to have children at all, yet millions of others decided to have children. Philip Morgan and Rosalind King have presented a provocative analysis of this issue. They argue that pronatalism has three major sources: behavioral genetics, social institutions and social coercion, and rational choice. According to Morgan and King, humans are "survival machines" whose genetic history favored those who "were able to have offspring and keep them alive." Thus, they assert that humans have "predispositions and capabilities," such as "a strong sex drive" and "altruism toward close kin." Morgan and King conclude that humans "are genetically predisposed to cherish and support" their own children. They cite McMahon's interviews in 1995 of new mothers who were amazed by how much energy and work their children required but also surprised by how completely they fell in love with them. Morgan and King suggest that the mothers' unexpected attachment to their first-born children would likely induce them to at least think about having another child.

According to Morgan and King, social institutions and social coercion also had a role in encouraging couples to have children. Traditional religious institutions, community norms, and family traditions and expectations, even in their weakened states, helped sustain a pronatalist cultural environment even in the West. Morgan and King also assert that children may also produce "rational" benefits that are subtle but nevertheless real. For example, having children can generate social capital by turning on social networks and giving parents new access to family and community support, although these networks have clearly been weakened in highly developed countries. In addition, making long-term commitments to children may offer parents a sense of meaning and order for their lives at a time when traditional sources of identity are being challenged.[25] Thus, in spite of the growing trend to have fewer children, surveys consistently showed that most people in the West continued to express pronatalist ideals about marriage, family, and children. This tension between ideals and behavior is essential to understanding the dilemmas and challenges faced by parents in 2000.

MEDIA CONVERGENCE

Demography may indeed be destiny, but it was not the only major force affecting children and families in 2000. A revolution had occurred in communications, with wide-ranging consequences for children and families in the West and around the world. The twentieth century saw the introduction of radio, television, and movies, and, late in the century, the Internet, personal computers, and numerous other mobile electronic devices. These innovations set in motion a series of changes in communication and learning that were unprecedented in their scope and unrivaled in their potential to shape the lives of children and families. In 1900, most children communicated with others by talking face-to-face or by writing. By the first decade of the twenty-first century, children in developed countries had a wide array of communication devices potentially available to them. On a given day, these children could send and receive text messages from friends, exchange e-mail, listen to music on an

MP3 player, play a video game, use the Internet to do research for a school project or check out a social networking site, listen to the radio, watch TV, and go see a movie. The contrast between the range of opportunities for children to communicate in 1900 and in 2000 is striking.

By 2000, the media revolution was dominant in developed countries and spreading rapidly in the developing world. Media services and products had become global commodities, and children were viewed as an important group of consumers to be eagerly courted by advertisers. It is estimated that by 2000 there were more television sets in the world than telephones, although the recent rapid spread of cell phone technology and the increasing availability of cheap computers may alter this comparison. Fifty television channels were created specifically for children during a two-year period in the late 1990s. By 2000 serious concerns were being expressed about the quality of programming for children and its possible harmful effects on them.[26] According to an American Psychiatric Association study in 1998, by the time children in the United States reached age 18, they would have viewed "16,000 simulated murders and 200,000 acts of violence."[27] Numerous academic studies pointed out the strong relationship between viewing violent content and antisocial, aggressive behavior. Objections were also raised about the relentless, exploitative marketing of an astonishing array of program-related products for children such as

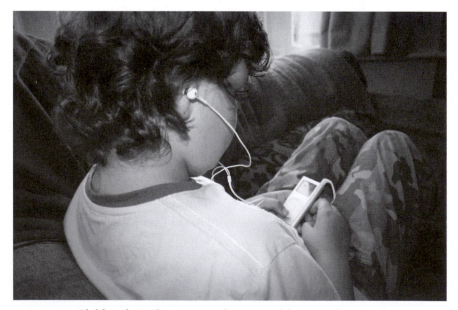

FIGURE 0.2: *Child with iPod.* Courtesy of Maria Kukhareva, photographer.

toys, food, drinks, clothing, and other items. The size of this media market for children was enormous, bringing billions in revenue to the seven media conglomerates that dominated this market, including four in the United States, two in Europe, and one in Japan. A good example of a product marketed to children that became a worldwide phenomenon was Pokemon, which originated as software on Nintendo's Game Boy. Pokemon quickly became the center of an array of products including "a comic book, a television show, a movie, trading cards, stickers, small toys," and other related products such as "back packs and T-shirts that swept across the globe" and "dominated children's consumption from approximately 1996 to 2000."[28]

Poor, undeveloped countries lacked the resources and infrastructure to develop their own programming for children or provide most of their children or adults with modern communication technology. However, even in poor countries, movies and TV were often accessible in cities, and cell phones were

FIGURE 0.3: *Child with Game Boy*. Courtesy of Maria Kukhareva, photographer.

beginning to become available. Internet use, however, was very rare or non-existent in most undeveloped countries. A deep digital divide existed between children in poor and rich countries.[29] From a communications and learning perspective, children in poor countries in 2000 had more in common with children living in 1900 than with children living in developed countries in 2000.

To summarize, the powerful media revolution that occurred by 2000 was incomplete and filled with paradox. Children, especially in the West, had unprecedented access to the new technology and therefore experienced greatly increased opportunities to communicate and the ability to exercise more control over their lives. However, they also risked commodification and manipulation by entertainment corporations more interested in profit than in their education. The media revolution also carried an implicit promise to create a global communication village in which all children would enjoy enhanced access to resources for communication and learning. To a great extent, this had happened by 2000 for children in developed countries, but millions of children in poor countries were excluded from this village and the opportunities it offered.

RIGHTS CONVERGENCE

Like media convergence, the convergence of rights for children was a highly promising but incomplete process. Children in 2000 were the beneficiaries of a century-long effort to create a legal framework to protect their basic rights.[30] In 1900 children's rights had no special standing in international law, but the extraordinary suffering and deprivation experienced by children during World War I stimulated a movement to protect their rights. Among the leaders of this movement was Eglantyne Jebb, a British woman who established the Save the Children Fund in 1919 and helped draft the language of the *Geneva Declaration of the Rights of the Child* adopted by the League of Nations in 1924, the first such document to be recognized by the international community. Unfortunately, the Geneva declaration was not legally binding. In 1948, shortly after World War II, the United Nations General Assembly approved the *Universal Declaration of Human Rights*. Article 25 stated, "Motherhood and childhood are entitled to special care and assistance." This article also lacked legal force, as did the much more explicit and extensive *Declaration of the Rights of the Child* approved by the UN in 1959. Children's rights advocates remained determined to establish children's rights in international law. Finally, in 1989, the United Nations General Assembly unanimously adopted the *Convention on the Rights of the Child*, which became legally binding the following year after twenty nations ratified the document. Eventually, only two nations failed to ratify the convention, Somalia and the United States.[31]

The adoption of the *Convention of the Rights of the Child* represented a historic convergence of efforts to extend legal protection to children around the world. The *Convention* is indeed a remarkable document in its comprehensive recognition of children's special needs and their implications for social policy. Among the scores of rights included in the *Convention* are life, identity, access to parents and family, expression, health care, education, play, and protection from neglect, violence, abuse, torture, military service, economic and sexual exploitation, and drug abuse. According to Article 3 of the *Convention,* the guiding principle for "all actions concerning children" should be "the best interests of the child."[32]

Any objective assessment of the actual situation of children and families in 2000 makes it clear that creating internationally sanctioned legal rights for children did not mean that these rights would necessarily be enforced, even in the West. Children in poor countries, especially, were too often denied basic rights guaranteed by international law. Poverty, armed conflict, and contagious disease often prevented them from receiving the protection and support they needed and deserved.[33] Even children in developed countries could have their rights denied or violated by the presence of poverty, neglect, domestic abuse, street violence, sexual abuse, and drug addiction. Still, it is important to recognize that real progress had been made in protecting children's rights. The *Convention on the Rights of the Child* represented a convergence of decades of advocacy and established a vital legal framework for making the reality of children's lives more consistent with the ideals and requirements expressed in the document. The rights convergence was real and significant, but in 2000 it was incomplete.

CONCLUSION

It is both provocative and sobering to reflect on the lives of children and families in 1900 and 2000. The differences between them were profound, the changes breathtaking, and the failures depressing. For the historian, these events and contrasts raise questions about how and why the situation for children and families in 1900 transformed into what existed in 2000. First, it is important to remember that during the twentieth century children were affected by a worldwide economic depression, five major military conflicts, including two world wars, and the cold war with its threat of nuclear holocaust. Virtually no child or family in the twentieth century escaped the effects of these traumatic events and other profound changes in family life, community, the economy, environment, education, life cycle, the state, faith and religion, and health and science that occurred between 1900 and 2000.

Thus, the purpose of the remaining chapters in this volume is to examine in more detail the processes by which the lives of children and families in the West were transformed during the twentieth century. Each author follows a topic or issue throughout the entire century. Maria Kukhareva and David Barrett focus on developments in twentieth-century Britain to illustrate how the Western family has changed. They emphasize the remarkable extent to which the family of the Victorian era has been replaced by complex, often contradictory arrangements that resemble a complicated puzzle or web that shapes personal, family, and kinship networks. As they explain, "the previously unacceptable is accepted, and what was unimaginable is now imagined and embedded people's lives."

Mona Gleason and Veronica Strong-Boag consider the implications of striking increase in the world's urban population for communities, children, and families. Among the topics they discuss are the attempts of middle-class reformers to control and shape youngsters, the diverse experiences of children in urban communities, and the culture of childhood and youth that was constructed in part by the participants themselves, including both girls and boys.

Lisa Jacobson and Erika Rappaport examine how the way Europeans and North Americans conceive of and arrange family life was transformed by economic change in the twentieth century. They argue that "men, women, and

FIGURE 0.4: *Pre-School Class. Quito, Ecuador.* Courtesy of Caitlin Fry, photographer.

children seized on economic change to renegotiate the boundaries between the family and the state and between family obligations and self-fulfillment."

In her chapter on geography and the environment, Pamela Riney-Kehrberg explains that the environments in which most children lived became increasingly urban rather than rural and that during the twentieth century children gradually lost their close connection to the natural world. Although urban children were not completely cut off from the natural world, Riney-Kehrberg concludes that urban children "increasingly chose indoor environments over the out-of-doors" in part because of "perceived dangers of the world out-of-doors, and the increasing temptations of the world indoors."

William J. Reese examines the process by which access to public schools increased in the United States during the twentieth century to the extent that around ninety percent of the school-age population was normally enrolled. This process was uneven and reflected the complex interaction among several factors, including economic change, war, immigration, urbanization, bureaucratization and professionalization, class conflict, religion, political conflict and reform, racial and ethnic discrimination, and the civil rights movement. Reese also notes that in addition to the change that has characterized education the twentieth century, traditional ideas and practices have also persisted.

Katherine Jellison points out that the "life cycle pattern" that was dominant among the urban middle class in the late Victorian era continued well into the early twentieth century. This pattern included marriage, independent households, birth control, and children in that order. Birth control permitted women to have fewer children who received relatively more attention and education. After completing their formal education, children usually left home, married, and set up their own households. As the century continued, this pattern expanded beyond the middle class, especially following World War II. However, by the 1970s political events and new cultural trends, including feminism and new divorce laws, challenged this traditional pattern, and "a greater variety of family life cycle choices and practices" became evident.

Kriste Lindenmeyer and Jeanine Graham focus on the United States as a case study in the evolution of the relationship between the child and the state. Although the twentieth century brought significant increase in the involvement of the state in the lives of children and families in the United States (and in most Western countries), this trend was uneven and often challenged by traditional patterns and assumptions about responsibilities for children. The areas where child and state issues were in question included children's legal rights, schooling, segregation, child labor, poverty, dependent children, divorce and child custody, family and juvenile courts, child health, and day care.

In his chapter on faith and religion Jon Pahl turns his attention to how young people have shaped their own religious experiences. To illustrate is point, he looks at Christian youth in Nazi Germany between 1933 and 1945, and of Christian youth in the United States from 1930 to the present. In addition, Pahl considers other global developments, including the attraction of youth to Mohandas Gandhi's movement for nonviolence, liberation theology and Pentecostalism in Latin America, Oaza (a Catholic youth movement in Poland), and others. Pohl concludes that in all of these cases, "religious youth and youth leaders" were "critical agents in determining historical developments."

Doug Imig and Frances Wright review developments in science and health that affected children in the twentieth century. They conclude that although the health of the world's children has improved significantly, many serious problems and inequities persist. For example, life expectancies for children born in developed countries have improved greatly during the twentieth century, but in some of the poorest and least developed countries, life expectancies remain less than half that in more developed countries. Even in the United States, which is the primary focus of this chapter, low income greatly reduces children's access to health care, and there is a troubling rise in the rates of asthma and diabetes. Wright and Imig conclude: "Today, across the developed and developing world, poverty remains the greatest threat to children's health."

In the concluding chapter, Jeanine Graham provides a global perspective on issues affecting children in the twentieth century. On the one hand, Graham points to positive developments for many of the world's children during this period: improved health, expanded access to public education, greater attention to and understanding of children's psychological needs, and last, but not least, the United Nations *Convention on the Rights of the Child*. Yet the twentieth century brought a depressing array of exploitation and suffering to children: the repression of dictatorships, discrimination and segregation, the physical and psychological trauma caused by countless wars, and the painful disruptions and displacement caused by conflict and famine. Although the twentieth century promised "a virtual world of possibilities," Graham concludes that the persistent presence of "conflict, poverty, and disease" makes these promises very difficult to achieve.

CHAPTER ONE

Family Relationships

DAVID BARRETT AND
MARIA KUKHAREVA

In *Through the Looking Glass*, Lewis Carroll wrote, "If I don't make haste, I shall have to go back through the looking glass, before I've seen what the rest of the house is like."[1] By peering through the looking glass once more, this chapter considers changes affecting family and society over the last 100 years, primarily through the British experience. The chapter emphasizes, among other developments since the turn of the twentieth century, the evolving roles of women and children, the effects those changes had on the role of men, the factors in a changing society that affected family life, and the way the new family influenced the community and social order. This chapter will focus in particular on changes in twentieth-century British society and on central pieces of legislation that reacted to and endorsed this change and helped form the contemporary family and the modern welfare state, including the importance of the Beveridge Report in 1942 and the launch of the National Health Service (NHS). In following British and Western families through wars, epidemics, and social structures in transition, the chapter will identify the factors that had the greatest effect on Western families, including changes that affected kin relationships and brought family units to their contemporary form. In its conclusion the chapter will consider the issues that traditional, modern, and postmodern families face in today's globalized environment.[2]

FIGURE 1.1: *Mixed European Family*. Courtesy of Maria Kukhareva, photographer.

AT THE TURN OF THE CENTURY

Formed and driven by the engine of the Victorian heritage at its inception, the twentieth century eventually transported Britain, northern Europe, and the United States into a totally new place, where the traditional and the modern coexist, where the gaps between social, sexual, and other differences widen and narrow simultaneously, where the previously unacceptable is accepted, and where what was previously unimaginable is now possible and embedded in people's lives.[3] Yet, after 100 years, have the assumptions and restraints of the Victorian era completely disappeared, or have they continued in new ways? As Smelser observed, "more than a century after the Victorian family's heyday, and when no one would seriously argue that the family is still essentially Victorian, that family still persists as a kind of ghostly model."[4] To trace the metamorphoses that family and society in Britain and the West have undergone in the past 100 years, one has to start at the turn of the twentieth century and the dark, narrow streets of the Victorian era and its aftermath.

At the beginning of the twentieth century, the family—the remarkable institution that symbolized stability, serenity, and even masculinity—was a crystallization of the Victorian era itself, with a strong and well-defined structure, clear-cut roles, and values and aspirations, especially those representative of the middle class. Timeless and cherished, the family provided prospective and existing members with security and guidance, but it also imposed formality and repressed any behavior that deviated from the sharply discriminative division between sexes.[5] However, the Victorian family as it was known in the West was mainly associated with the values nurtured and practiced by the middle and upper middle classes, leaving the working class to live more according to the conditions they were placed in rather than the norms set by the higher society. Women struggled in working-class families, having to work as well as care for the children, although theirs was not the type of work that the feminist movement would later demand. Lack of qualifications and educational opportunities overall determined the type of labor these women would be able to perform.[6]

Early twentieth-century Britain, as well as northern Europe and the United States, experienced decreased levels of child labor as a result of technological changes and wider access to education in general. This in turn led to a vast increase in the number and range of low-level service occupations and thereby to increased income for working-class adults. Greater financial independence and broader opportunities for the working class, especially for children and women, opened up new horizons and raised aspirations. Furthermore, the roles of the father, the mother, and the child—as well as kin relations in general and interaction between family members, both nuclear and extended—were continuously shifting from absolute to relative, conditional, flexible, and fluid. The dialogue between the interdependent institutions of family and state acquired a new character, and changes that would look insignificant to a citizen today were a breath of fresh, almost foreign, air to children and women, as well as to men and the elderly.[7]

It is important to remember, however, that no matter how powerful these changes were, the Victorian family achieved remarkable persistence by allowing other family forms to coexist alongside it, by deviating and expanding, by adopting new elements, and by omitting others. This process involved accepting new forms without completely replacing the old ones. These new forms and approaches would manifest themselves in the coexistence of modern and postmodern families alongside traditional counterparts, all of them sanctioned by law and recognized by society.

THE FAMILY AND SOCIAL CHANGE

The social change that followed the Victorian era can be understood as a reaction to its rigidity. The period from 1900 to World War I was a classic age of social policy change and policy debate in the United Kingdom, as well as in northern Europe and the United States. The relationship between the individual and the state was emerging on the social and political agenda, from issues such as the role of mothers and free school meals to the maintenance of incentives to work for those on welfare. This debate continued after World War I. Poverty and inequalities in the application of rights and the distribution of wealth, as well as class division (with the working class at its core), came to the center of the discussion throughout the 1920s and 1930s. Significantly, the issue of the rights and duties of women, including birth control, came into question. Working-class femininity and sexuality were compared to their traditionally middle-class counterparts, with a link being drawn between birth control, family size, and economic deprivation. This resulted in the family planning movement, among other measures, and was reflected in major legislation including the 1930 ministerial memorandum.[8] Education presented another example of inequality between women and men or, rather, between girls and boys. Although the 1944 Education Act laid the foundation for free education for all British children from primary to secondary school, children over eleven years of age were still subject to quotas for admission to grammar school; such quotas allowed only the brightest students to pass on the basis of entrance exams, thus excluding many from basic educational opportunities. Still, efforts to expand educational access were continued in England, as well as in other European nations and the United States.[9]

The process of addressing these disparities developed over the course of the twentieth century in Britain and was supported by the women's movement in the 1960s and the NHS legislation in 1973, which both promoted not only further equality for women but also the health of unborn children.[10] Gradually the family as a productive unit in Britain and the West became more nuclear, with a decreasing number of births, increasing numbers of single-parent households, and older members living separately from their children, either on their own or cared for by the government and community care institutions. Similar to its Victorian counterpart, the twentieth-century British family represented an economic entity, one whose members had to generate income. The irony, however, is that while the average household diminished in size, the number of kin earning a living increased.[11]

The status of the family as a caregiver for its members—from children to older people and the ill and disabled—has been undergoing a change that perhaps has brought the most controversy into the discussion. In Britain, though much less so in the United States, the growth of the welfare state and the Beveridge reform to some degree obviated the family's so-called duty of care—that is, the responsibility of the family as a social institution to care for the vulnerable, the sick, and the elderly. Looking after the vulnerable and those in need increasingly became the government's priority, sharing and even shifting the care role from the parents and children to designated professionals. Social services, the NHS, schools, and local authorities began to take responsibility for cases in which the family members were not be able to perform their traditional functions of care. It is important, however, to note that the concept of duty of care was itself transformed several times in the last 100 years. Never before, perhaps, had the interconnection between family and society been advocated so strongly by government policy, local authorities, media, and charitable organizations as it was during, and especially at the end of, the twentieth century. Even so, individualism has not been replaced by a communal approach; rather, the two expanded and merged, with responsibility being placed on the state as well as on the family.[12]

None of these changes would have happened were it not for the transformation in role of women during the twentieth century. In Britain and in other Western countries, legislation, reflecting the social change at the time, played a significant role in this transition, legitimizing new norms and new rights, endorsing reform that had already started in the heart of the society—that is, in the family. The 1960s was a decade of considerable historic distinction in the twentieth century: several pieces of legislation marked this period, affecting family life and family structures on various levels. With nine legislative acts relating to families enacted in Britain over a period of less than five years—including the Family Provisions Act of 1966, the Abortion Act of 1967, and the Sexual Offences Act of 1967, among others—the period of reform greatly improved the status of women as members of society and as members of their families. The most revolutionary of all these reforms was perhaps the Divorce Reform Act of 1969, which eliminated many of the hindrances that characterized the earlier divorce procedures. Similar legislation was enacted in continental Europe and the United States in the 1960s.[13]

The new acts not only affected the way women could lead their lives and be perceived by the community, they also changed the position of children by reducing the adulthood and citizenship age to eighteen, which served to recognize their rights and needs as being different from those of adults. The 1970s followed, along with the implementation of the new legislation, as well as with major changes in the social and behavioral sciences. The focus was on the human development, and the child was at the center of it. With the new postwar "embourgeoisement," new views on the status of women and children, and the new legislation, child and adolescent development were seen as important in the growth of the society and the family. For some, the changes were so profound that they felt that twentieth-century society was witnessing "the destruction of the past, or rather of the social mechanisms that link one's contemporary experience to that of earlier generations."[14]

The world does not stand still. Throughout the West, growing divorce rates, increased maternal employment, and lower overall birth rates (but higher rates of teenage parenthood) attracted increasing attention from governments, media, and local communities. In the second half of the twentieth century, stronger emphasis was placed on aspects of children's lives such as education, recreation, and the development of key life skills. Multiple programs and initiatives supported by government policy, local authorities, and related institutions were established to support parents in their main duties.[15]

Caring for the elderly and attitudes toward this duty of care also underwent significant changes in Britain, continental Europe, and North America. The evolving role of women meant that the duty of care, once clearly assigned to the female member of the family, had to be shared and perhaps even shifted to other members of the family or, as it happened, to the community and the state. For example, in Britain the National Health Service Act of 1946 not only launched the NHS but also introduced the concept of community care, an approach that caused disputes between politicians, doctors, nurses, and social workers for decades. At first designed with chronically ill mental health patients in mind, this solution was gradually expanded to include older family members, most of them at home. High on the political and social agenda, community care proved to be a controversial subject for discussion. Not having been clearly defined in key legislation and thus allowing confusion about responsibility, funding, and strategy, this approach to supporting the family's caring functions has been the focus of much debate among researchers and in the media. The debate also highlighted differences in opinions about the respective responsibilities of what were known as the public and private spheres of society.[16]

Although in the last decade of the twentieth century Britain established a clearer and more consistent approach to community care through the passage of the Community Care Acts of 1990, 1996, and 1998, the dispute between the NHS and local authorities regarding the ultimate responsibility for the provision of care remains. And as the people in Britain and the West live longer, the need for appropriate care for older and frail family members stays on the agenda. Availability, the right to access the service, and its scale and quality are of direct or indirect concern to every household and every family in Britain and the West.

Overall, the late twentieth century became known as the age of social engineering in Britain, although less so in the United States.[17] The ideology underlying government policy became more explicit with respect to family issues, and the impact of public policies and services on family relationships was widely acknowledged as significant, from issues such as housing and social security to education, health care, and welfare. This period was marked by changes in legislation as well as in social attitudes about older people's roles and expectations, the status of women, and the boundaries among kin and between the family and society.[18]

KINSHIP, FAMILY, AND MARRIAGE

Kinship, family, and marriage have undergone a major transformation in the last 100 years. Although kinship and kin relations in early twentieth-century Britain were relatively undefined when compared to other cultures, they still had much clearer and more well-defined boundaries than they do today. The highly idealized nuclear family, with clear-cut gender roles and inequalities, provided a strong model for the citizens of Victorian Britain and elsewhere. Parenting and domestic duties were defined primarily as the wife's prerogative, whereas the breadwinning function was assigned to the husband. Marriages in those days could not be easily broken, whether for reasons of financial dependency, law, or stigma. The family equaled marriage, and marriage equaled family, making its roots in blood ties, legality, and the romantic exclusivity of the love/ sex interrelationship between partners, which was often idealized.[19]

The indissoluble character of marriage-based kin relationships in Britain and the West was shaken by major wars, especially World War II. Security and stability were lost, families were destroyed, and new families were formed quickly. Women and children presented themselves in a new light supporting the war effort. The second half of the century saw the emergence of the companionate family with interpersonal relationships, not implicit contracts between the spouses, as the core of the relationships. The reforms that followed this change were designed to reinforce the new ideology and to face postwar challenges: low birth rates, increasing divorce rates, and higher numbers of delinquent youths with single mothers trying to earn a living on their own. New policies were expected to bring stability back into family life. At the same time, new notions appeared, such as new forms of birth control and education programs for women. In this way, society looked to novel solutions for familiar problems while hoping to retain and regain what it could of the family's traditional structure. However, the rise of companionate marriage announced a small but necessary shift in the way in which the partnership between a man and a woman was conceived. It added a new element to family's accepted structure: a personal relationship with the ability to bring fulfillment into an individual's life. However, the new right to strive for fulfillment, once it had been recognized and accepted, ironically contributed to increasing disillusionment and lack of fulfillment, thus advancing the rise of the divorce rates later in the century, especially in the post-Divorce Act decades.[20]

The growing number of divorces gave hundreds of men and women an opportunity to remarry and form what would be known as a reconstituted families, the ethos for which was still strongly based on evidently gendered practices of parental care and economic support typical of conventional marriage. A huge change in the lives of many people, this process represented a significant symbolic shift: the existing moral code, which saw lifelong marriage and living in sin as the only possibilities, was lifted. In terms of their importance to society, individual relationships were replacing the traditional institution of marriage as an abstract idea.[21]

Children and their development in a fully functioning family were also seen in a new light: remarriage now meant forming another family, possibly one more successful in supporting the child. In Britain, the Children Act of 1989 redefined parental responsibilities: the duty of parenthood would now be retained by both parents, replacing the former right of custody awarded to only one parent at the time of divorce, thus making parenting more inclusive not only within but also outside and beyond marriage. The right of children to have legally recognized relationships with both parents was been sanctioned in law in the late 1960s with the Family Law Reform Act and later acts. The process of legitimizing nonmarital parenthood was underway in Britain and the United States, biological ties outside of marriage or alongside a broken marriage were more frequently recognized as legitimate, and children could still have a relationship with a father or mother even after a divorce or separation.[22]

The last decades of the twentieth century saw the family, once viewed as a stable, clearly defined, nondeviating unit, presented as a new ideological construct. In recognition of the unique parent-child connection as well as parental responsibilities, the preservation of biological ties between parents and their children was increasingly placed at the center of the family and family relations. The maintenance of this relationship overrode the substitution model provided by the reconstituted family: with the greater independence of women, and men increasingly fighting for their parenting rights, caring for the children became paramount, irrespective of the parents' marital status and their place in the family cycle.[23]

The new ideology was designed in part to inspire divorced or separated parents to share financial responsibility as well as the obligation to care for their children through a set of postseparation arrangements that would function across more than one household. This change, among others, led society to look differently at the increasing number of same-sex partners and their child rearing rights—another step toward the postmodern family.[24]

The new ideology acted as a powerful regulator of the social and economic environment in family life after divorce. In Britain particularly, the more problematic side of this philosophy, however, was its enforcement through the family justice system and the Child Support Agency and its administrative structure. After a divorce, the nuclear family would become split into a binuclear formation, thus changing the language that surrounded it. Legal separation would no longer be the end of the family. For many, divorce came to represent a stage, often a burdensome one, to get through in one's extended life course. However, there was growing concern among some about the possible damage divorce could cause to children's emotional well-being and overall development. This concern found its way into the legal, political, and wider discussion and contributed to the misconception that postdivorce children would become a social liability that would then have to be addressed by government policy.[25]

Another important change in family relationships was related to the connection between grown children and their parents. In Britain and much of the West, the introduction of community care as a service for aging family members who wanted to continue living on their own made it more possible for women in nuclear and single-parent households to further their careers as well as look after other family members. However, these new arrangements could also weaken ties between children and parents because the traditional duty of care, whether forced or voluntary, held families together, for better or for worse. The complexity of the issue is further evident in that although the newer concepts of marriage and family are consistent with the current, rather individual-focused mentality of British and North American society (especially the growing preference for independence and living on one's own), the striking increase in longevity may require current approaches to care to be modified again to suit new conditions.[26]

FAMILY BREAKERS AND FAMILY MAKERS

The twentieth century was among the most war-ridden centuries in history, not only in terms of deaths but also in terms of impact that wars had on those who survived. In the words of Ronald Fletcher, "in Britain, as in other countries of Europe, two entire generations were torn out of the settled contexts of their families and communities and subjected to the disruptive influences of these two world wars."[27] Wars, especially World War II, involved not only the country's military but also the whole society, including families. No family remained unaffected by the war. For those at home, the war brought food shortages, exhausting labor to support the war effort, and, too often, the tragic loss of loved ones. For soldiers, the war brought profound uncertainty, excruciating combat conditions, and sometimes a close proximity to death. The war changed families forever. Children being moved away from home; men joining the armed forces; women, children, and older people working to support the war effort; and women forming their own regiments were all a basic part of life during the war. These experiences affected adults and children for the rest of their lives, from the way they rebuilt their families, raised their children, and cared for their partners and parents to how they cared for the elderly.[28]

In contrast to prewar times, "family" and "home" ceased to refer to the same thing, and rightly so: thousands of people found themselves in a literally new family because of family members who had died or never been found, and even if a new family was composed of some of the same members, it required new functions to rebuild itself, to forget traumas, and to regain a lost sense of stability. The home that children of war had to leave behind and the address they came back to after the war were never quite the same place. The world itself was a different place; nothing could ever be the same again.[29]

Paradoxically, one could also say that the war influenced the development of the family and its members in positive ways. The rapid industrialization in the West brought by the war meant that the role of women and children on the home front was very important. While men were at the front, women, children, and older people were all involved in the direly needed labor on farms, in factories, and at home. Patriotism, citizenship, and the common goal of a united people made families and individuals stronger.[30]

The war offered a sudden chance for many women to establish their equality to men: by caring for the wounded and dying in hospitals and at the battlefront, and by fighting the enemy in their own impromptu units, the so-called weaker sex proved to be a strong partner to men, supporting them during the war and welcoming them home afterward. The war, though tragic and unmerciful, presented women with an opportunity to get involved in jobs traditionally performed by and associated with men.[31] It also should not be forgotten that throughout the century British women were proactive in founding and developing pacifist organizations to promote peace (and facing hard criticism for it), though perhaps less so during World War II. Throughout the century, from the Women's Social and Political Union (and later the Women's Party) founded and run by Emmeline Pankhurst to Greenham Common Women's Peace camp (founded to oppose nuclear weapons), the role of these organizations in the social history and development of women's rights should not be underestimated.[32]

The postwar period brought a great deal of hope to families in Britain, Europe, and North America, despite the great losses and damaged futures that were suffered. It was the time to rebuild for the future, to reconstruct and reunite families, and to form new relationships, raise children, run households, earn money, and receive education. In Britain, alternative policies were suggested to tackle poverty and deprivation that would align with the three key generic principles described by Townsend as "(a) conditional welfare for the few; (b) minimum rights for many; and (c) distribution justice for all."[33] The new welfare state policy, with the Beveridge Report at its center, was supposed to revive the family by supporting men as breadwinners and women as housewives. Advocates hoped that by fulfilling these traditional roles, men and women would create strong foundations for a postwar family.[34] The Butler Education Act, also known as the "educational Beveridge" (1944) and the NHS (1948) were also intended to support the family, respond to its needs, and ensure that individual families, supported by the state, would contribute to a stronger, healthier, more educated nation.

Wars and their effects, however, were not the only events causing disruption in the family life cycle. From the early twentieth century, the social behavior of individuals became the focus of the state's concern about public health: individual intervention was viewed as the key to controlling the quality of the population and ensuring national efficiency. Thus, establishing the NHS was a logical step taken by the government to tackle illness if not to instill wellness.[35]

Epidemics and illnesses, both physical and mental, have always played a key role in bringing families together as well as pulling them apart. Illicit drug abuse (which reached its peak in Britain in the 1960s), alcohol addiction, genetic illnesses, old recurring epidemics like typhoid during the years of World War II, and previously unknown viruses like hepatitis C or HIV in the 1980s shook the foundations of hundreds and thousands of families. Moreover, in Britain, Europe, and the United States, family members often suffered from four major illnesses sometimes linked to lifestyle—cancer, heart disease, strokes, and lung disease—especially in working-class families. Important factors included behaviors such as improper diet, smoking, and alcohol consumption.[36]

Religion as a part of family life brought families together and broke them apart. Stepping further and further away from their Victorian heritage, Britain and the West have become increasingly secularized since the 1960s, although late-century opinion polls revealed that the majority of the population considered themselves Christian.[37] With growing multiculturalism as a key feature of British society, families increasingly had to deal with different religions—sometimes similar to their own but sometimes quite unfamiliar and different. Children or parents marrying into a different faith not only affected the immediate family; they potentially affected further generations and future relatives. And, not surprisingly, religion affected other social interactions such as belonging to a circle of friends, a common interest group, and children's education. For decades Britain welcomed those practicing many faiths, supported faith communities, promoted tolerance, and protected families' rights to send their children to religious schools. Government policy, media channels, and education promoted a growing awareness and tolerance of others' faiths. However, another factor in the changing make-up of the family in Britain was Britain's historic connections with other countries, especially those of the former Commonwealth. The substantial influx of immigrants from Commonwealth nations after World War II added to Britain's diversity and resulted in the creation of new family units and the separation of siblings and generations across the world.[38]

Another paradox that characterized family life in twentieth-century Britain and the West was the greater financial independence of women and, to an extent, children. An opportunity to support oneself as well as the family began strengthening many families, as well as aiding separation, especially after the complete legalization and simplification of the divorce procedure in Britain in 1969. This shift was followed by a wider recognition of parenting rights of fathers in the successive decades. Further, the introduction of the concept of community care for the vulnerable members of the family and society added a new dynamic to the evolution of the British family as a social institution.[39]

FAMILY IN A GLOBALIZED SOCIETY

The world is coming together in a metaphorical way: major events like the breakup of the Soviet Union, the rebuilding of a united Germany, and the formation of what is now the European Union have affected migration patterns. Also, international organizations like the United Nations were able to impose unified laws and norms on whole groups of countries. As a result of the maturation of the social and intellectual capital of the whole human nation, scientists and researches are able to gather more data on families and children in countries across the globe and draw comparisons and recommendations to make the world aware of its own diversity. Policies and communications on the international level have become more transparent, and the world is viewed as a much smaller place by politicians, scientists, and the general public, especially in developed countries.[40]

Britain has long occupied, and continues to occupy, an important strategic place in the world. With its rich history and diverse cultural make-up, British society today is a product of not just decades but centuries of migration, resettlement, and assimilation that were encouraged by political and industrial changes. Although large Dutch, Jewish, and black communities lived in Britain long before the Industrial Revolution, new opportunities have attracted new waves of immigrants that helped transform the British economy. The Nazi regime left its mark in the book of international migration patterns: thousands of Jewish families with children fled to Britain from central Europe in the hope of finding safety and peace. The war that followed forced hundreds of thousands of others to seek refuge, many of them settling in the United Kingdom. The country kept expanding its population by attracting families from the former Commonwealth countries that were arriving in the search of new job opportunities. Postwar Britain faced the imposing task of rebuilding the country, and partly for that reason welcomed immigrants. Families from the West Indies, India, Pakistan, and former colonies in Africa that once formed a vast British Empire, and whose citizens were still technically British subjects, were making new homes on British soil. The 1948 British Nationality Act aided this process and simplified this resettlement by granting favorable immigration rights to many families that were coming to the British shores.[41]

The 1960s, however, marked a new era in the immigration and migration history of Britain and the West. A series of acts across several decades restricted immigration access into Britain, from the Commonwealth Immigrants Act of 1962 to the "partiality principle" added in 1968. Legislation enacted in the 1980s and 1990s increased these restrictions further. Similar patterns affected refugees and asylum seekers in the twentieth century: following the United Nations' agreement of 1951, higher number of families were trying to escape to the United Kingdom, and the legislation was being adjusted accordingly. In the early 1990s, new, stricter procedures were introduced to handle refugee and asylum seeker cases that consequently resulted in lower migration rates at the turn of the twenty-first century. British identity is multidimensional, and the British family is not a homogenous institution.[42]

The new freedom in Britain's social life brought both new dangers and new responsibilities. The twentieth century was expected to become the *Century of the Child*.[43] Indeed, during this period, human rights, particularly the rights of women and children, were widely endorsed by the state and key international organizations. Certain types of crime, such as garroting, declined or disappeared. However, other forms of crime, such as mugging, seemed to flourish in the conditions of the globalized world. Encouraged by improved links of communication between continents and countries, higher awareness of other cultures, and developed infrastructures of the criminal underworld, human trafficking, drug distribution, and other types of transborder crime have spread. The world trade market, driven by the most developed countries, has created new business opportunities for criminal groups around the world and has affected thousands of families, destroyed the lives of family members, and brought fear and uncertainty to others, affecting both living and future generations.[44]

Britain occupies a rather unique position in the world. A relatively small island for its population and placed geographically to be able to absorb influences from different parts of the world, the United Kingdom has been acting as a host to clans and families representing not only different cultures but also different stages of historical development. Therefore it is possible to speak of the three family types coexisting in British society—the traditional, the modern, and the postmodern—not in pure form, but manifesting themselves at various times and situations. Compared to its mainland European Union comembers, Britain, one of most ethnically diverse countries in Europe, represents a complex mix of coexisting cultures, living side-by-side and expanding each other's culture and knowledge of the rest of the world.[45]

When one takes into account several migration waves throughout the last century, including both people born in Britain and those who came from elsewhere, one sees how a multiplicity of cultural and family norms and customs have enriched the British culture and changed it forever. The change has been strongly enhanced by international and UK media including the Internet and new forms of technology, which have facilitated the secularization of family life, freedom and independence, higher awareness of the human rights issues, changing domestic and social roles and responsibilities, and other trends.

British families, like those in Europe and the United States, have become more diversified, and not only in terms of ethnicity. Class divisions are shifting and changing in character as well.[46] The British government is doing more to encourage higher aspirations among children from minority groups and underrepresented backgrounds. In addition, the Victorian class system has been affected by striking ethnodemographic changes. Each culture has brought its own understanding of class and thus has changed the way class divisions are perceived in Britain. Birth rates and their distribution have been affected by the migration patterns over the years and have changed the way families look today. For example, families of Indian and Pakistani origin tend to have more children, with extended families living as one household, which tends to counterbalance declining birth rates among nuclear (and even binuclear) white British families, especially in larger urban areas. The rising affordability of travel and more transparent migration policies and agreements among countries made it possible for thousands of British citizens to move to other countries; however, the British population grew as newcomers from other countries were able to settle in the United Kingdom.[47]

CONCLUSION

The family as a social institution went through major changes in the last 100 years. In this chapter we have looked at how the family left the Victorian era behind and entered the new development cycle powered by the changes in the society as well as shifts in individual attitudes. Although powerful, the transition was not even, smooth, or painless for every partnership and household. A multiplicity of factors, both external and internal, affected the family revolution. Moreover, no government or legislation will ever be able to standardize these metamorphoses completely. Diversity is becoming a key feature of modern society, and a variety of forms of cohabitation are now widely

FIGURE 1.2: *Family, Cape Town, South Africa, Christmas 2000*. Courtesy of Henry M. Trotter, photographer, who is a member of this extended family. Available at: http://commons. wikimedia.org/wiki/Image:Coloured-family.jpg (accessed on October 22, 2008).

recognized. All that governments today can do is to support these new structures and institutions via flexible, up-to-date family policies.

The family, once a relatively rigid structure, has broken into different parts, only to form a fluid web of partnerships and practices that now define what we see as our personal, familial, and kinship networks within the life course of a family and its members. This major development has been enriched by numerous geographical, cultural, ethnic, religious, and other differences, on one hand, and by reforms in the world of employment and production, technological revolution, gender relations, and sexual orientation, on the other.

Social reconstruction and social reform played a major role in the British social history, with the welfare state at the center of these processes. Government intervened to secure equal rights for all members of the biological family as well as its extended structures my supporting minimum standards of living, health, and housing and by expanding access to education and employment. In other words, efforts were made to meet the basic human needs necessary to form and maintain a healthy society. Modern British society, with its new, revised values and updated ethos, is inextricably bound up with the emergence of the modern British family.

In Britain and the West, the causal relationship between family, marriage, and kinship has undergone an inversion. It has become more and more clear that "marriage is rooted in the family rather than the family in marriage."[48] The shift in attitudes toward marriage has transformed the way that society treats partnerships, parenthood, and domesticity. Partnerships are occurring more frequently outside marriage, and parental responsibilities reflect these changes. Birth control, paired with reproductive technologies, has given society a greater range of parenthood choices. The modern family offers its members a wide range of approaches to relationships, from serial monogamy to step families, single parenthood, same-sex partnerships, and adoption. Families are now dispersed and layered spatially and economically, both vertically and horizontally, with the welfare of the child and children's rights enshrined in formal legislation.[49]

All that said, the family is still the key component, whether in a reordered form or other manifestation. It remains the base in the formation of modern society, with its values and core aims less tight and rigid but as crucial as ever. What Ralph Linton wrote in 1959 might have been written yesterday: "The ancient trinity of father, mother and child has survived more vicissitudes than any other human relationship. It is the bedrock underlying all other family structures." Thus, Linton concluded, "Although more elaborate family patterns can be broken from within or may even collapse of their own weight, the rock remains. In the Götterdämmerung which over-wise science and over-foolish statesmanship are preparing for us, the last man will spend his last hours searching for his wife and child."[50]

We are, after all, our parents' sons and daughters. Society is reinventing itself by adding new to old—not rejecting the past but rather using it as a starting definition when embracing change. If one were to predict the future of the family in Britain and the West by observing recent history through the looking glass of the twentieth century and beyond, one might wonder, if, in the words of Lewis Carroll: "what could be seen from the old room was quite common ... all the rest was as different as possible ... And if I hold [the looking-glass book] up to a glass, the words will all go the right way again."[51]

CHAPTER TWO

Community

MONA GLEASON AND
VERONICA STRONG-BOAG

A critical development for children and youth in the twentieth century has been the ten-fold increase in the world's urban population.[1] After 1900, Europe, North America, and Oceania experienced the fastest urban growth. By 2000, 79.1 percent of the population in North America, 72.7 percent of that in Europe, and 47.15 of that in the world at large was urban.[2] That challenge and opportunity worked with the other big stories of the century—recurring immigrant waves and nativism, inadequate urban infrastructures, world wars (1914–1918; 1939–1945), the Great Depression (1930s), the cold war (1945–1989), and end-of-the-century globalization—to set the critical landscape of modern childhood in the West. This chapter takes up the ongoing question of community in a world where adults and youngsters endeavored in various ways to come to terms with urban life. The first section addresses the efforts of middle-class reformers and professionals to manage youngsters, first by moving them into rural areas and then by organizing urban lives. The next section turns to what diverse urban communities offered their members, especially children. The final section concentrates on what Canadian historian Neil Sutherland calls "the culture of childhood."[3] These discrete sections portray children and youth engaged with community in diverse but related ways, forging their own experiences but also encountering adults both as formal managers of options and as more informal participants in their lives. While North America supplies a major focus, the West more broadly also figures here.

FIGURE 2.1: *Teenagers, Toronto, Ontario.* 1949. They are meeting in the beanery owned by the father of one of their number. L. Jacques/National Archives of Canada/PA-128763.

MIDDLE-CLASS RESPONSE TO URBAN CHILDREN AND FAMILIES

By 1900, middle classes everywhere had long involved themselves in the oversight, uplifting, and discipline of families. Some initiatives, such as child emigration schemes, orphanages and other live-in institutions, the settlement house movement, and children's clubs were highly organized. In response to recurring concern about the urban youth problem and the loss of cultural/moral values in the encounter with modernity, such initiatives proliferated in many parts of North America, the United Kingdom, Europe, Australia, and New Zealand as one expression of adult agendas.

The emigration schemes that spread from Britain to Canada and the other colonies of European settlement in the late nineteenth century and the relocation of American youngsters from cities to rural areas in much the same period emphasized shifting refugees from urban distress to the salvation of rural homes. Rejecting its southern neighbor's Poor Law solutions to poverty, Scotland made an early start in dispatching suspect city youngsters to its own remote locations.[4] In England, philanthropists, such as Dr. Thomas Barnardo, similarly rejected institutional remedies, choosing instead to help send some 80,000 British "Home Children" to Canada between 1870 and 1914. Closely associated with Britain's churches and charities, child emigration programs received government endorsement in the United Kingdom, Canada, Australia, and South Africa. In 1967, the final installment of nine children was dispatched from Britain's Barnardo home to Australia.[5] In 1853, the Protestant reformer and minister Charles Loring Brace initiated the major American effort at juvenile relocation. After founding New York's Children's Aid Society, he set in motion the so-called orphan trains that carried more than 100,000 youngsters to farms in the American west between 1854 and 1929. In the latter year, the last shipment, three boys, went to Sulfur Springs, Texas.[6] Rural destinations sometimes included institutions. Even as about one half of Parisian street children in conflict with the law were returned to their families, others were transferred to residential settings such as La Colonie Agricole established in Mettrai, France, where it was hoped they might emerge as industrious farm laborers.[7] The same hope motivated the establishment of reformatories and industrial schools in wilderness and rural areas everywhere in the West. Agricultural settings were assumed to offer discipline, useful skills, and better health.

Rural life was never the only solution to distress. Youngsters in many nations were also confined to urban institutions. While sometimes intended to provide an interlude before placement in families, as with England's Barnardo homes, orphanages and shelters also provided shelter for months or years at a time. Care for coreligionists has regularly prompted Mennonites, Jews, Catholics, and Protestants to maintain children's residences. While modern child study professionals generally criticized institutional options, some of these institutions provided otherwise unavailable shelter, support, and education and provoked a strong sense of shared community. Wars and economic disaster—not to mention the preference of many birth families for care from which youngsters might be recovered in better times and the continuing difficulty of finding substitute homes for boys and girls defined as mentally or physically abnormal—kept institutions in operation. By the close of the twentieth century, orphanages in Russia, Romania, and Bulgaria seized headlines for further disadvantaging children in their care.[8]

State intervention into indigenous families also regularly involved residential institutions in the United States and Canada, beginning in the late nineteenth century, and in Australia, early in the twentieth century. These so-called schools persisted in nonurban settings until the 1980s in the latter two nations, where they operated hand in glove with Christian churches.[9] Like the emigration schemes used for the poor more generally, such institutions attempted to deracinate youngsters from traditional practices, beliefs, and languages. Reformed pupils were meant to return to improve Aboriginal communities and often to work as domestic and agricultural laborers for white employers. The white majority viewed the movement of aboriginal children and adults into cities as dangerous to public order and morality. For some years Canada's notorious pass system insisted that natives receive Department of Indian Affairs permission to leave reservations, thereby effectively excluding them from economic opportunities offered in towns and cities.[10] By World War II, soaring indigenous urban populations in North America, Australia, and New Zealand nevertheless confirmed that these groups were unwilling to remain in isolated communities.

While girls and boys occasionally benefited from migration and institutionalization, many fared badly and encountering indifference, abuse, and even death. Some never lost the sadness and confusion of permanent separation from relatives. Hazelle Latimer, sent west on the orphan train at age eleven, summed up loss with steely clarity: "my mother and I were very close because I was all she had and she was all I had. On January 7, 1918 my mother came to the school and she had a suitcase. She was going to go and ... see why she was having these awful headaches. And that was the last I saw of her."[11] Such experiences inevitably shaped children's ability to form subsequent relationships.

Even as experiments with migration and institutions reaped questionable outcomes, reformers turned to other urban solutions to child and youth problems. The rural devastation of the Great Depression and the migrations occasioned by World War II and its aftermath confirmed cities and suburbs as the ongoing focus for voluntary and philanthropic efforts. Hopes for rural salvation that inspired early migration and residential programs largely disappeared. One dominant response to working-class and immigrant children in burgeoning cities was compulsory school attendance legislation. Classrooms became critical centers of socialization for many pupils, offering them opportunities to compare their lives with others and to learn facts and skills unavailable in their families. Some youngsters, such as those variously known as Gypsies, Travelers, and Roma, remained, however, hard to serve and indeed often unwelcome by mainstream populations. For them, schools remained too often at odds with the core values of their adult communities and represented sites that threatened their well-being.[12]

In the English-speaking world, the settlement house movement emerged as a key remedy for urban youngsters believed to be out of control. Modeled after Toynbee Hall, a British Anglican charity established in London's East End in 1884, settlement houses expanded into other English cities but found fullest expression in North America where rising numbers of non-Anglo-Celtic migrants panicked elites. By 1918, 400 settlement houses operated across the United States.[13] In Canada, the movement thrived in Toronto, but Montreal and Winnipeg supplied other centers of earnest endeavor.[14] The most famous American example, Chicago's Hull House, cofounded in 1889 by Jane Addams and Ellen Gates Starr, typically provided a home-away-from-home for disadvantaged youngsters and their families.[15] Many girls and boys found their first introduction to stimulating worlds beyond their families in such settings.

Settlement houses everywhere emphasized community regeneration. Progressive reformers viewed poverty as a result of the unequal distribution of wealth and inadequate social support, not of innate depravity, incompetence, or indifference, explanations often favored by conservative social critics. The early twentieth-century social gospel inspired many settlement activists to apply a practical Christianity to social ills.[16] Girls and boys stood near the center of the larger struggle for democracy. Yet, for all its sympathetic orientation to urban diversity, the settlement movement ultimately promoted middle-class standards of health, education, and family life.

Charitable camps for the urban poor, such as those run by New York's Fresh Air Fund starting in 1877, Vancouver's Alexandra Orphanage (Camp Alexandra) starting in 1918, and Toronto's Family Service Association (Camp Bolton) starting in 1922, were similarly inspired by desires both to promote youngsters' well-being and to control their behavior. Public recreation programs took up the same challenge. In 1906 the Playground Association of America was founded in Boston, and American cities increased their playgrounds from 100 to 4,000 between 1905 and 1914. Many influences were international. German experts informed recreational planning in the United States and elsewhere.[17] Such efforts aimed to assimilate newcomers, reduce ethnic conflict, and instill an appreciation for managed play and teamwork.[18]

After the 1930s and World War II, individual settlement houses frequently survived, but offerings also evolved or became incorporated in municipal and grassroots initiatives such as the Vancouver Kitsilano War Memorial Community Centre (starting in 1951). Such neighborhood-based facilities, offering an unprecedented range of public services, were hailed as grassroots expressions of invigorated postwar democracy, and leisure rights slowly emerged as one part of full citizenship.[19] While notions of appropriate behavior continued to inform initiatives, local input encouraged a broader range of responses to populations whose diversity increasingly included Asian- and African-origin residents.

Throughout the century, clubs and organizations, organized locally, nationally, and internationally, also enlisted girls and boys. The Boy Scouts,

Girls Guides and Scouts, Young Men's Christian Association (YMCA), Boys' Clubs, and Young Women's Christian Association (YWCA) sprung up to offer sanctioned alternatives to urban temptations. Some, such as the Hiter Jugend (Hitler Youth) proved to be especially dangerous experiments in producing what Kenny Cupers sums up as "governable subjects."[20] A wide range of progressive, liberal, and deeply conservative initiatives set out to capitalize on the gang instinct identified by experts like G. Stanley Hall, the influential American psychologist of adolescence.[21] As Cynthia Comacchio has shown, "adult-supervised, community-based, Christian-influenced, and often church-affiliated organizations" focused on character education, lessons in citizenship, and wholesome recreational activities.[22] Related initiatives, including the North American middle-class summer camp movement, were similarly divided along class, race, and gender lines.[23] As Margaret Tennant has demonstrated as well, in the case of New Zealand's children's health camps, gender, ethnicity, and class were calculated as national problems that required collective solution.[24]

Recurring racial and religious prejudice contributed to the need for separate youth groups and organizations. The first Native American Girl Scout troop was founded in the 1920s in New York State's Onondago Nation.[25] In the 1930s, the Chinese Presbyterian Church in Victoria, British Columbia, established its own Boys and Girls Club.[26] Groups of Jewish Guides and Scouts, and sometimes Muslim as well, that appeared over the course of the twentieth century in many settings promised integration for suspect identities. At their best, they broadened understandings of citizenship and maintained elements of traditional culture. For some urban youngsters, they also promised rare entry into wilderness settings and broader views of their place in the world.

Working in tandem with class and race, gender informed clubs and organizations. One history of American girls' organizations demonstrates how enthusiastic social and professional leaders did more than merely imitate boys' groups. At the founding of the American Camp Fire Girls, one Boy Scout chief executive assuaged anxiety by explaining that "the aim of the Camp Fire Girls of America is to develop womanly qualities in the girls of an entirely different character from those arranged for the boys."[27] Yet if they reinforced mainstream femininity, clubs could also offer subversive moments. Participants treasured experiences that valued active womanhood and sisterhood.[28]

Rural youth, often consumed with work on family farms and physically isolated from peer groups, were less likely to be closely scrutinized by reformers. To alleviate their feelings of isolation, they nevertheless also joined clubs. Opportunities for external affirmation, as Lone Guides and Scouts demonstrated, could be highly valued. Longings for peer groups were movingly revealed in Canadian agricultural newspapers between 1900 and 1920 when five- to sixteen-year-old readers requested membership in the Maple Leaf Club, the Legion of the West, the Young Canada Club, and the Beaver Circle.[29] In the United States, Canada, and beyond, 4-H ("Head, Heart, Hands, and Health") Clubs spanned the entire century, marshalling farm girls and boys behind commitments such as, "I pledge my head to clearer thinking, my heart to greater loyalty, my hands to larger service and my health to better living, for my club, my community, my country, and my world."[30] Some sensibilities also shifted. For example, by the beginning of the new millennium, Manitoba's 4-H Clubs contradicted a long history of European dispossession of native farmers by partnering with aboriginal young people in a pilot project coordinated by Assembly of Manitoba Chiefs' staff.[31]

While increasingly urban-dwellers, the number of youngsters slowly dropped as a proportion of national populations everywhere. Some older initiatives, including many clubs, were devastated by loss of numbers. Other forces, however, increased their purchase on young minds and bodies. Girls everywhere confronted recurring belittlement in expressions of popular culture. Post-World War II France was typical in supplying distorted representations of young women.[32] Corporate advertising that promised to correct supposed deficiencies, whether of weight, skin color, or hair texture, infused many messages. Throughout the century, fears about popular culture fuelled public panics about everything from Victorian penny dreadfuls to Hollywood gangster films, horror comics, and electronic gaming as worried adults attempted to control aesthetics and morality.[33] Radio, film, television, and the World Wide Web nevertheless offered their own forms of community. Young consumers developed common knowledge and interests that would have horrified philanthropic champions of migration, urban settlements, native residential schools, and traditional clubs. At their best, traditional efforts to create communities had aimed to produce active and informed citizens. At their worst, however, adult efforts at indoctrination in mainstream values were not ultimately all that different from the goals of corporate capitalism endeavoring to sell Pepsi, Maybelline, and the Gap.

INSIDE COMMUNITIES: MUTUAL AID AND SURVEILLANCE

Middle-class whites were not the only adults with firm ideas about how youngsters should grow up. Families and wider community members of every class had ideas of their own. Typical of their age group, Viennese working-class youth were expected to put the welfare of their families above workplace, class, gender, or political loyalties.[34] Indigenous, immigrant, and other groups kept watchful eyes on their young and offered other ways of making sense of the world. Elders formed part of networks of surveillance. Indigenous girls and boys learned traditions of their ancestors and suspicion of imperial intruders from aunts and grandmothers. Progressive communities, like their more conservative counterparts, employed practices, from hootenannies and choirs to storytelling, prayer, Sunday schools, and camps to warn youngsters about capitalism and secularism. Native, black, and Hispanic children laboring in North American hop, tobacco, and cotton fields, like Gypsy girls and boys scavenging in continental Europe and elsewhere, learned hard lessons about what childhood meant on the margin. By the end of the twentieth century, Muslim youngsters similarly encountered rival cultural agendas demanding their allegiance. Disadvantaged youngsters often found themselves torn between mainstream and parental expectations of their future.

Adults regularly employed surrounding resources to bolster family survival. Community members could tell tales, warn, and advise. News of jobs, as well as truancy and promiscuity, or more minor improprieties, could be reported, especially in relatively homogeneous enclaves. Many mothers drew on the informal childcare of aunts, grandmothers, and neighbors. Support was commonly conditional on reciprocity and behaviors that met customary expectations. As Neil Sutherland has shown, youngsters were routinely embedded in a "wider environment of care."[35] Despite powerful domestic ideologies in the West that championed the patriarchal nuclear family as the only proper and normal arrangement, the permutations by which responsibilities for children and childcare have been allocated have been legion.[36] The shifting boundaries of households and the regular inclusion of nonkin meant that "for most of its history ... the Western family system has functioned with an imaginary that has enabled individuals to form familial relations with strangers and to feel at home away from home."[37] When life was uncertain, it behooved all to extend communal obligations to as many potential guardians as possible.

Often unfairly embedded in social contexts of prejudice, censure, and inadequate kinds of public support, unwed mothers have always been especially dependent on assistance from others.[38] That harsh reality lay behind the choice in 1925 of one Canadian mother. "Obliged to earn her living by her own exertions" and finding "it impossible to do so and at the same time to care for, nurse, bring up and educate the said child in a proper and suitable manner," she signed away her newborn. Although her province had an adoption law, she and the adopting couple used a form much like older indentures. New parents contracted to treat the boy "in a proper and suitable manner" and the surrendering

mother agreed not to disturb their "possession." As with many traditional arrangements, she did not disappear. The contract permitted "access to the said
child occasionally and visit[s] for the purpose of seeing him."[39] Such links, like
the shift to open adoptions at the end of the twentieth century, testified to the
possibility of continuing community even in very difficult circumstances.

Although relatives and neighbors from every culture have substituted for
birth parents when circumstances demanded, the indigenous peoples of North
America, Australia, and New Zealand and North Americans of African origin have been especially identified with kinship care.[40] In British Columbia,
Canada's westernmost province, women like Mary John, sometimes known
as the "Stoney Creek Woman," depended on aunts to help in the birth and
upbringing of children. Her older stepsister taught her the skills to make the

FIGURE 2.2: *Examination in Newfoundland School, Nfld.,*
1949. Atlantic Guardian/National Archives of Canada/
PA-128016.

moccasins, jackets, and mitts that she traded for children's clothing.[41] Other native women's ability to find employment in fish canneries or hop fields depended on grandmothers and aunts providing child care.[42] Immigrant communities displayed similar patterns. In New York's Lower East Side, Jewish and Italian mothers and their American-raised daughters tenaciously protected home country traditions while creating new practices of community survival.[43] In demonstrating multigenerational and multifamilial parenting after World War II, Toronto Italians echoed such patterns. Often in defiance of social workers, teachers, and parenting experts who encouraged mimicry of middle-class practices, immigrants clung to useful traditions even as they innovated.[44]

Twentieth-century social workers' advocacy of paid kinship foster care and child welfare acts that endorsed placement with relatives or friends testified to the familiarity of community networks.[45] Between 1922 and 1963, some 2.5 percent to 8 percent of recipients under the provincial Mothers' Allowances program lived with other kin in Ontario, Canada's most populous province.[46] In 1999, between 1.3 million and 4.3 million American children resided with relatives, usually older women. Such kin care represented twenty to thirty percent of all fostering in many countries. Duties were rarely shared equally. In Britain, some seventy percent of such caregivers have typically been reckoned to be grandmothers, and another twenty percent were aunts, and duties fell much more frequently to maternal relatives.[47] Such commitments are not new, as Anna Davin has demonstrated of early twentieth-century London.[48]

For families raising disabled children, caregiving has presented special challenges. Institutionalization was rarely the first step. The disability camping movement that emerged in the aftermath of Canada's post-World War II polio epidemics revealed recurring kin involvement in care and in political movements for improved supports.[49] One exploration of an Ontario hospital for patients with intellectual disabilities in the early twentieth century found that "lower-class families (the majority of those using the asylum and accessing prior treatments) and rural families did not view intellectual disability in as fatalistic a manner as the medical profession."[50] Handicaps such as deafness or blindness might be similarly incorporated within households and neighborhoods. Family stories of loved ones with cystic fibrosis and multiple sclerosis demonstrate enduring commitments.[51]

The benefits of cooperation inspired membership in fraternal orders, such as the Loyal Order of Moose and the Independent Order of Foresters, that initiated pensions, allowances, orphanages, and children's boarding homes. Between 1890 and 1922, such groups founded 71 orphanages in the United States alone.[52] Girls and boys at Mooseheart, a home for children of deceased members of the Loyal Order of Moose, begun in 1910 and still in existence in Aurora, Illinois, took mothers in as caregivers, imposed curfews, and established extensive educational and recreational programs that produced a "bumper crop of college students" in the 1930s.[53] The Jewish Children's Home in Rochester, New York, like similar Canadian endeavors in Winnipeg, Toronto, and Montreal, similarly produced "stern patriarchal control and regimentation" alongside a sense of an extended family and a "hub for religious ritual and prayer."[54] Determination to protect their own also prompted African Canadians to support Nova Scotia's Home for Colored Children in the aftermath of the great Halifax Explosion of 1917. For decades it affirmed a community that white Canada too often considered inferior.[55]

Alternative clubs similarly reinforced original identity. In the United States, Jewish and African American Scouts offered distinctive versions of mainstream initiatives. In the late 1930s, middle-class black mothers in Philadelphia started the first Jack and Jill Club to supply social and cultural alternatives. By 1968, 120 chapters flourished in 33 cities.[56] Other efforts went further. In 1939, Jewish adults in the United Kingdom and the United States created the Bnei Akiva and the North American Federation of Temple Youth respectively to promote study and support for Israel. Evangelical Protestant youth groups offered other versions of resistance.[57] Political minorities set up their own antidotes to elite directives. Progressive internationalists and pacifists founded the Order of Woodcraft Chivalry (1916) and the Woodcraft Folk (1925) in England to challenge the perceived militarism of Guides and Scouts. Other movements such as the Kibbo Kift Kindred (1920) "promoted non-Christian egalitarianism, socialist values, and/or idealized the Soviet Union."[58] In movements of every persuasion, family ties were frequently critical to their initiation. Of the seven founders of Glasgow's Young Communist League before World War II, six were not yet in their teens when the eldest, at seventeen, became the secretary. As one initiate recalled, "Mother had by this time become a keen communist," a not uncommon choice in a port city (Clydeside) hard hit by the economic turmoil of the 1930s.[59]

The meanings attached to community membership remained complex and contingent over the twentieth century. Communities could fail or make life more difficult. Working-class parents unhappy with disobedient offspring sometimes used courts, police, and the child welfare system to impose order.[60] Deaths and mistreatment also supply ample evidence of alienation and brutality as well as unmindful or indifferent neighbors. Some tragedies sometimes attracted intense public scrutiny, as with the case of the murdered ten-year-old Aurore Gagnon in 1920 Quebec and end-of-the-twentieth-century investigations of government handling of wards in New Zealand.[61] Cruelty to youngsters, particularly

FIGURE 2.3: *Roman Catholic School, Pouch Cove, New-foundland*, September, 1948. C. Lund/National Archives of Canada/PA-128004.

infants, has long been a sign of collective failure.[62] As Linda Gordon demonstrated in her pioneering study of Boston, violence was a commonplace feature of working-class and immigrant life.[63] The graves that surrounded many residential schools for indigenous youngsters in Canada, like the cases of infanticide everywhere, provide other reminders of the limits of concern.[64] Despite romantic notions of villages raising youngsters, communities, like states, are not always able or inclined to be generous or even-handed.

CHILDREN AND YOUTH MAKING CULTURE

However large adults figured in local landscapes, there were many other players. In the schoolyards, back alleys, front stoops, or in clubs, schools, and other organizations, girls and boys constructed their own critical relationships, often well beyond the range of older ears and eyes. In the culture of childhood, as Neil Sutherland has argued, "youngsters learned how to be children, to become members of both the almost timeless world of childhood and their own brief generation within it."[65] Those counted as friends or as enemies informed the day-to-day and the future.

For many twentieth-century children, whether working-class Londoners, residents of Canadian native reserves, or Maoris in New Zealand, the space beyond family dwellings provided pleasurable and dangerous interactions.

Ethel Spencer, one of seven children born to a white, upper-middle-class sub-urban Pittsburgh family at the turn of the twentieth century recalled, "though relatives were an integral part of life during our childhoods, they were not, since they were mostly grown-ups, on quite the same level of importance as the friends of our own age with whom we played every day."[66] A woman in Sutherland's study testified "we had a gang if you want to call it that … we would hang out under the lamp on the corner. We didn't do any harm; mostly we just talked."[67] Of her neighborhood friends in Brookdale, Nova Scotia, Shirley Dawn McKim remembered, "we all went around together like one person. We were out together almost every day. We played at our house or we played at their place … nobody ever looked after us … nobody checked up on us."[68]

Fond reminiscences of independence are matched by equally strong memo-ries where adult needs came first. A Vancouver boyhood was described in just this way: "You come home from school and you could tell what they were cooking, their big pots of borscht, or spaghetti, or gefilte fish, or whatever it was. Everybody seemed to know what they were having for dinner before they got home … at 9 o'clock you'd hear all the neighbors' whistle. Everybody knew their parents' whistle, and then by 5 after 9 there wasn't a kid on the street, they were all home … It was a curfew; but it was a curfew that was natural. They were all working people, went to bed early, so the kids had to be in."[69] While boys could find serious restrictions placed on their free time, girls, based on their liability for domestic labor as well as assumptions about their sexual vulnerabil-ity, were very often held to closer account by adults. As girls matured, these restrictions often became powerful internalized forces of surveillance. As one Canadian summed up her teenaged years in the 1940s, "the main reason that I'd never [have sexual intercourse] before marriage, is that my mother told me she'd throw me out of the house if I ever got pregnant outside of marriage."[70] Degrees of independence and surveillance ultimately varied enormously, reflecting di-verse cultural preferences and the exigencies of the day. During both world wars for example, many adults were gone, whether as military recruits or conscripts, in longer hours of paid employment, or in labor and concentration camps. In times of depression and recession, they might be similarly absent in search of wages or different options, though they might also be more available to monitor youngsters. The nature of the times always mattered.

Whether preciously short or seemingly endless, time spent with peers was the major preoccupation defining cultures of childhood. Girls and boys everywhere learned (mis)information about topics families often considered taboo. Some New Zealanders remembered that the so-called facts of life were of considerable interest but that details were unreliable. Cloaked in a "milieu of silence," sexuality traveled everywhere through gossip.[71] Having snooped through her mother's copy of Margaret Sanger's *Happiness in Marriage*, Mary Peate, who grew up in Montreal, Quebec, in the 1930s, favored her own sources. "For one thing," she later recalled, "I wasn't too convinced of Mrs. Sanger's authority on the subject ... she didn't really seem to know as much about it as the girls we sat with on the front steps."[72]

Youngsters also long turned to the popular media for information and companionship. In early twentieth-century Canada, letter-writing clubs provided antidotes to distance and isolation. They enabled young people to share opinions. Nine-year-old Sylvia Mitchell, from the prairie province of Saskatchewan, wrote in 1915, "we are twenty miles from the nearest town, and it takes up to three hours to get there. When we came here first there was no trail, so we had to make one."[73] In 1914, "Every Inch a Boy" wrote anonymously from Manitoba that "misbehavior in Sunday school" was an individual matter. "Each one of us," he explained, "has a responsibility that cannot be shouldered by anyone else."[74] News could be shared ("there has been great excitement over the train robbery!"), peers educated about family traditions ("I am an Indian girl. My father is a trapper and hunter") or appeals for companionship initiated. Margaret Wintemule, a twelve-year-old from Ontario wrote, "I have infantile paralysis and have not walked for nearly four years. I cannot go to school and find it very hard sometimes to find amusement. I would like very much to have a postal shower."[75]

While letters could be accepted as an innocuous expression of communication, youth gangs, in effect another type of club where adults were not presumed to be in control, were everywhere less welcome. They were nevertheless commonplace. One 1997 study of eighth-graders in eleven American cities discovered that nine percent were current gang members and that seventeen percent had been members at some point.[76] Another study reported that twenty-three percent of American Indian communities surveyed at the end of the twentieth century were dealing with youth gangs.[77] Such expressions of youth culture were featured in popular films such as *West Side Story* (1961), *A Clockwork Orange* (1971), *Colors* (1988) and *Boyz N the Hood* (1991). Involvement in gangs often drew on local loyalties and provided critical support, as James Howell's overview of American youth gangs suggests. The unprecedented visibility of female, immigrant, and native gangs in many Western nations at the close of the twentieth century further demonstrated the diversity of resistance to prevailing messages about suitable behaviors, as well as possible dangers to young people.[78]

FIGURE 2.4: *Quebec Family.* June 1959. National Film Board
Series—Four Families.

Children themselves routinely enforced ideas about who fully belonged
and who did not in the culture of childhood. They oscillated between behavior
that would win the approval of elders, such as sharing, cooperating, and com-
peting, and behavior that brought disapproval, such as teasing weak or disabled peers or those judged to be in some way "different."[79] Like British-Sikh
teens at the end of the twentieth century, many tried to find a workable blend
of old and new customs.[80] Within even seemingly homogeneous groupings,
hierarchies of leaders and followers, and bullies and victims, existed. While
pickup hockey, baseball, and soccer, not to mention, gossip, skipping contests,
tea parties, and even gangs might well be positive, they ranked youngsters.
Those who appeared to possess envied qualities as natural athletes or gifted
cartoonists or harmonica players or hunters and trappers might be popular.
The less fortunate learned repeatedly of their lesser value. Prejudice often hit
hard. In Vancouver in the 1920s and 1930s, Wo Soon Lee routinely endured
neighborhood white children chanting, "Look out! Chinky, chinky Chinaman! Stinky, stinky Chinaman!"[81] Despite reassuring classmates that she was
"a Canadian, from Saskatchewan," Fredelle Bruser Maynard's Jewishness
kept her frequently on the sidelines of the Anglo-Celtic Protestant majority.[82]
The 1997 murder of fourteen-year-old Indo-Canadian Reena Virk by other
socially marginal teens, like the suicides of gay/lesbian/bisexual/transgender
teens bullied by their peers, supply a similar corrective to any romanticization
of youth cultures.[83]

The modern era inspired, destroyed, and reconstructed communities of every sort. Girls and boys made central contributions to the multiple expressions of community over the course of the twentieth century. Many young people did so not simply in response to the demands of adults but to seek to realize their own ambitions, to slip away from any too-ready supervision, and to resist the will of others. This has not always been to positive effect, but truancy, shoplifting, and joyriding, while sharply different than the more socially approved options of academic or athletic prowess, also reflect young people's efforts to negotiate different realities for themselves.

CONCLUSIONS

Youngsters were centrally implicated in the great events that shaped the twentieth century. Wars displaced them, compromised their nutrition and health, made many of them vulnerable to sexual predators, and deprived them of elders. During the economic turbulence of the 1930s, children everywhere also struggled to make sense of brutal conditions and social disparities, and more than 200,000 American children became vagrants.[84] During the London Blitz of 1940–1941, they counted for one in ten deaths.[85] In 1945, Anne Frank's death in the Bergen-Belsen concentration camp captured the worst of the century's possibilities. Bomb shelters promised protection but also embodied the century's recurring threat. By the end of the century, some youngsters survived without families and in impaired communities, in migrant and refugee camps established in Australia, Great Britain, and the United States.[86] The collapse of the global economy in 2008 further added the peril in which many girls and boys everywhere lived.

Memories of twentieth-century childhoods regularly underscore the difference that social identity made to individual experience. Raised in Melbourne, Australia's eastern suburbs in the mid-1930s, Moira Lambert recalled happy, carefree hours of "perpetual sunshine" in which "we all implicitly accepted the fact that everybody lived in the station to which it had pleased God to call them."[87] For Native North Americans confronting the continuing European colonization, recollections might well differ. Tyendinaga elder Eva Maracle described an Ontario native reservation in Canada in the 1920s:

> the grown-ups always spoke the [Mohawk] language to one another, and they did to us kids until we went to school ... [later] they were afraid to talk to the children in Mohawk for fear of what might happen ... maybe the kids would be taken away, or punished.[88]

Despite vulnerabilities often made worse by adults, youngsters frequently learned to cope. Recollections of the Kamloops Indian Residential School in British Columbia, Canada in the 1920s and 1930s show that "students found time and space to express themselves and to produce a separate culture of their own within the school ... build around opposition to the severity of the rules and regulations guiding their lives."[89] As 2008 American presidential success story Barack Obama remembered, "At least on the basketball court, I could find a community of sorts, with an inner life all its own. It was there that I would make my closest white friends, on turf where blackness couldn't be a disadvantage."[90] Adele Wiseman, later a leading Canadian author, remembered how reading offered her a critical antidote to the 1930s and to the exclusions she experienced as a Jew growing up in Winnipeg, Manitoba.[91]

As adult elites attempted to direct youngsters over the century, urban neighborhoods supplied the mainstay of much experience. Most girls and boys learned who they were and might be through local individual and collective interactions. For the more fortunate, commonly those closest to the mainstream, life often seemed full of promise. Some disadvantages slowly lessened. White middle-class girls benefited notably from feminist struggles. When birth control became more readily available and feminism surged once more in the last decades of the twentieth century, girls emerged as savvy critics of their negative portrayals in popular culture.[92] Female cultures judged transgressive became especially visible—for example, in such popular 1990s TV productions as *Buffy the Vampire Slayer*—and provided a space where teens challenged patriarchy.[93] While so-called glass ceilings and other impediments, such as the beauty myth, with its encouragement of anorexia and bulimia, and recurring sexual violence, survived, girls could take hope in national leaders like Margaret Thatcher (United Kingdom), Kim Campbell (Canada), Vigdis Finnbogadottir (Iceland), Mary Robinson (Ireland), Helen Clark (New Zealand), and Angela Merkel (Germany) and in the dramatic increase in women's numbers in prestigious professions.

Girls and boys sometimes took leadership roles as community activists. In both world wars, thousands collected fats and metals to aid their soldiers; in peacetime many joined antiwar marches. The 1960s and 1970s mobilized teens in diverse community protests against injustice and inequality. In 1989, Canadian Severn Cullis-Suzuki, the nine-year-old daughter of a leading environmentalist, started the Environmental Children's Organization; at twelve she addressed the Rio Earth Summit and later received the UN Environment Program's Global 500 Award. In 1995, twelve-year-old Craig Kielburger and friends in Toronto founded Free the Children, the "largest network of children helping children through education." In 2006 he was awarded the World Children's Prize.[94] Such activists embodied recurring youthful efforts to make a difference in their world. Other children could not, however, so easily see themselves in the national imagination. By the new millennium, indigenous people were still reminding the West that good news for children depended on justice. While the identity politics of immigrant, racial, and sexual minorities was feared by the right (the very group that also threatened the child welfare gains of the twentieth century), it offered the respect and meaning that was crucial to children and youth everywhere.

CHAPTER THREE

Economy

LISA JACOBSON AND ERIKA RAPPAPORT

Economic change in the twentieth century has transformed how Europeans and North Americans have organized and conceived of family life. The ascendance of large-scale corporations and global capitalism, the economic crises of the Great Depression and the two world wars, and the growth of mass consumer societies gave rise to new habits of consumption and new patterns of work both inside and outside the home. All have had a profound bearing on relations of power and authority between husbands and wives, parents and children, and the family and the state. This chapter analyzes the ways in which economic and political change altered the experience and meanings of motherhood and fatherhood, love and marriage, and childhood and youth. It also explores how men, women, and children seized on economic change to renegotiate the boundaries between the family and the state and between family obligations and self-fulfillment.

Although race, class, gender, age, national cultures, and national political economies created vast differences in how families and children experienced economic change, several dominant trends in Western societies emerged in the twentieth century: the increasing participation of married women in the paid workforce and the decreasing participation of preadolescent wage earners; the erosion of boundaries between the public and private spheres; the growing distinctiveness of youth and children's culture; and the increasing competition between parents and the mass market over the socialization of children. These developments have often produced contradictory results.

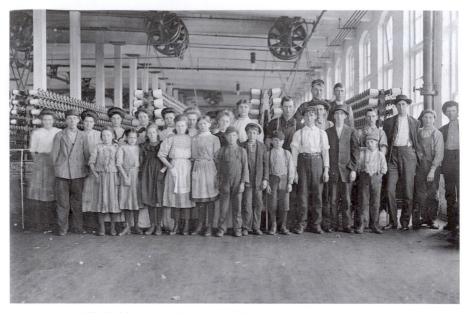

FIGURE 3.1: *Mill Children in Whitnel, North Carolina (1908)*. Lewis Hine, photographer. Records of the National Child Labor Committee, Library of Congress, Prints and Photographs Division (reproduction Number: LC-DIG-ncle-01552).

Women have assumed greater responsibility for breadwinning, but the unequal sexual division of labor within the household in many Western societies has stubbornly persisted—even in communist regimes that initially attempted to abolish the private family. Paradoxically, consumer culture has cemented family ties and divided family allegiances, simultaneously bolstering the cultural salience of the private family even as it has weakened the boundaries between the public and private spheres. It has united family members in shared pleasures and shared rituals, but it has also intensified conflicts over spending and drawn family members into their own separate worlds of leisure.

FAMILIES AND CHILDREN IN THE AGE OF INDUSTRIALIZATION AND MASS CONSUMPTION

Industrialization and the expansion of mass consumption in the early twentieth century sharpened class and racial distinctions in the ways families defined gender and generational roles, allocated resources, and raised children. The greater earning power of middle-class men enabled middle-class children to experience a prolonged childhood free from the responsibility of work. Middle-class women devoted themselves to raising children, and their unpaid labor as thrifty budgeters, housekeepers, cooks, and caregivers sustained the illusion that male breadwinners were solely responsible for the family's economic stability and social mobility. Most working-class families could not subsist on the earnings of a single male breadwinner and often relied on the wages of women and children to make ends meet. Many married working-class women engaged in some form of paid homework, which included taking in sewing and other finishing work. Wives' ability to stretch the family budget, barter goods and services, and access credit through pawnshops and local merchants sustained working-class families. However, many wives hid this labor from their husbands to protect the fiction of the solitary male provider. Arguments and domestic violence were all too frequent reactions to husbands learning of their wives' deceptions.[1]

The collective contributions of men, women, and children to the family economy also sustained millions of Europeans, Mexicans, and Asians who

FIGURE 3.2: *Doll, Newberry, South Carolina (1908)*. This doll was made by a five-year-old child while playing in the knitting mill where her mother worked. Lewis Hine, photographer. Records of the National Child Labor Committee, Library of Congress, Prints and Photographs Division (reproduction Number: LC-DIG-ncle-01475).

immigrated to the United States between 1890 and 1920. Industrialization, the commercialization of agriculture, and a global agricultural depression had displaced many peasant farmers and skilled craftsmen from their home countries, but the unskilled jobs in factories, sweatshops, and domestic service that awaited them in the so-called Land of Dollars required families to pool the earnings of several family members.[2] Although the challenges of adapting to an industrial economy and new culture strained family relationships, recent immigrants developed strategies to preserve ethnic customs and traditional gender and generational hierarchies. Italian immigrants, for example, maintained patriarchal authority by making sure that wives only accepted work such as making artificial flowers or sewing dolls that could be done at home.[3] The conventional balance of power between parents and children, however, was more easily disrupted because children learned English and American customs more quickly and often questioned the relevance of Old World ways.[4]

Racism magnified the challenge of adapting to a new economic order in the United States. Black sharecroppers, eager to create an independent family life denied them under slavery, attempted to keep both women and children out of the fields so that mothers could devote more time to childcare and housework and children could attend school. Some succeeded in preserving a traditional division of labor, but limited returns on crops and exorbitant interest rates kept many indebted to white planters and local merchants. Like many immigrant families, most black families relied on the economic contributions of both the husband and wife as well as networks of extended kin and churches for mutual assistance.[5]

Much as immigration to the United States disrupted traditional power relations within families, internal migration in European countries threatened to undermine the hierarchal structure of the peasant family. In late-imperial Russia, for example, huge numbers of primarily male peasants migrated to the new factories and cities, leaving their families in the countryside. Local authorities reported that "when the junior members of the family become the main breadwinners in the peasant household, their role in the family also changes. Elders have already ceased to enjoy the absolute authority they wielded in earlier times."[6] Many elders worried that newly independent wage earners learned new consumer habits in the towns, spending unnecessary income on luxurious clothes, shoes, and drink.

Gender ideology and the particular nature of labor markets had a profound effect on wage structures, definitions of skill, as well as attitudes toward male breadwinning and women's participation in the paid workforce. European countries that industrialized early and rapidly, such as England and Germany, saw a greater increase of women in the formal economy than in southern European nations such as Italy and Spain.[7] In northern Germany, for example, rapid industrialization and severe labor shortages in the textile industry encouraged a relatively high proportion of married women to enter the paid labor force. In 1899 married women made up nearly a third of the female factory workforce. Transformations in the American economy also brought increasing numbers of women into the paid workforce. Previously most women had found employment as domestic servants, agricultural laborers, loom operators in textile mills, and teachers, but the rise of big business, the expansion of factories, and technological innovation created more jobs and new fields for women. Women joined the workforce as retail clerks, typists, and bookkeepers—jobs that offered better pay and conditions than factory work or domestic service—as greater numbers graduated from high school with the requisite literacy and math skills. By 1920, in the United States women comprised nearly half of all clerical workers, and the number employed as domestics had dropped sharply from sixty percent of all employed women in 1870 to twenty percent in 1920. Increasing numbers of college-educated women became social workers, factory inspectors, nurses, home economists, and librarians. A few broke into the ranks of medicine, journalism, and the law. Most women in the United States, however, entered the workforce as unmarried adolescents and left upon marriage—a testament to the broad acceptance of the dictum that married women belonged in the home. Employers paid women about half of what men received for the same work because they assumed, in keeping with breadwinning ideology, that women worked merely for so-called pin money—money for frivolous purchases like a new hat—and were not required to help out with family expenses. The pattern of women leaving work upon marriage reinforced the perception that they were not serious members of the labor force, thus providing additional justification for their lower pay.[8]

The influx of women into the labor force generated considerable sexual antagonism and new efforts to shore up the male breadwinner. Working-class men, like their middle-class counterparts, subscribed to idea that men should be able to provide the sole economic support for their families. In the United States, unions campaigned for a family wage large enough to provide a decent standard of living for their family without the supplemental wages of women and children.[9] The German labor movement went one step further and supported state-sponsored efforts to encourage domesticity and motherhood. The conservative government limited child and female employment, extended maternity leave, and established housekeeping schools for working-girls—all in the name of protecting the *familienväter* or family father.[10] Such reforms established a model followed in much of Europe and maintained in welfare and labor legislation throughout twentieth-century German history.

Ironically, the idea that men and women properly occupied separate spheres of home and work eventually helped to legitimize women's participation in the workforce. Defenders of women office workers, for example, argued that women's nature fitted them for jobs that demanded subservience and unflinching devotion to their boss in much the way a wife served her husband. Women's office work seemed even less threatening as men came to see such jobs as dead ends rather than as stepping stones for higher positions. Describing their secretaries as "office wives" or "office housekeepers," some businessmen even argued that office work prepared women for marriage and motherhood by teaching them organizational skills and general lessons about human nature.[11] Social workers, teachers, nurses, and even physicians emphasized that these jobs were natural extensions of their roles as mothers and sympathetic caregivers. While some women professionals stressed their intellectual equality with men, the language of separate spheres created the shortest path to legitimacy.[12]

World War I brought more women into the workforce and into higher paying jobs than ever before. By 1918 the British workforce was thirty-eight percent female, a fifty percent increase during the war years.[13] A new iconography of the nurse, female munitions worker, and transport driver celebrated women's capabilities and redefined citizenship as derived from one's patriotism rather than from gender or property.[14] However, these advances were tempered by a conservative gender ideology that represented women as wives and mothers who had sacrificed their men to the war effort. Stories of atrocities committed against women and children emphasized women's need of male protection, while the figure of the mourning widow legitimized new forms of social insurance and became one of the lasting ways the war was remembered. Thus, women's war work was minimized by the idea that they worked only for the duration and by an ever-present cult of motherhood and female sacrifice.[15]

The war nevertheless politicized domestic labor and consumption, especially in places like Germany and Russia where severe food and other shortages forced women to stand in long lines and petition the state to help them feed their families.[16] Female-directed food strikes erupted in many nations, and in some places these street protests helped overthrow rigid autocratic states that could not adequately provide for their people. The war hastened the demise of the domestic servant and transformed the middle-class wife into the modern-day consumer housewife who did most of her own household labor and therefore was now eager to use labor-saving technologies, packaged foods, and birth control, even if these advances did not actually reduce her work within the home.

While World War I valorized the politicized consumer housewife, it also fueled a growing backlash against the New Woman, an unmarried and glamorous consumer who eagerly embraced new fashions and identities. Some women could now live outside of marriage and the nuclear family and support themselves by their labor.[17] Early twentieth-century popular culture minimized the threat these women posed by portraying working girls as savvy consumers who dreamed of marriage and family.[18] Conservatives, however, tended to see the New Woman in a different light: as desexed or oversexed and uninterested in the institution of marriage.[19] Soldiers returning from a war ostensibly fought to preserve the sanctity of the family were particularly troubled by the continued specter of women as competitors in the workforce. In Germany, the loss of the war, European territories, and overseas colonies led to a crisis of masculinity and provided fertile ground for the growth of a particularly misogynistic culture determined to eradicate the New Woman of the Weimar era. After the Nazi takeover in 1933, the New Woman was increasingly seen as a foreign import overly devoted to French fashions and American mass culture.[20] A similar rhetoric emerged in Mussolini's Italy as the fascists presented themselves as defenders of Italian womanhood against the threat of the "crisis woman," the "False and alien ... product of Paris, Hollywood, and Italy's biggest cities, Milan and Rome."[21]

Much like the New Woman, the child consumer and the child laborer became lightning rods for broader concerns about the sanctity of the family and the authority of the market. Children's participation in the economy as wage earners and consumers raised troubling questions about their vulnerability to commercial exploitation. Middle-class reformers pressed for compulsory education laws and anti-child labor laws, hoping to extend the sheltered childhood ideal to the working class by keeping children in school, off the streets, and out of factories. Although many unions opposed child labor, a position consistent with their demands for a family wage, some working-class parents saw child labor as crucial not only to the family economy but also to children's training and future prospects. They resented such laws as an unjust interference with parental rights.[22] In the late nineteenth and early twentieth century, several European nations and states in the United States mandated school attendance and banned child labor, but prohibitions against child labor did not become federal law in the United States until 1938.[23]

Children's spending also became a focal point of family conflict and public concern. In the early twentieth century, wage-earning children in working-class and immigrant families turned over most, if not all, of their pay to their parents but retained some say in household spending decisions. Working-class and immigrant parents often permitted wage-earning sons to retain a small portion of their pay for discretionary spending, but they typically required wage-earning daughters to hand over all their earnings in an unopened pay envelope.[24] Most children complied with these expectations, but not solely out of duty or under threat of punishment. Parents rewarded working children by allowing them greater input in family spending decisions and a larger clothing budget, and by subjecting them less to physical punishment than their nonworking siblings.[25] The bargaining power of wage-earning sons and daughters was especially high in families headed by single mothers, who depended even more on their children's income for economic survival. Some working-class parents, however, disciplined wage-earning adolescents who asserted too much economic independence by reporting them to the juvenile courts for not contributing enough to the family's income and for spending their earnings foolishly.[26]

While working-class children leveraged their economic capital to bargain for a greater share of family resources, middle-class children relied on their cultural capital within increasingly child-centered and democratic households to achieve similar ends. In the 1920s and 1930s, mass marketers noted that middle-class children enjoyed greater assertiveness and spending freedom (thanks partly to allowances) and began to target children and young adults through magazine and radio advertising.[27] Some commodities, such as cigarettes, became especially associated with modernity and youthful rebellion. Although the health risks of smoking were as yet not well known, many still sought to suppress the spread of this habit by forming groups such as Britain's Hygienic League and Union for the Suppression of Juvenile Smoking.[28] Despite, or perhaps because of, such efforts, young men and women began to associate the purchase and use of some commodities as a sign of their newfound independence and maturity.

Mass marketers recognized children and adolescents as consumers in their own right, but they also enlisted their pester power to influence family spending even on big tickets items like radios, cars, and bicycles. Although wary of alienating parental goodwill, advertisers also shamelessly supplied children with sales ammunition that appealed to parental concerns. Child rearing experts recommended allowances as a means to regulate children's stepped-up consumer demands and teach them to spend wisely within fixed limits. Some adolescents, in fact, preferred not to have an allowance, calculating, as some Muncie, Indiana high school girls did, that "you can get more without one."[29]

THE GREAT DEPRESSION AND WORLD WAR II

The national and international crises of the Great Depression and World War II greatly disrupted traditional family patterns. Though there were similar problems in the United States and European nations, responses to economic failure and falling birthrates diverged in these years. In the United States, unemployment hovered between 15 and 20 percent throughout the 1930s, reaching a staggering 25 percent during the depths of the crisis in 1933. Many working-class men now depended on wives and children as the sole wage earners and suffered deep humiliation from their loss of status as the family's chief breadwinner. In the face of prolonged male unemployment, patriarchal authority began to break down. Family relationships became strained, with mothers nagging at fathers, parents nagging at children, and children refusing to obey their unemployed fathers. Although divorce rates declined in the 1930s, the desertion rate rose, and many unhappy couples stayed married because they could not afford to do otherwise.[30]

Some women who assumed primary breadwinning roles also began to assume a more dominant role in the family. As one Polish wife explained, "You know, who make the money he is the boss." She reported that the children were fonder of her than their father, a point affirmed by her daughter: "I certainly like my mother lots more, for she buys me everything."[31] Breadwinning mothers may have gained their children's approval in the short run, but this was not a lasting legacy. In fact, children who grew up in families where traditional gender roles

FIGURE 3.3: *How Jimmy Got His Bike*. Cartoon in *American Boy* (December 1939). Like many juvenile advertisers, children's magazines sanctioned the practice of lobbying parents for goods by offering children tips on bargaining strategies, as this cartoon does.

were disrupted were more likely as adults to embrace more traditional gender arrangements. In the 1950s, surveys of children who lived through the Depression found that less than half of the daughters had positive views of mothers who had assumed dominant roles in the home during the 1930s. By contrast, eighty-six percent approved of their mothers' wage earning so long as fathers retained their authority as family decision makers. This study suggests how the 1930s set the stage for two seemingly contradictory postwar trends in the United States: the resurgence of domesticity and the increased participation of married women in the workforce. Although the Depression appeared to generate little excitement for gender role reversals, it may have produced greater acceptance of married women as supplemental rather than primary breadwinners.[32]

Although married women sometimes provided the sole source of economic support for their families, in the face of public hostility to married women's employment, several states, cities, and school boards in the United States prohibited or limited the employment of married women. In 1932, 1,600 married women lost their federal jobs thanks to a new federal law prohibiting the employment of married women if the government already employed their husbands. New Deal programs reinforced the idea that government could best strengthen the family by employing men and keeping women home. Men filled the vast majority of jobs in work relief programs, which men accepted as an entitlement, while relief for single mothers, typically cash payments and food stamps, remained stigmatized as welfare and did little to promote female economic independence. Ironically, the sex-segregated labor markets that had long disadvantaged women actually benefited them during the Depression. Women rarely displaced male workers, but they did hold onto their jobs more often than men because pink-collar jobs in offices and service industries disappeared more slowly and reappeared more quickly than the jobs in male-dominated sectors such as steel and automobiles.[33]

During World War II, public hostility toward married women workers and independent working women eroded in the United States. Instead of barring women from jobs, the government now actively recruited them to take so-called men's jobs and supported equal pay for women. Economic gains for women were considerable, especially for black, Mexican, and Asian women who left jobs as domestic servants for better-paying factory jobs. Many women gained satisfaction and a greater sense of their capabilities from working and left their war jobs reluctantly but determined to see their daughters achieve greater independence.[34] Although World War II transformed women's self-conceptions, it did not represent a dramatic change in public attitudes toward women and work. Government propaganda cast women's work as a temporary crisis measure and patriotic duty, not a permanent transformation of gender roles, and pressured women to give up their jobs for returning soldiers. The government also made little effort to ease women's dual burden of work and childcare. Most of the 1.5 million working mothers with children under the age of ten relied on family members for childcare, but a survey done by the Women's Bureau in 1944 found that sixteen percent of mothers in war industries had no child-care arrangements at all. The federal government did not fund day care centers for defense workers until 1943, and even then only provided space for ten percent of the children who needed such care. The United States lagged far behind Great Britain, where the government constructed central kitchens and public nurseries, and required employers to give women workers an afternoon off each week to do the family shopping. The U.S. government's failure to provide adequate support services to relieve the double burden of wage earning and child care underscored the continued ambivalence about working mothers and had a detrimental effect on the war effort. The rate of absenteeism among women workers was fifty percent higher than that of men, and their turnover twice as high.[35]

In the United States, the experience of deprivation during the Great Depression and World War II paradoxically strengthened the public's association of the American way with consumer abundance and a sheltered childhood. The Fair Labor Standards Act (1938) abolished child labor and enshrined the ideal of sheltered childhood in law—yet the hardships of economic depression and a world war meant that a sheltered childhood, with all its implications of protected innocence and freedom from worry, remained out of reach for many children. Child experts, bolstered by the New Deal's emphasis on boosting purchasing power, promoted children's allowances and consumer training even more aggressively. Now the excessively thrifty child, not the spendthrift, aroused suspicions of psychological maladjustment.[36] Wartime advertising and government propaganda also raised expectations for a postwar future of consumer abundance, even as Americans scrimped and saved to buy war bonds and conserve scarce resources. Norman Rockwell's *Freedom from Want* painting of an extended family gathered to enjoy a lavish Thanksgiving dinner became the war's perhaps most iconic illustration of the family-centered, consumer-oriented lifestyle that American soldiers were fighting to defend.[37]

In Europe, the collapse of markets, the experience or threat of revolution, and the looming possibility of war made the interwar years a period of prolonged economic hardship and political instability. Europeans began to worry about the threat of Americanization, and many associated the New Woman, the Jew, and certain forms of mass culture with the growing hegemony of U.S. companies and international commerce.[38] Governments, whether liberal, socialist, or fascist, worried about dropping birthrates and began experimenting with social policies designed to reinforce the family, the economy, and the nation. Organized labor and feminist movements as well as conservative pronatalists enacted measures to improve the quantity and quality of the population. Between the 1930s and 1950s, European governments instituted programs for prenatal care, maternity benefits, day care, subsidized food and housing programs, and state-funded child allowances—payments to parents dependent on the number of children they produced. Governments typically did not pay these often-modest benefits for the first child and sometimes paid the father rather than the mother. Such policies boosted income and domestic demand without increasing wage rates. They did not stem the tide of declining birthrates or markedly change the number of women employed in the formal economy.[39]

In Great Britain, the 1920s witnessed the collapse of older textile, steel, and mining industries and intense labor struggles. The short-lived Labour governments of 1924 and 1929–1931 accomplished little, but women achieved a few striking advances. Feminists intensified their push for some form of state endowment for women and children but were divided over whether a family allowance would pose a threat to the family wage. Some even argued that paying women for motherhood might deprive fathers of the incentive to work.[40] During the interwar period, the image of the starving, overworked British housewife became a major focus of public debate and ironically helped legitimize the expansion of social welfare and certain forms of mass commerce and leisure, such as paid holidays and the holiday camp, an affordable form of the family vacation that appealed to working-class notions of community and collectivity.[41]

In contrast to Great Britain's troubled but relatively stable political system, other European governments could not survive failing economies. Germans experienced an acute housing shortage in the 1920s and the collapse of the mark wiped out middle-class savings and faith in a liberal state. Though diplomatic measures stabilized the European economy, the crash of 1929 led to skyrocketing unemployment and eventually to the Nazi seizure of power. Nazi family and economic policy built on trends of the Weimar era. In the 1920s, the German state and advertisers had already promoted a profitable and patriotic body culture.[42] In Nazi Germany, however, racism and sexism became fused as the government worshiped the Aryan mother and punished those who did not conform to "scientifically approved" forms of racial health. Legislation, prizes, and punishments forced women to direct their efforts toward *Kinder, Küche, Kirche* (children, kitchen, church).[43] In 1934 the newly created State Health

Offices with Departments for Gene and Race Care carried out a program of forced sterilization of people deemed unfit to have children. The 1935 Law for the Protection of the Hereditary Health of the German People required people to obtain a certificate from the state before they married that ensured they did not have any infectious diseases or hereditary illnesses. Also in 1935, the Nuremburg Laws forbade marriage between Aryans and non-Aryans. Nazis forced Jewish families from their jobs, schools, and social clubs, boycotted their shops, and subjected them to state-organized violence.[44]

Family policies in the Soviet Union boldly reimagined the relationship between the private family and the state in the interest of promoting gender equality and marital satisfaction. In the early 1920s, the new Soviet Union tried to create an entirely new family and economy. As one Soviet sociologist wrote in 1929, "[The family] will be sent to a museum of antiquities so that it can rest next to the spinning wheel and the bronze axe, by the horse drawn carriage, the steam engine, and the wired telephone."[45] Indeed, as early as October 1918, the Bolsheviks ratified a code on marriage, the family, and guardianship that encouraged women's equality and a "withering away" of the family.[46] The Bolsheviks argued that capitalism had placed women's family and working demands in tension and that under socialism household labor would move into the public sphere and cease to be a woman's private burden. Once that happened, theorists predicted marriage would become satisfying and based on shared interests and mutual affection. The Bolsheviks did not encourage men to do their share of women's work, but instead rewarded women who did "men's" work outside of the home and dramatically altered the legal framework for marriage, divorce, and inheritance. In 1920, the Soviet Union became the first country in the world to give women a legal and cost-free means to terminate a pregnancy. Pervasive famine and economic ruin, however, hindered efforts to create gender equality during the early years of the revolution. Some critics argued that the new family legislation undermined the peasant economy, while others noted it allowed men to abandon their families. As one critic put it, "We made a revolution in such a manner that it benefited only men. Women have remained in a tragic position."[47] Nevertheless, rapid industrialization dramatically increased economic opportunities for women, who comprised forty-two percent of the industrial workforce by 1937. This change led party leaders to introduce more facilities for childcare and socialized dining. In the mid-1930s, Soviets enacted additional laws to strengthen the family and combat the problem of unsupervised, out-of-control children who dabbled in petty crime and mingled with mature criminals. New laws reinstituted abortion bans and forced men to support and control their families. As one scholar has put it, the "Party designated the family, along with the militia, and the courts ... to enforce social order on the streets. Far from withering away, the family was becoming an indispensable unit in the state's control of its citizenry."[48]

World War II affected the European family and economy even more than World War I had. Once again women entered the paid work force in record numbers; a few countries, including Britain and the Soviet Union, even conscripted women into military service as soldiers and in support positions.[49] In Britain, an estimated eighty percent of married women and ninety percent of single women joined the war effort. Throughout the war, advertisers and government propaganda reminded housewives that their small economies and everyday purchases had tremendous political, perhaps even global, repercussions. Extreme food and housing shortages necessitated early and widespread rationing and encouraged a culture of bartering, hoarding, and making do. Women's skills aided survival as the war eradicated any secure divisions between home and war zones. Sexual favors became important currency for women with little else to bargain for food and shelter, and in occupied zones rape became a full-fledged weapon of war.[50] These experiences intensely politicized everyday life and ultimately ushered in much more extensive and thorough change in the nature of the European economy.

POSTWAR YEARS

The disruptions and strains of the Depression and the war sowed the seeds of postwar gender conservatism. Returning to a family ideal centered on a breadwinning father, a stay-at-home mother, and children's happiness offered security and fulfillment to those who had struggled economically during the Depression and had lost loved ones or been separated from family members during the war. French president Charles de Gaulle captured the mood of the moment when he urged women to produce in ten years "twelve million beautiful babies for France."[51] Postwar prosperity—fueled by economic expansion, North America's competitive advantage over war-ravaged Europe, unionization, and rising real wages and home ownership rates—buttressed these developments in the United States. By the mid-1950s, sixty percent of Americans had attained a middle-class standard of living, in contrast to only thirty-one percent just before the Great Depression. For the first time in U.S. history, the family patterns of the middle class and working class converged, as many working-class men earned a family wage that enabled wives to opt out of the paid workforce. The federal government bolstered economic security by subsidizing low-interest rate home loans, funding college education for returning veterans through the GI Bill, and easing the burden of elder care through Social Security and Medicare.[52]

The black middle class also expanded dramatically in the second half of the twentieth century, thanks to improved job opportunities during and after the war, civil rights legislation, affirmative action, and antipoverty legislation. Between 1940 and 1970, five million African-Americans, many displaced agricultural workers, left the rural South for Southern and Northern cities, where they found better jobs and schooling, purchased homes, and sent their children to college. Despite these postwar gains, many blacks remained concentrated in the lowest income brackets and lowest-paying jobs. Continuing job discrimination created black unemployment rates twice those of whites. Because blacks and Latinos were last hired in unionized industries, they were often first laid off when the economy soured. Racist housing policies and lending practices excluded racial minorities from suburbs where housing values were likely to rise.[53]

In certain respects, the dramatic increase of married women who worked outside the home seemed to belie postwar gender conservatism. In Europe, many women remained in the workforce simply because their husbands could not fully support them and because rising divorce rates necessitated some women to support themselves. By 1970, more European women were in the paid labor force than in the 1940s, though many still believed that doing so was a necessary evil. In some countries, such as England and Belgium, women made up nearly forty percent of the industrial workforce.[54] In the United States many women worked part-time in pink-collar jobs and justified their work not as a quest for self-fulfillment but as a sacrifice for family well-being and children's advancement that would fund children's college education, the family vacation, or perhaps the second car. However conservatively justified, married women's larger presence in the paid workforce marked an important transformation: families no longer associated their work with being lower class or in dire financial straits.[55] Women's paid work, however, did not reduce expectations that women bore primary responsibility for managing the home and caring for children. Postwar advice literature even warned fathers not to help too much with the dishes or caring for infants because children needed "manly men and womanly women" as proper role models.[56]

The spread of affluence and permissive childrearing and the growing economic clout of teenage consumers made the baby boom generation an especially appealing target for advertising. Radio and magazines remained the favored venue in the mid-1950s for reaching teenage consumers, but the advent of television gave advertisers a new means to reach children en masse. The postwar years also saw greater age segmentation within the children's market, as mass marketers developed scientific techniques for discerning the interests and desires of teens, preteens, and grade school children.[57] Many young Europeans and Americans consciously adopted a personal style and forms of consumption to reject the politics and lifestyle of their parents' generation. As Ray Gosling, the television broadcaster, filmmaker, and gay rights activist, recalled, "We wanted a new world, where you weren't hidebound by class and etiquette and by having to follow your betters and where you could respond to basic instincts and have some fun and be free like the Americans were."[58]

Between the mid-1950s and mid-1970s, Europe's economy boomed, and even places like Italy became a mass consumer society, thanks partly to the Marshall Plan, which aided economic recovery, falling birthrates, and state welfare. Governments rebuilt their cities, economies, and their populations by

FIGURE 3.4: *The Children's Hour—1951 Style*. Teddy Hoff, 9, a Hollywood, California schoolboy, and his friend Paula Simonton, also 9, watch space-suited explorers on television. Teddy wears a space patrol haircut, a new fad of the growing number of space drama fans. Eddie Hoff, photographer. Shades of L.A. Archives/Los Angeles Public Library. http://jpgl.lapl.org/pics46/00042887.jpg. Courtesy of Los Angeles Public Library.

promising citizens sweeping welfare provisions, such as subsidized housing, free health care and schooling, family allowances, and other maternity benefits. In postwar West Germany, for example, child allowances or *kindergeld* encouraged women to stay home and produce more children and defrayed the costs of rearing a family to the next generation.[59] Moreover, the rational consumer housewife who was efficient and thrifty and made proper shopping choices became positioned as the key to economic recovery.[60]

POSTMODERN FAMILIES

During the 1960s and 1970s, the so-called traditional family began to lose its supremacy. Divorce rates climbed, birthrates fell, and more men and women delayed marriage. By the 1970s, formerly deviant family patterns—working mothers, divorce, premarital sex, and lengthy bachelorhoods for men and women—began to affect a majority of the population. Since 1970 European fertility rates have fallen below replacement levels, and out-of-wedlock births have risen sharply. In 1997 nearly one-quarter of all children in the European Union were born outside of marriage. Countries with the most extensive welfare states, such as Sweden, Iceland, Denmark, and Finland, registered the highest rates.

Some critics, particularly those on the left, have argued that the logic of consumerism—with its emphasis on creating new wants and discontents—weakened commitments to family and contributed to rising divorce rates.[61] Conservatives in the United States blamed feminism for rising divorce rates, working mothers, and the liberalization of sexual norms, but these trends preceded feminism's resurgence in the late 1960s and 1970s. Married women's increased participation in the workforce began in the 1950s when many discovered they needed two incomes to fund the consumer lifestyle promoted in the media. Dual incomes became even more essential in the 1970s and thereafter, thanks to rising inflation and declining real wages.[62] Indeed, a majority of Americans experienced a family wage for only a short period in U.S. history—the two and half decades following World War II. Some couples adopted a more equitable sexual division of labor within the home, but in many families, women's work outside the home little altered existing arrangements or notions of family obligation. Men proved more willing to give up exclusive breadwinning than to relinquish its privileges: being excused from housework and the day-to-day childcare. To be sure, late-twentieth-century husbands changed more diapers and washed more laundry than their predecessors had, but the sexual division of child rearing and household labor remained far from even.[63] Most Americans have focused on private solutions to the problem of the so-called Double Day, but Europeans have more widely embraced public solutions to this dilemma, including flextime, day care, and paid maternity and paternity leaves.

The movement of manufacturing jobs in North America and Europe to Asia and Latin America in the last quarter of the twentieth century had a major impact on families at the bottom of the economic ladder. During the mid-1970s, deindustrialization in Northern and Midwestern U.S. cities eliminated many manufacturing jobs that had fostered economic advancement during the 1940s, 1950s, and 1960s. The steel and auto industries, where racial minorities had made the biggest postwar gains, were especially hard hit. Between 1979 and 1984, half the black workers in durable-goods manufacturing in the Great Lakes region lost their jobs. The loss of blue-collar jobs also removed important avenues to social mobility for Latinos and other racial minorities. A range of adaptive family strategies, including extended kinship networks and collective child rearing, sustained lower-class black families through economic hardship. Strong kinship ties made African Americans more likely than other urban Americans to care for elders, paupers, and orphans instead of placing them institutions but also led families to sacrifice their own individual economic mobility in the interest of helping extended kin.[64]

Mass marketing to children and youth became more aggressive and intrusive as companies dispatched market researchers to teenagers' homes and fourth graders' slumber parties to learn what makes kids spend.[65] One mark of the pervasiveness of children's consumer culture is its increasingly global scale. Children in Shanghai, China were sufficiently acculturated to consumer abundance that they readily grasped the moral dilemma of *Toy Story*—a "Disney tale about the conflicts aroused when a new glossy purchase replaced an old favorite." Children's uneven access to consumer culture, however, has sharpened divisions of race and class among children even as consumer culture has broadened children's range of common cultural references. Unlike their middle-class counterparts, who generally regarded allowances as discretionary income to spend as they pleased, poorer children understood the trials of making ends meet. Knowing the costs of rent, groceries, and their birthday gifts, inner-city black children spent their allowances on basic necessities like socks and school supplies and used the remainder for inexpensive snacks.[66]

Consumer culture has created new challenges for parents who want to provide children with a childhood sheltered from corrupting influences. Both conservatives and liberals have innovated new family arrangements to limit children's exposure to consumer culture, including schooling children at home, restricting their media consumption, and embracing countercultural simplicity as an alternative to mainstream consumer culture. The Christian conservatives who currently dominate home schooling in the United States might seem miles apart from the secular countercultural leftists who pioneered home schooling in the 1960s, but both groups share a disdain for mainstream consumer culture and a desire to shield children from acquisitive values and degrading images of sex and violence.[67] To a remarkable degree, parents have actively consented to the dramatic expansion of children's consumer freedoms. Some argue that children's expanding consumer freedoms compensated for the increasing discipline demanded of children from vigorously enforced school attendance and lengthy homework assignments.[68] Others contend that parents willingly acceded to an expanding children's consumer culture because it allowed adults to participate vicariously in the playful, even primitive, pleasures of childhood that adults had long ago learned to repress and control.[69] Parents have also yielded to an expanding children's consumer culture because doing so has made it easier for mothers, especially those who work outside the home, to accomplish the daily tasks of rearing children and managing a home. Busy mothers have often relied on toys, videos, and television to keep children occupied and entertained while they cooked and cleaned. Some parents, especially those in two-income households, buy their kids more things to assuage their own guilt for not spending more time with their kids.[70]

Over the course of the twentieth century economic change has transformed relations of power and authority in the family in both subtle and striking ways. Although the experience of economic change varied widely by class, race, immigrant status, age, and gender, some broad generalizations apply. Hierarchies of gender and generation have softened and sometimes broken down as married women entered the paid workforce in greater numbers and as children and youth embraced consumer culture to try on new identities and articulate peer-based interests and aspirations. Moments of economic crisis have dramatically transformed the relationship between the family and the state, though paradoxically many interwar state interventions further buttressed gender conservatism. New Deal work relief programs, the Nazi emphasis on *Kinder, Küche, Kirche*, pronatalist programs in liberal welfare states—all aimed to shore up faltering families by restoring the primacy of breadwinning fathers and domestic mothers. Communist governments set out to eradicate the private family and the gender inequalities it perpetuated, but Soviet women, despite achieving some equality in politics and the workplace, suffered from extreme shortages of everyday commodities and continued to labor under the double burden. Wars have produced even more dramatic change as rapid economic and military mobilization drew unprecedented numbers of married women into previously male occupations and prompted experiments with state-funded daycare and other programs to ease women's dual burden of breadwinning and child rearing. Such wartime changes were sometimes cast as temporary expedients, but the doors to bolder change only partially closed. Even as a more expansive state and consumer culture have eroded the boundaries between the public and the private spheres, the private family has retained its cultural salience—in part because it remains a primary site of ritual and identity formation and comfort as well as strife. The dilemmas that families confronted at the beginning of the twentieth century—the challenges of balancing work and family while making ends meet and the challenges of protecting children while still preparing them for the outside world—remained unresolved at the end.

CHAPTER FOUR

Environment

PAMELA RINEY-KEHRBERG

The twentieth century was one of transformation in the relationship of Western children to the environments in which they lived. At the beginning of the century, many or most children in the United States, as well as a large number of European children, lived in rural or nearly rural village environments, in intimate and daily contact with the natural world. By the century's end, the vast majority no longer lived in close contact with the natural world, and their homes were no longer on farms or in villages, but in suburbs and cities. Gone was a regular and intense experience of nature and its effects. In its place was a nature vastly mediated by distance, development, and technology. Children, for the most part, no longer lived in natural environments but became observers of and visitors to them.

The years of the twentieth century saw enormous changes in the ways that people lived. Increasingly, adults worked in factories and other employments outside of agriculture, and they brought their families to live with them in urban environments. Although many urban developers incorporated parks and green spaces into their plans, relative to the countryside there was a conspicuous absence of trees, grass, underbrush, and other wild spaces, especially in crowded inner city locations. People's distance from nature grew in other ways as well. Urban housing stretched upward toward the sky. Adoption of gas and electric lighting meant that families relied less and less on natural sources of illumination. In the United States in particular, central heating challenged the winter cold. Nature and its effects

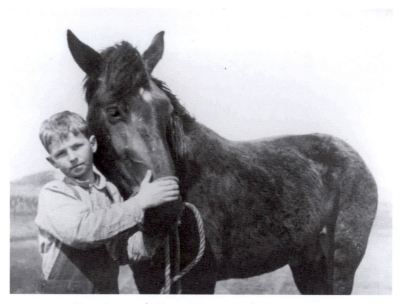

FIGURE 4.1: *Farm Boy with Horse.* Courtesy of Mary P. Riney.

receded farther and farther into the distance. Nevertheless, at the dawn of
the century, many children still lived on farms or in villages, in close daily
contact with natural environments. The land was all around them, their
families often made a living working the land, and nature often determined
the degree of economic success or failure that a family would experience in
a given year.

FARM CHILDHOOD: GIRLS AT WORK

Farm girls generally spent most of their working lives in and around the home,
aiding their mothers with the many chores associated with homemaking.
Nonetheless, they could hardly escape close and daily contact with the effects
of nature. Girls pumped and hauled water into the house. They gathered fire-
wood and kindling. They ventured into the garden and the barn, to aid with
fruit and vegetable production, as well as gathering milk and eggs. Girls hung
laundry on lines outdoors, often even in the coldest of weather. Although work
varied with ethnicity, most girls spent some time out of doors, working in the
fields (German and Scandinavian immigrant girls in the United States more
so than the native born). Girls on new farms in sparsely settled areas often
spent a good deal of their time working out of doors.[1] Because she lived in

an undeveloped frontier area, Viola Pospeshill, whose family homesteaded in western Nebraska, spent more time out of doors than the average girl. In a 1912 letter to a children's publication, she described her work: "when we first came to our ranch we had to herd cattle to keep them away from the stacks of hay. I always rode a white horse named Daisy."[2] Viola Pospeshill's herding, however, involved closer contact with nature than many girls experienced in their daily working lives.

FARM CHILDHOOD: BOYS AT WORK

Farm boys' working lives, on the other hand, almost always involved close and daily contact with the natural world. Whereas girls generally worked inside with their mothers, boys usually worked outside with their fathers. In the spring, summer, and early fall, it would not have been unusual for a boy to spend nearly all of his waking hours outside, working. Boys hauled water, cut and hauled wood, did chores in the barn, and attended to the fields. They plowed, planted, cultivated, and harvested. They, like Viola, often worked as herders, sometimes staying out with the cattle overnight.[3] Arthur Single, whose family ranched near North Platte, Nebraska, wrote to the editors of the *Nebraska Farmer* about his daily life: "This spring we had to herd cows. We had lots of fun too. We have an old cow that I like to ride. When I first got on her she ran a long ways, and I tried to round up the cows but I could not do it. We have another old cow that I tried to ride, but my brother twisted her tail and she pitched me off. It made me mad."[4] Single, like many boys, could not resist turning his work into an opportunity for play. Hunting, fishing, and trapping were among the favorite activities of many rural boys. These pastimes allowed boys to intermingle work with play, all in a pleasing natural environment. Families relied on the results of these hunting and fishing activities for food, and boys often turned trapping into an opportunity to earn some precious spending money. Each of these pastimes afforded boys the opportunity to spend many unsupervised hours out of doors, often in the winter, when others were at home, huddled around the stove. They learned about wildlife habitat and habits and became deeply familiar with the world around them.[5]

FARM CHILDREN AT PLAY

In their play, especially, both boys and girls immersed themselves in the natural world. Farm homes were generally small, and mothers were often occupied with their own chores. When given the opportunity to play, children generally amused themselves with unsupervised outdoor pursuits. Boys and girls valued the opportunity to explore, hoping to find their own personal hideaways and other treasures in the land around them. When the horses were done working for the day, children often enjoyed horseback riding. They played with domestic animals and observed wild ones. Children spent many an hour building playhouses out of whatever material was available. That material was often derived from the natural world. Children particularly prized stumps and hollow logs as playhouse locations. In the summer, they swam in streams, rivers, and lakes. In the winter, children engaged in other outdoor amusements, such as sledding, skating, snowshoeing, and skiing. They also perceived the built environment as a playground, making use of the barns and other outbuildings.[6] Imagination and open space made a potent mixture.

CONFRONTATIONS WITH NATURE

Children's relationships with the land, however, were not always playful. Sometimes they were antagonistic. Writer Sanora Babb's childhood, spent in part on an impoverished farm in far eastern Colorado, illustrates the extreme hazards facing ill-prepared families settling on frontiers. Her father moved the family from St. Louis, Missouri, to a piece of land near Two Buttes, Colorado. A more remote or harsh farming environment could hardly be found on America's Great Plains. The family lived in a dug out, really just a cave, below ground. Babb wrote, "Standing on a box, we could look out the window on the ground and feel a part of the miniature life of ants and beetles and anything that crawled."[7] The family watched the weather carefully, knowing that their livelihood depended on it. Babb observed, "Our broomcorn matured without mishap of prairie fire or drouth. There were days of scorching winds and fierce sun when it seemed that the crop would burn up, but the fertile soil had stored its winter moisture well."[8] Babb, like the adults around her, went into the fields to harvest the crop. Unfortunately, however, once the crops had paid the bills, there was little left to see the family through the winter. By winter's end, the family was barely surviving on "salt and red and black pepper. From these we made 'pepper tea,' which was hot water with a sprinkling of pepper to deceive the taste buds, a last-resort recipe for the 'starved out.'"[9] The children contributed to the family's meager meals by fishing for minnows, which their mother added to the pepper tea to make a very thin "minnow soup."[10] The frontier environment of eastern Colorado offered the family the barest of livings; consequently, after much hardship, they abandoned it in favor of life in town.

GEOGRAPHIC CONSIDERATIONS

While these examples are specific to the United States, the generalizations based on these examples are not. Frontier farming conditions such as those the Babbs faced were more common to agricultural life in the United States and Canada, and particularly on the prairies and plains. In the early years of the twentieth century, few other locations in the Western world were as remote. In these places, rough terrain and sparse settlement often added to the hardships that children in farming families faced. But differences of degree aside, farm children's encounters with the natural world, and their impact on the everyday business of work, play, and farm survival, were common to agricultural life worldwide. Children chilled themselves doing early morning chores in fall, winter, and spring weather, no matter where they lived. The rhythms of the seasons defined all farm children's work. Boys and girls played out of doors, and became acquainted with the flora and fauna of their family's farms. They also adapted their leisure activities to the land, making use of the resources available to them.

No matter the location, in the early years of the twentieth century, farm living implied a certain, earthy closeness to nature; a contemporary French description of rural childhood illustrated this perfectly. Pierre-Jakez Helias, who was born in 1914 and grew up in rural France, "pointed out that the beaten-earth floor of his Breton house was cold for a child learning to walk, especially if you sat down with a bare bottom, but easy to look after. If he peed on it, a handful of sawdust and a few sweeps of a brush were the end of the matter."[11] Historian Harry Hendrick's discussion of British childhood illustrates the commonalities of leisure pursuits between those children and their peers in the United States and Canada: "Rural children, besides playing hiding and chasing games such as 'fox and hounds,' 'sheep come home' and 'a night's lodging,' would spend time birdnesting, climbing trees, damming streams and cruelly harassing small animals. Much of their leisure was seasonally determined as with skating, sledging and snowballing, and going to the annual traveling fair and zoo."[12] Equally, a description of peasant children's activities in Russia could just as well be a description of farm children's lives in Nebraska. "In the winter, the children's favorite activities are sledding and skating. They spend entire days running on frozen puddles, ponds, and streams, skating on their feet."[13] For farm and village children, a close, daily relationship with the realities of the rural environment was inevitable.

PHILOSOPHIES OF FARM CHILDHOOD

A farm childhood represented life lived close to nature, and the opportunity to experience all of its wonders. Removal to the city implied the loss of a vital childhood experience. This sentimental poem by Eleanor C. Hull, appearing in the American publication *The Farmer's Wife,* in September of 1915, captured this perceived divide between the experience of rural versus urban childhood.

> Oh, little city boy and girl, I wonder if you know
> The beauty of the countryside when cherry blossoms blow?
> I wonder if you've felt the thrill that comes with spring's beginning,
> Or know the woodsy autumn smell when all the leaves are thinning?
> Oh, little city boy and girl, I wonder if you've heard
> The shrill and slender piping of some dawn-awakened bird
> That deepens into melody so pure and sweet and clear,
> There is no more beautiful a little child could hear?
> Oh, little city boy and girl, I wonder if you've seen
> The willows' still reflection in the brook they overlean;
> Or have you watched the lovely light that lingers everywhere
> When all the fields are gray and brown and all the limbs are bare?
> Dear little city boy and girl, I hope some day you'll come
> To know and love the countryside where every spot is home
> Things fair and fresh and wonderful are waiting for you there,
> And such a hearty greeting there's enough and some to spare![14]

Rural environments represented beauty, health, and wholesomeness presumably unavailable in urban locations.

Children, however, did not always perceive the countryside as a superior environment, especially if they had lived their entire lives in a city. Annual hop-picking expeditions lasting from August to late September afforded working-class London children the opportunity to compare their urban homes with the countryside. Sarah Shears, who grew up in a village in Kent, observed the young urban visitors. The youngsters evinced a fascination with their temporary environs, disappearing into the woods when they should have been working. "Irate mothers would yell, 'Alfie!' 'Maudie!' 'Frankie!' 'Katie!' and threaten the most awful punishment if they didn't return to work, but the woods echoed with their cheeky cockney voices, their rough play, and the latest songs from the London music halls."[15] But as much as the children enjoyed their weeks in the wilds of Kent, "they tired of Eden and, like Adam and Eve, were glad to evacuate." To them, the city was preferable, and an environment they could better understand. "Country lanes were a nightmare after dark. Who could make them understand that a rabbit was more frightened than they, or a cow mooed suddenly only when she was startled, or the screech in the barn was not somebody being murdered but merely an owl?"[16] Environmental preferences were learned, and to the city child, the countryside could be threatening. As a result, many adults advocated educating children to appreciate the natural world.

PHILOSOPHIES OF CHILDREN AND NATURE: NATURE AND MASCULINITY

In the early years of the twentieth century, Theodore Roosevelt found himself advocating vigorous exercise and competitive athletics for boys, in the absence of regular physical labor done in the fresh air. Still, he longed for a day when boys had partaken in what he called "natural outdoor play." Roosevelt wrote, "In the Civil War the soldiers who came from the prairie and the backwoods and the rugged farms where stumps still dotted the clearings, and who had learned to ride in their infancy, to shoot as soon as they could handle a rifle, and to camp out whenever they got the chance, were better fitted for military work than any set of mere school or college athletes could possibly."[17] Raised in the right environment, boys became real men. The nation would have to train those without the benefit of a farm background and the appropriate understanding of the natural world to take on vigorous physical tasks. A nation without such training for the young would surely go astray. G. Stanley Hall, an influential psychologist and educator, theorized along the same vein. He believed that a too-civilized childhood made boys unfit for the rigors of adulthood. In fact, he believed that it made them both mentally and physically ill.[18] The development of organizations such as the Boy Scouts stemmed from fears that youngsters, and particularly boys, would fail to develop into competent, healthy, and vigorous men in the absence of fresh air and hard work.[19]

BOY SCOUTING AND MASCULINITY

Robert Baden-Powell, the British founder of the Boy Scouts, placed the knowledge of the natural world at the center of his philosophy, and at the center of the requirements for scouting. First and foremost, a scout was to know woodcraft. "WOODCRAFT means knowing all about animals, which is gained by following up their foot-tracks and creeping up to them so that you can watch them in their natural state, and learn the different kinds of animals and their various habits."[20] Woodcraft included the knowledge of animals, their tracks and other signs, as well as the knowledge of wild plants and their uses. Scouts were also to master campaigning, or "living in the open; they have to know how to put up tents or huts for themselves, how to lay and light a fire; how to kill, cut up, and cook their food, how to tie logs together to make bridges and rafts; how to find their way by night, as well as by day, in a strange country, and so on."[21] Chivalry, life-saving, endurance, and patriotism rounded out the lessons of scouting. But lessons about the natural world and living in it came first, and Baden-Powell presumed that most boys would have to learn those lessons by way of structured scouting activities rather than by exposure to nature on a daily basis by way of their residence on farms and in villages.

URBAN GAMES

Perhaps the biggest difference between rural and urban children's relation-ships to their environments was in the organization of their games. While rural children entertained themselves with exploration and "harassing small animals," urban children played hopscotch, marbles, soccer, and cricket.[22] It was when children's urban pastimes became more creative that adults began to worry. Children did not confine themselves to the easily understandable and respectable games that adults wished. Progressive-era researchers in the United States made the disturbing discovery that children playing in the city streets were not always amusing themselves innocently. On June 23, 1913, researchers in Cleveland made a census of children's behavior, observing 7,799 children, 5,241 boys and 2,558 girls. The observers found the vast majority of children in yards, vacant lots, and alleys. While some children applied them-selves diligently to working, housekeeping, minding a baby, or gardening, most were playing. Some played baseball, flew kites, or rode bicycles, but the vast majority engaged in "just fooling around," or "doing nothing." The category of "doing nothing" included "breaking windows, destroying houses, chalking suggestive words on buildings, throwing mud at street cars, touching girls, looking at pictures of women in tights ... stealing, gambling and drinking."[23] The urban young were making themselves at home in their environment, and often in ways that disturbed and distressed adults.

A study of Inwood, which was from 1915 to 1930 a developing urban neighborhood at the tip of Manhattan, showed that children in that era had considerable freedom to explore their environment. Development was trans-forming Inwood from rural to urban, and many families with middling incomes found their way to the area. Children played vigorously in a community under construction. As one individual remembered, "We still had a lot of room to move around about. We ran up and down the buildings where the hills used to be. There were no locks on the doors downstairs, no locks on the doors to the roofs. You could go from roof to roof."[24] Abandoned barns and other remnants of the area's rural past offered play spaces for children as well. Children particularly enjoyed vacant lots. Recollecting his boyhood, one man remembered "since there were a lot of empty lots, we played there mostly. There was a lot of wood and old trees around, and we would make fires and cook potatoes."[25] Girls remembered building and furnishing playhouses using scraps of wood found on building sites. The Hudson and Harlem rivers offered opportunities for wading and swimming as well. The community had yet to build many playgrounds, and children made their own play places.[26] "Inwood … was not so much a stable, nurturing environment indulging children, as it was one that constantly *challenged* them. … children met their urban environment head-on; they were not presented with an array of pleasant alternatives, but rather derived much of their enjoyment through discriminating between what was to be enjoyed and what was to be avoided."[27]

URBAN WILDLANDS AND INTELLECTUAL DEVELOPMENT

The importance of vacant lots and other undeveloped urban spaces persisted well into the middle years of the twentieth century. In the 1950s and 1960s, entomologist and naturalist Robert Michael Pyle grew up near the High Line Canal, a sixty-six mile irrigation ditch running from the foothills of the Rocky Mountains through Denver and its suburbs. The High Line (also this author's childhood haunt) offered green space and numerous opportunities for childhood adventure. Pyle wrote, "I sought out the winding, cottonwood-shaded watercourse for purposes of exploration and play alone and with friends; discovery of crawdads, birds and butterflies; sulking and kicking the dust through a troubled home life; hiding, camping, fort building, stealing corn, cooking out, and pretending every kind of life in the out-of-doors; and ultimately, walking and parking and petting with girlfriends."[28] Pyle credited his career as a biologist to his early years on the canal, and the curiosity and familiarity with nature that his experiences inculcated. "It was the place that made me." He wrote, "Had it not been for the High Line Canal, the vacant lots I knew, the scruffy park, I'm not at all certain I would have been a biologist. … The total immersion in nature baptized me in a faith that never wavered."[29] Unfortunately, those open, undeveloped spaces hidden within urban and suburban areas had become relatively rare by the late twentieth century, whether in the United States, Canada, or Europe. Vacant lots and other waste spaces such as bomb sites had become housing, industrial and commercial buildings, and parking lots, and parks had been manicured and developed, leaving little wild space for the enjoyment of children.

THE ORIGINS OF THE PLAYGROUND

No matter what children thought of their surroundings, many reformers, both in the United States and Europe, came to believe that public spaces had been compromised and that children belonged in the home and other supervised places, away from the city's evils. The streets were too brutal for children.[30] But many reformers also believed that homes, especially the homes of immigrant and working-class children, were inadequately supervised and unstructured. Historian Howard Chudacoff has also argued that children's games "unnerved" adults, with their appropriation of sidewalks and streets meant for other purposes. There was hardly room for children in an urban environment of commerce and automobile travel, and children's presence increasingly disrupted the adult world.[31]

The answer was for adults to provide children with alternative environments. Following the German example, American city planners and educators began to develop playgrounds for urban children, particularly in the Northeast and Midwest. In the ideal, reformers believed that adult-supervised, adult-planned spaces should take the place of streets, alleys, stoops, vacant lots, and crowded homes.[32] The degree to which children complied with these adult-made plans is questionable. In the early years of the twentieth century, studies found that among school-aged children in Milwaukee and Cleveland, only about four percent actually played on playgrounds; only a slightly larger number used playgrounds in Chicago.[33] Later in the twentieth century, many children's antipathy for playgrounds remained, since most playground designers had "gone in the direction of pleasing adults, rather than children." While parents, insurance companies, and parks and recreation officials preferred sculpted, carefully designed play places, children tended to prefer more unsightly locations for play. A Danish invention, the "adventure playground" generally included "a number of hand-made shanties, some two-stories high, rickety forts, rope-walks across water, mud slides. There may be individual flower or vegetable plots being tended by youngsters and a crude grill for cooking hot dogs. Typically each youngster is assigned a small plot of land on which he can do whatever he pleases."[34] While this innovation flourished in Scandinavia, it never really caught on in the United States, perhaps because it so successfully mimicked the very elements of unstructured, vacant lot play that worried parents.

SOCIAL CLASS AND THE EXPERIENCE OF THE ENVIRONMENT

There were definitely class differences in children's experiences of the environment surrounding them. As Harry Hendrick commented in relation to childhood in the United Kingdom, the continuation of children's outdoor play and familiarity with the world beyond the home was a function of class more than a function of geography. While middle-class parents confined their children to backyards, playgrounds, and playrooms, poorer children familiarized themselves with the city's streets. For most working-class and poor children, "there was little free room indoors in which to play, so that 'playing out' was a vital feature of the social organization of domestic space."[35] Historians of France have noted the same phenomenon. "Working-class children in the towns were also thrown back on their own devices, with little money for toys or outings, compensated for by games with other children on the streets."[36] The situation in the United States was the same: "Privacy was as treasured and rare in the working-class districts as fresh air and light."[37] Games played out of doors gave parents, as well as children, a chance to breathe.

As a result of parental reactions to the dangers of the streets, and probably as a result of having more private space indoors and out as well, middle-class children lived more confined lives and had far less experience of the environment in which they lived. Their parents did not encourage them to run in the streets or play in vacant lots but to play in fenced yards, playgrounds, and playrooms stocked with toys and books. By the 1930s, many middle-class families in the United States had brought the playground, essentially, into their own backyards, purchasing swing sets and sand boxes for their own children.[38] Middle-class children's activities also received far greater scrutiny than those of rural children or poorer urban children. "Traditionally middle-class children had much less freedom than their social inferiors as their leisure time was spent indoors, or in the garden, under the supervision of parents, nannies and governesses."[39] Increasingly, their experience of the natural world came in the form of adult-organized and supervised activities, such as camping or scouting.

THE ORIGINS OF THE SUMMER CAMP

By the late nineteenth century, urban adults were trying to find ways to expose city children to the wonders of the natural world. In 1876, Swiss pastor Wilhelm Bion took sixty-eight impoverished Zurich youths on a summer vacation to the Alps. In the 1880s, French reformers adopted Bion's model and began taking groups of needy schoolchildren to the countryside for summer vacations in peasant households. Reformers' primary concern was to remove children from the deleterious effects of the urban environment.[40] Working-class children suffered disproportionately from tuberculosis and "homelier ailments as well—anemia, rickets, bronchitis, and a generally lethargic, or overly nervous air, owing to chronic malnourishment and childhoods spent curled in the cramped, damp, and generally unclean housing of the urban poor."[41] Over time, this became a publicly run, publicly funded annual event. By the end of World War II, France's *colonies de vacances* had grown into a nationwide movement, involving tens of thousands of working- and middle-class children, who spent four to six weeks in the summer enjoying fresh air and sunshine in children's collectives. It would not be until after 1968, and the institution of family vacations for a larger and larger proportion of the French population, that the colonies began to fall out of favor.[42]

Some American reformers also adopted this model. In New York City, for example, the Fresh Air Fund sent (and continues to send) impoverished city children to the countryside in an attempt to improve their physical and moral health. Begun in 1877, by the late 1980s the program had sent approximately 1.5 million children to camp and to sojourns in rural homes. Children visited more than a dozen different states, as well as Canada.[43]

SUMMER CAMPS IN THE UNITED STATES

In the United States, summer camp was a somewhat different affair, generally run by private organizations. The first American camps originated in the late nineteenth century, largely for the benefit of relatively well-to-do boys. Interestingly, their development proceeded from east to west. The camps first developed in eastern states, with large urban populations, and spread only gradually to less urbanized locations.[44] By the 1930s, organizations ran between three and four thousand camps, serving a wide variety of children and interests. Boy and Girl Scout camps focused on training young outdoorsmen and women and good citizens. Charity camps brought the children of the urban poor to the countryside to improve their health. Other camps mirrored the religious and political interests of parents. As historian Leslie Paris aptly put it, "In an increasingly postagrarian economy, camp advocates aimed to return children to rural environments, not in the context of productive labor but productive leisure."[45] All of the summer camps offered children the opportunity to spend a week or several weeks enjoying the benefits of fresh air and sunshine.[46] Although different camps stressed nature study to different degrees, a central feature of many children's camping experiences was to "cultivate friendships" with the various elements of the natural world.[47] These connections could come in any number of forms: taking nature walks, observing plants and animals, collecting specimens, and sleeping under the stars. Camping experiences provided children with a structured, supervised experience with the natural environment, a far different experience than that of youngsters in rural areas, who lived in close proximity to nature.

NATURE STUDY AND THE SCHOOLS

The schools, too, acted to keep urban and suburban children in contact with the natural world. In the United States, many schools adopted nature study as part of their core curricula in the hope of fostering in children a love and appreciation of nature. According to historian Kevin Armitage, educators hoped that "nonhuman nature would become a consistent part of the individual's practical and moral considerations. ... sympathy for nature would harmonize the individual with his or her natural surroundings and in so doing would increase the quality of life, foster scientific inquiry and prompt an ethics of conservation."[48] An important component of nature study was fostering a love of the natural world. Developed in 1894, Bird Day gave children one such opportunity. Bird Day "was a teach-in for the conservation of birds,"[49] a day in which students wrote about birds, celebrated them in song and story, and improved wildlife habitat. Properly educated children would (the naturalists and educators hoped) become small conservationists.[50] Whether this actually happened, of course, was another question altogether. But throughout the twentieth century, educators attempted to inculcate children with a love and understanding of the natural world, through nature study, environmental education, outdoor education, and conservation and environmental events, from Arbor Day to Bird Day to Earth Day.

Inevitably, much of the twentieth century story of the relationship of children to environment and geography is a story about control. Children who had often run free (more or less) in their environment, be it rural or urban, found themselves increasingly constrained. Parents removed their children from country to city. Parents, reformers, and educators attempted to relocate children from the street to the playground and park and to provide children with struc- tured experiences with nature, such as trips to camp and nature study in the classroom. Rightly or wrongly, adults perceived unmediated environments as dangerous places and sought to filter children's experiences of nature.

GEOGRAPHY AND ENCOUNTER WITH NATURE: WORLD WAR II AND ITS AFTERMATH IN EUROPE

As much as parents and other adults attempted to mediate the relationship between children and their environment, the twentieth century was one in which geography played an incredibly important role in determining the con- tours of children's lives—especially in relation to two world wars and the bleak periods of recovery immediately following them. The experience of those years re-imposed on children in war zones many of the more questionable joys of living close to nature—cold, lack of shelter, and lack of food, without the implied pleasures of camping out. There would be no escaping these condi- tions. Nearly 400,000 children braved the siege of Leningrad, enduring horrific conditions. They experienced cold, starvation, homelessness, and all of the other environmental challenges of war. Nine-year-old Tania Savicheva's diary illustrates the grim reality of living in that place and time.

> Zhenia died 28 December, 12:30 in the morning, 1941.
> Babushka [Grandmother] died 25 January, 3:00 in the afternoon, 1942.
> Leka died 17 March, 5:00 in the morning, 1942.
> Dedia [Uncle] Vasia died 13 April, 2:00 at night, 1942.
> Dedia Lesha, 10 May, 4:00 in the afternoon, 1942.
> Mama, 13 May, 7:30 in the morning, 1942.
> Savichevs died. All died. Only Tania remains.[51]

The war, and Tania's location in it, had taken a terrible toll. Whether Tania survived or not is unknown; she is presumed to have perished.

These hardships persisted into the postwar years. In the course of World War II, Stuttgart, Germany, for example, lost fifty-seven percent of its build- ings to fifty-three air raids. The postwar housing scarcity was acute. If families had not been able to tunnel into the city's hills, the situation would have been considerably more desperate. Postwar food rationing also deprived children of necessary nutrients. Individuals received meat rations of roughly a quarter of a pound per week, and other supplies came in equally short quantities. The police reported that children had begun to appear in bakeries, begging for bread.[52] In postwar Berlin, the situation was equally grim. Many who experienced these years as children judged conditions to be more difficult than those during the war. These were the Hungerjahre, or Hunger Years, where the lack of housing, heat, and food plunged children into misery.[53] It would be years before food and housing supplies reached adequate levels across Europe.

NATURAL DISASTERS: THE AMERICAN DUSTBOWL

Geography could intervene in the lives of children in other ways as well. Natural disasters disrupted children's lives much in the same way as war, robbing them of resources and making them refugees. Perhaps the best example of this was the Dust Bowl, which affected the Great Plains of the United States throughout the 1930s. The drought began around 1930 and extended through the growing season of 1940. Dirt storms of massive proportions accompanied the drought in many locations. It was one of the most significant environmental disasters in U.S. history, and it affected children's lives in many ways. First, farm poverty accompanied the drought. Families faced the double disaster of inadequate moisture and poor prices for what little they could grow, due to the economic depression that also occurred during those years. This, in turn, affected children's well-being. Public health nurses visiting area schools found poorly nourished, underweight children, whose parents could not adequately provide for them. Additionally, blowing dirt caused dust pneumonia, a condition that particularly affected children and the elderly. Dust-related conditions were a leading cause of children's deaths throughout the middle years of the decade. Families facing the drought and persistent dust storms often chose to migrate to other areas of the United States, such as California, that were not facing drought and dust storms. Unfortunately, this exposed children to other stresses, such as parental unemployment and underemployment, and unwelcoming public officials who refused to provide aid to Dust Bowl migrants. Many would be reduced to living in tents and other makeshift accommodations.[54] Ultimately, parents in these locations had very little control over the way in which the natural world affected their children.

CHILDREN DIVORCED FROM NATURE: THE INNER CITIES

These difficult interludes aside, by the end of the twentieth century, most children seemed to have lost much of their ongoing relationship with the natural word. Rural and urban, poor, working class, and well-to-do all had retreated to the confines of their homes. On the one hand, many of the most impoverished urban environments had become increasingly unsafe for children. Journalist Alex Kotlowitz titled his book about two boys growing up in inner-city housing projects in Chicago *There Are No Children Here*. Although the subjects of his book, Lafayette and Pharoah Rivers, did venture out of their family's apartment regularly, the environment did not encourage extensive exploration. In the Governor Henry Horner Homes, the families lived in high-rises, and the playground was paved in concrete, as was the baseball diamond. Only six functional basketball courts remained for 4,000 children's use. Uncomfortable metal benches provided the only place to sit outside. Being outside made children susceptible to stray or deliberate gunfire. The only thing close to a natural environment nearby was along the railroad tracks, where profuse weeds and a thicket grew, and the occasional butterfly or snake made an appearance. The trains, of course, made this a hazardous place for children's play. This environment, clearly, was no place for children.[55]

PARENTAL FEARS AND NEW DIVERSIONS

Even in areas where the conditions were not so grim, poorer urban children retreated from the street. Harry Hendrick has written about the relationship of technological and cultural change to British children's retreat from the world outside of the family home in the period since the 1970s. "Thereafter, however, the 'out of doors' faced serious competition for the working-class child's loyalty from television, the video and supervised recreation such as local football teams, swimming and athletic clubs, piano lessons, dancing class, and so on. Nowadays, not only is children's leisure time more organized by parents, but cities are seen to represent a threat to children from cars and from dangerous adults, even though the figures for road accidents were much higher in the 1930s and children are far more at risk from adults whom they know than from strangers."[56] Modern families came to live lives that were "centered inside the house" and its environs; homes became "private islands."[57] Parents organized children's leisure in order to keep them safe, with potentially serious consequences: "fewer children than ever are allowed out on their own either to travel or to play, and many researchers fear that they have fewer opportunities to learn about local geography, distance, time, climate and the reading of street names and signs and, therefore, are becoming less independent and less confident in their own abilities."[58] And more and more, they became dependent on the television, the computer, and other technologies to entertain them. They relied less and less on their own imaginations and on what those imaginations made of the environment surrounding them.

POTENTIAL LOSSES

Some observers believed that children had lost other important life experiences and possibilities to this change as well. They had lost the opportunity for much free and unstructured play. They had lost an understanding of the natural world. They had also lost intimacy with it. Children had fewer and fewer opportunities to know and appreciate nature, and to come to that appreciation by their own devices. Becoming a self-taught naturalist was increasingly an experience of the past.[59] By the 1990s in the United States, even the schools had given up much of their emphasis on the natural world. Outdoor education programs often focused more on building self-confidence and group dynamics than on allowing children time for quiet contemplation of nature.[60] Teachers increasingly abandoned the field trip, long the standard insertion of nature into the academic year, for virtual activities. Electronic field trips and television specials took children to the ends of the earth but did not allow them to observe nature in its unmediated, raw state. Virtual field trips, unlike the real thing, were far less messy and dangerous and did not open school districts up to the kind of liability that more natural adventures might. Entomologist Richard Michael Pyle lamented these developments, believing that "displays of extravagant animals behaving dramatically in captivity and on the television can spoil the young for the real thing outside their door." Who would want to sit in a field, observing monarch butterflies or cabbage moths, for instance, if polar bears and penguins were available on the television?[61]

THE EXAMPLE OF A SMALL CITY: AMES, IOWA

By the end of the twentieth century, one only had to observe the use of parks and playgrounds to see that children's relationships to nature had become radically different than in years past. The pictures in Figures 4.2 and 4.3 are of a public park in Ames, Iowa, a Midwestern college town with a population of roughly 50,000. While more than 100 acres of Inis Grove Park are manicured grass, there are also many wooded acres and a trail leading down to a public walking path along the Skunk River. The park is also home to two playgrounds. Like many modern playgrounds, there are molded plastic slides, swings, and climbing structures, all intended for the use of pre-adolescent children. Clearly, this is not an adventure playground. Even so, the park is well used. On weekday mornings and afternoons, small children of preschool age come to the park with their parents and other caregivers. In the afternoons and early evenings, school-aged children make their appearance, either to make use of the playgrounds or to play soccer on marked fields. Usually, they are accompanied by their parents. On the weekends, families make use of various park facilities. It is very unusual for an unaccompanied child to visit the park.

FIGURE 4.2: *Urban Park 1*. Courtesy of Richard Kehrberg.

FIGURE 4.3: *Urban Park 2*. Courtesy of Richard Kehrberg.

It is almost as if an invisible fence separates the playgrounds and marked playing fields from the wooded areas. Either because of their parents' instructions, or their own inclinations, children do not wander outside the developed areas of the park. Despite the temptation of wild blackberries growing at the edge of the grass, they remain unpicked. Perhaps the park's frequenters do not even recognize that the plants bear edible fruit. In spite of the ravine, hills, woods, water, rocks, wildlife, and all of the other temptations of nature, children rarely venture into the undeveloped areas of the park. If they do, it is to accompany their parents on very occasional walks along well-worn trails. The adults are perhaps reluctant to allow their charges to wander through the underbrush; the ravine is very steep and poison ivy grows in abundance in wooded Midwestern environments. Adults, walking for their health, make far more use of the less developed areas of the park than children do. The exceptions to the rule are small groups of adolescents whom observers may see scurrying off into the woods, presumably to enjoy the privacy from prying adult eyes that the dense trees and river banks offer.

Occasional adolescents aside, what youngsters generally take away from their outdoor experiences in this park is a mediated, supervised experience of the natural world. Fresh air, sunshine, and a possible roll down a Kentucky bluegrass–clad incline is the extent of their direct contact with the substance of the earth; parents, of course, will forbid the roll down the hill if it has rained recently. These children, like the majority of those in the Western world, are urban children. Their parents, like the majority of those in the Western world, are busy, working people. Most of them have come to believe that an unsupervised child is an unsafe child and that unsupervised experience of the natural world is particularly unsafe. They have a lot in common with their medieval and early modern counterparts, who believed that evil lurks in wild and untamed places. Parents consider the interiors of homes, manicured backyards, and carefully tended playgrounds the safe places, and the right places, for children to play. If these children have the opportunity to experience the wilds at all, it is usually in the form of another type of supervised activity, such as scouting or summer camp. While it is highly probably that some children escape into the ravine and woods and subvert their parents' intentions for orderly play in this urban park, these activities are largely invisible compared to the more orderly activities of the majority. The way in which children more regularly subvert their parents', and playground designers', intentions is by using the provided equipment in unanticipated ways. Children walk up the slides, slide down the climbing walls, and walk over the top of the plastic tubes they are supposed to climb through.[62] Although much play has moved indoors,

FIGURE 4.4: *Justin's Tree House, West Virginia, October 1995.* Lyntha Scott Eller, photographer. The Coal River Folklife Collection (AFC 1999/008), Library of Congress, Archive of Folk Culture, American Folklife Center. Digital ID: afccmns lec05803. Accessed on October 22, 2008, at http://hdl.loc.gov/loc.afc/afccmns.lec05803.

and parents exercise much more control than did parents of an earlier generation, children still approach their environments with a degree of creativity and independence.

CONCLUSIONS

In the course of the twentieth century, children drifted away from regular and intimate contact with the natural world. Families moved from farm to city, changing employment, and leaving behind agriculture, with its implied daily contact with the land. But children whose parents had removed them to the city did not necessarily have to lose contact with the natural world, even if in a somewhat diluted form. Vacant lots, the courses of waterways, ditches, and railroad embankments all offered opportunities for adventurous youths, should their parents allow it. Middle-class children often faced restrictions on their activities that poor children did not. Parents with resources often expected their children to stay in and play rather than roam outdoors. Adults also introduced controlled experiences with the environment, such as nature study and summer camp. Children were to enjoy the benefits of nature, without the dangers associated with more free experiences. That is not to say, however, that parents were always in control of these situations. Children living in the path of the twentieth century's wars and major natural disasters were often immersed in natural environments in uncontrolled and highly uncomfortable ways. But over the course of the twentieth century, it would seem that the forces of control won. Or, perhaps, their influence became irrelevant. Children increasingly chose indoor environments over the out-of-doors. Between the perceived dangers of the world out-of-doors, and the increasing temptations of the world indoors, the distance between children and personal experiences of the natural world has increased significantly.

CHAPTER FIVE

Education

WILLIAM J. REESE

The twentieth century brought a revolution in access to schooling for children and youth around the world. In the nineteenth century, Germany, France, Sweden, Great Britain, and the United States took the lead in making primary education available to all their children. Thus, by 1900 most children in western Europe and the United States had access to primary education, although only a small minority were able to attend secondary schools and even fewer could go to college or university. Outside the West, access to schooling was generally restricted to children of the elite. By 2000 access to primary and secondary education had become virtually universal in most developed countries and was increasingly available in developing countries. Even higher education, previously restricted mainly to the elite, was becoming mass education, especially in western Europe and the United States.[1]

This extraordinary expansion in access to schooling during the twentieth century was a global phenomenon, but it was a complicated, uneven process that reflected the particular conditions, character, and traditions of each society in which it occurred. Western Europe and the United States continued to be prominent in this educational expansion throughout the twentieth century, but it was the United States that led the movement to provide universal secondary education and greater access to higher education. Indeed, the expansion of opportunities for postprimary education "occurred almost a generation earlier" in the United States than in Europe.[2] Claudia Goldin has observed that in comparison with Britain and France, "the United States by the 1930's was three to four decades ahead in post-elementary education and educational gaps remained large at least to the 1950's."[3] During the last half of the century, the countries of western Europe greatly increased opportunities for secondary education, which by the end of the century approached or in some cases exceeded those available in the United States. Even so, the United States remained a leader in providing access to higher education.[4]

The reasons for U.S. educational leadership during the twentieth century are too varied and complex to explain in this brief chapter, but considerable insight can be gained from an examination of how public schools became a central institution in American life. Expected to respond to the vast social changes that made America a modern nation, they consistently enrolled around ninety percent of the school-going population and dramatically expanded their social functions. The nation's school system, born in the Northern states in the antebellum period, had long had an expansive, sometimes utopian, mission. Horace Mann, the most famous school reformer of that period, had proclaimed that schools could teach character, uplift the poor, make students productive adults, and, coincidentally, help train the minds of the young in basic academic subjects.[5] That broad mission was never abandoned

FIGURE 5.1: *Students in Clarke School*. 1909. DN0007051, *Chicago Daily News* negatives collection, Chicago History Museum.

and actually grew larger in the modern age, as citizens turned to the schools both to preserve the values of the past and help address the pressing issues of the times.

Every popular cause that could attract enough reform-minded citizens seemed to become the responsibility of the school. From the feeding of hungry children to medical inspection to training youth for the work force to entertaining the community at athletic events: there was little that the local schools were not expected to do. Schools were also the site of major battles over academic standards, curriculum, religious and moral training, and racial justice. In the process, public education often became all things to all people, a mirror that could be held up to the nation to expose its flaws without always showing how to remove every social blemish, large or small. Schools became familiar if often beleaguered institutions, whose growth and adaptability nevertheless remained their distinguishing feature by the early twentieth-first century.

During the first half of the twentieth century, the schools faced major criticisms related to such concerns as progressive education, academic standards, and racial justice, concerns that have hardly disappeared today. As the high school became a mass institution, the old dream of many school reformers—that all children would go to school, and for many years of their lives—had become a reality. The high school enrolled around seven percent of the adolescent population in 1890 but nearly everyone in that age group in 1950.[6] But the expansion of school going also meant that more citizens knew more through personal experience about the inner workings of the system, which, when joined with rising expectations of what schools could do to promote the good life and common good, only increased public scrutiny and criticism. And yet the schools proved durable in the coming decades, faced with the serious demands of a many-sided, expansive civil rights movement and the major social upheavals that transformed America generally after World War II. For all the complaints about the failures of different aspects of public education—that (in the 1980s) the schools had helped place the nation at risk and that (in the early 2000s) they had left too many children behind academically—the system adapted and survived despite being asked to do the impossible: to make everyone more equal while respecting individual differences, and to ensure that students were equal and excellent too.[7] Like a boxer battered and bruised, teachers and administrators took many a good punch; some found it impossible to meet the many, sometimes contradictory demands of their opponents, and some were left woozy but stayed in the ring.

SCHOOL ENROLLMENTS

One of the greatest issues facing schools in the early decades of the twentieth century was how to house the sheer number of students seeking admission. Nearly nineteen million immigrants, often from central and southern Europe, arrived in America between 1890 and 1920, bringing a diversity of languages, religions (often Catholic, sometimes Jewish), and cultures to the nation.[8] Principally settling in the North in industrial areas, newcomers from the empires of Russia, Germany, Austria-Hungary, and from Italy transformed the nature of many urban schools. Towns and cities struggled to add enough classrooms and build enough schools for the newcomers and also to provide more social services, from free meals for poor children in some elementary schools to guidance counseling in the higher grades.[9]

The number of children and youth accommodated was staggering. Between 1900 and 1950, elementary and secondary enrollments boomed from a combined 15.5 to 25.7 million pupils, an increase of two-thirds, despite the end to heavy immigration in the 1920s and the declining birth rate registered during the Great Depression.[10] Total enrollments in high schools skyrocketed as full-time jobs disappeared for teenagers. During the same half-century, as communities built more and more schools and as urban and suburban populations expanded, per capita spending on public education as a percentage of national income grew impressively, from 1.2 to 2 percent.[11] Local control of schools (and financing based on property taxes) ensured that huge inequalities existed in terms of access to quality, well-funded education. Rural areas often faced hard times and declining populations, and many individual states had to increase their share of funding when home owners could not pay their property taxes during the hard times of the 1930s. This problem was exacerbated in the South, the poorest region of the nation, since its states operated segregated, Jim Crow schools, essentially running two systems on less money than what wealthier regions used to run one system. Overcoming racial disparities in the schools, North and South, remains an unresolved, perennial problem.[12]

Growing enrollments during the early decades of the twentieth century were undergirded before the 1920s by the phenomenal growth of the American economy, as the nation became a major industrial power and child labor overall declined. Centered largely in the urban North, the industrial revolution not only attracted immigrants from across the sea seeking a better life and standard of living for themselves, and their children, but also African Americans and poor whites who in the post-Civil War period labored in often servile working conditions in the rural South. The movement of rural Southerners northward grew by World War I and notably expanded in the coming decades, as sharecroppers and tenants were displaced from farms and sought the promised land of better jobs for themselves and better schools for their children.[13]

What immigrants and white and black native-born newcomers to Northern urban areas encountered was a school system that itself was undergoing dramatic change. Northern cities had long been home to the most innovative ideas in education. As Carl F. Kaestle demonstrates, in the nineteenth century, cities established the first age-graded classrooms, more uniform and standard curricula, and free high schools.[14] Cities had the concentration of wealth and pupils to try to make school organization rational and efficient. Even when the ideals were not matched by reality, reformers would continue to tout the advantages of urban models until at least the 1960s, when complaints about bureaucracy, failing schools, and the ills of the city proliferated. Most children in 1900 were, however, still attending ungraded or partially graded one- or two-room schools in rural areas or small schools in villages and towns. But the cities served as the model, as reformers pressed forward, guided by their urban vision and plans to professionalize education.[15] And industrialization and immigration (before the 1920s) drew more people to the cities, which swelled the numbers of children, enabling more urban-oriented reformers to wield greater authority in the world of education.[16]

ORGANIZATION AND LEADERSHIP

Historian David B. Tyack and other scholars have demonstrated that, at the turn of the twentieth century, civic leaders, whether businessmen or professionals, often wanted schools to imitate the organizational patterns and structure of industry.[17] School boards were therefore streamlined and the basis of board membership altered; as the size of school boards was cut dramatically, ward-based elections (which had ensured neighborhood representation) were often replaced by at-large, nonpartisan elections, which ensured that elite citizens usually triumphed and thus controlled the educational purse strings. Historians such as Samuel P. Hays and Robert Wiebe similarly show that these elite board members often admired expertise, whether in schools or in other sectors of the economy.[18] Newly empowered, elite board members granted more decision-making authority to superintendents, who in the nineteenth century had functioned more like clerks than educational titans. Superintendents, who in urban areas usually had college degrees and even advanced graduate training, often admired the efficiency and productivity of big business, and they sought suitable means to make local schools under their control operate as efficiently and productively as possible.[19] Fearful of competition from industrial Europe, especially Germany, school reformers often championed the cause of vocational education to ensure a strong national economy.

Often dominant in major professional organizations, urban superintendents, armed with the latest ideas drawn from industry and science, tried to construct a smoothly functioning system. Scientific management of industry, epitomized by the influence of Frederick W. Taylor, had its counterpart in the schools.[20] By the 1930s, as the nation reeled in the face of economic depression, urban schools had assumed a distinctive character that would be emulated to a large degree as rural schools consolidated and smaller ones increasingly disappeared in the coming decades. Since the early 1900s, for example, superintendents had labored to make age-graded classrooms more of a reality than simply an ideal. In addition, homogeneous ability grouping—grouping together children who have similar measured ability or attainment for instruction—became more common in the elementary grades.[21] In small schools, children were separated by ability within a class of a particular grade; in larger schools, children were placed in separate classes of the same grade. The slowest pupils, in whatever type of arrangement, typically covered less academic material and had more drill and didactic instruction. Placing children in homogeneous groups in elementary grades made simpler the later placement of students in different tracks in the high schools, whose expansion was the wonder of the age. Intelligence tests and achievement tests, commonly used in many schools to help sort children into appropriate ability groups or tracks, were in their infancy in 1910 but within a few short decades had enabled administrators to impose greater efficiency on their systems.[22]

Ability groups were premised on the age-old assumption that children were different, and lay people as well as educational experts argued passionately about whether individual differences were inherited or a product of environmental factors. Many early advocates of intelligence testing believed in eugenics, a term coined in the 1880s by an English polymath, Francis Galton, who stressed the genetic bases of human differences, including intelligence.[23] So did later champions of intelligence testing such as Lewis Terman, a psychology professor at Stanford who popularized the belief that whites had more native intelligence than the children of most immigrant groups, African Americans, Mexican-Americans, American Indians, and so forth.[24] Critics of this view included John Dewey, Walter Lippmann, and William C. Bagley, who openly attacked the claims of Terman and his professional allies in the 1920s.[25] Even if the overtly racist views of psychologists sometimes softened or disappeared, standardized tests, once adopted, remained important in enabling teachers and administrators to monitor, assess, and evaluate student achievement and performance. Test scores, along with grades and other data, helped determine which children were sorted into ability groups or tracks in the burgeoning system.

EDUCATION REFORM

While scientific testing forever transformed how Americans assessed student outcomes and academic performance, schools, especially on the elementary level, also had some characteristics reminiscent of the nineteenth century. Reforms entered schools in different communities and regions at varying rates. Most importantly, many rural areas before the 1950s refused to consolidate their schools. There were still 130,000 one-room schools as late as 1942, when approximately half of America's school children still lived outside of urban areas.[26] These schools often resembled those of the nineteenth century and did not have classrooms found in contemporary Chicago or Atlanta. In these rural schools, age-graded instruction remained difficult if not impossible. There is no doubting the ultimate influence of urban models of school organization—the spread of ability grouping, testing, and tracking, for example—after mid-century, once rural schools consolidated and small schools more rapidly disappeared. But reforms sometimes took decades to implement. Even in the cities, traditional practices often coexisted with other changes deemed modern by urban school leaders.

For example, in many if not all schools in the first half of the last century, whether in the city or countryside, the school day often began with a non-denominational, Protestant prayer. Most elementary school children studied the basic subjects—the so-called three Rs, plus some geography, history, and science—and teachers continued to base their instruction on textbooks, often supplemented with additional teaching aids such as maps, charts, and globes. Schools also tried to accommodate the majority when enough people complained about an unpopular teacher, or discussions of unpopular ideas, whether the topic was evolution or communism. After the Scopes Trial of 1925, for example, the subject of Darwinian evolution often disappeared from biology textbooks in a bow to evangelical Protestant critics.[27] Moreover, as in the past, schools had multiple responsibilities, extending far beyond the teaching of subject matter. They continued to emphasize moral behavior, punctuality, and good citizenship, qualities commonly noted on the report cards sent home to parents, which continued to record grades in academic subjects. In the South, where African American schools were grossly under-funded, states reacted to civil rights groups that fought against segregation by better equalizing funding. White supremacists used the law and the courts in every way possible—and sometimes employed violence and terror—to pre-vent integration, and they also narrowed but never eliminated the funding gap between black and white schools in the 1940s and early 1950s.[28] They in-creased funding to prevent the death of Jim Crow by showing, unsuccessfully, that separate could be made equal and thus would meet the standards set by the U.S. Supreme Court in the famous *Plessy v. Ferguson* decision of 1896, the legal basis for racial segregation.[29]

Everyone familiar with rural black schools also knew that parents were often conservative when it came to the classroom. Like many white working-class parents, African Americans usually wanted their children to focus on academics and the basics, not on the vocational subjects that some reform-ers espoused for other people's children. At a time when rural agricultural economies were unraveling, black parents were rightly suspicious of the value of nature study and shop class over English and arithmetic.[30] Other aspects of elementary schools, wherever they existed, frustrated reformers who com-plained about the hidebound nature of education. In particular, child-centered progressive reformers throughout these decades wanted to bring new experi-mental methods and subjects to the classroom and to undermine tradition.[31] At the opposite end of the reform spectrum, vocational educators complained loudly that academics remained too important, and overvalued, in the typical school everywhere in America.[32] Schools never seemed to change fast enough for those who sought rapid educational change.

Fighting traditional practices was not easy. Since the nineteenth century, classroom practice had long emphasized teacher authority, the centrality of textbooks as an instructional tool, pupil memorization and recitation, and the importance of order and decorum.[33] This was challenged, in every generation, by proponents of child-centered education, who favored more freedom for the child, less testing and competition, and more experimental forms of pedagogy, such as cooperative learning. Without question, some of these ideas helped soften some authoritarian practices and alter some as-pects of the traditional elementary classroom. While school desks, as Larry Cuban has shown, were often still bolted down in the 1930s and 1940s, more flexible seating arrangements, smaller class sizes, and innovative teaching methods ultimately entered some classrooms.[34] Nature study, field trips, arts and crafts, and other alternatives to the traditional curriculum became more common.

At the same time, however, so did contrary efforts that emphasized uniformity and reinforced student passivity. Workbooks became ubiquitous in urban systems in the 1930s, and the growing popularity of multiple-choice tests reinforced the notion that there were right answers to every question. School room competition for grades and gold stars hardly disappeared once desks were more comfortable, when students enjoyed more airy, pleasantly decorated rooms, or if teachers talked the talk of child-centered instruction. Even in the most famous suburban system—that of Winnetka, Illinois, in the 1930s and early 1940s, which embraced a version of progressive education—pupils had to master the basics and perform well on tests before savoring some of the joys of child-centered instruction, whether building teepees or engaging in other group projects.[35] Adults everywhere believed that pupils should master the basics.

Conservatives and other critics of public education often claim that schools were transformed for the worse over the course of the twentieth century, thanks to what John Dewey and his progressive followers had championed, more freedom for the child. Dewey had established an experimental school, the Laboratory School, at the University of Chicago in the 1890s, and he helped popularize (though not uncritically advance) the various educational experiments underway in the nation in a variety of books, including one he wrote with his daughter, Evelyn, titled *Schools of Tomorrow*, which was published in 1915.[36] Most public schools, however, never fully embraced child-centered instruction, a concept incapable of uniform definition, and Dewey spent considerable time distancing himself from those who thought that children should do as they pleased, only learn by doing and not from books, or wanted teachers to abdicate their authority or proclaim that all learning was fun.[37] And he realized that testing, routine, and familiar practices remained fairly common in most public schools, in all regions and most school systems. Ability groups and tracks, work books, and standardized tests, proved far more influential than anything child-centered advocates proposed, such as nature study or field trips or the elimination of tests and grades on report cards.

Contemporaries, then as now, certainly worried about whether standards were eroding thanks to modern liberalism, which some critics feared was creeping into the schools. Though the practice was hardly universal, efficiency demanded that more children win promotion from grade to grade, and promotion rates did overall rise after the 1920s.[38] This likely resulted more from the realization that holding children back did not usually yield the desired academic results, and cost taxpayers many millions of dollars annually trying to make everyone conform to the same standard, than any presumed influence of progressive tenets on school practice. But critics were right to see that elementary teachers, who relied on textbooks (and workbooks) to organize and guide instruction, were despite their essential conservatism far more receptive to innovative pedagogical ideas than were the more subject matter–oriented teachers found in the high school.[39]

HIGH SCHOOLS

Many observers noted that high schools faced severe problems in the early twentieth century. Secondary enrollments skyrocketed as full-time jobs increasingly disappeared for teenagers.[40] To maintain the essentially academic character of the modern high school was viewed as an impossibility by many educators, who assumed that working-class pupils who increasingly attended could not effectively compete with the native-born middle classes.[41] African Americans in the rural South often lacked any access to high schools, though their enrollments also boomed in the 1930s and 1940s as parents fought for more schools and labored to help their children prepare for a world with declining numbers of farms, their traditional site of labor.[42] As high schools nearly everywhere embraced more pupils from more social backgrounds, the question nevertheless remained: could everyone master academic subjects? Professional administrators and leading educators, especially in the cities, responded in the negative and built more vocational programs, which were usually aimed at pupils from poorer social backgrounds. Urban high schools in particular no longer were exclusively academic institutions.

Efficiency in the industrial sector was synonymous with low costs and high productivity, and efficiency in education meant limiting academic instruction to those who presumably could benefit from it. Many urban school administrators, especially those with graduate school training, doubted the capacity of young people from families bereft of educational credentials. In graduate school, future superintendents immersed themselves in professional educationist literature, which emphasized the importance of human differences and praised hierarchical, corporate models of industrial organization. Educational psychology stressed statistical methods and measurement and taught that not every child had the talent to succeed in academic classes, which helped reinforce the idea of ability groups in the elementary schools and formal tracks in the high school.[43] The traditional belief that high school students, whatever their destination in life, should study academic subjects, was seriously weakened, especially in larger cities that were able to afford larger buildings, hire specialized teachers, and equip schools with the apparatus needed to train pupils in vocational subjects.

Comprehensive high schools were often touted in professional educational circles as the hope of the future. Offering something for everyone became the modern democratic ideal in the schools. At the comprehensive high school, pupils enrolled in one of several tracks: academic at one extreme, vocational at the other, or in a so-called general track (a mix of weakened academic courses) in between.[44] Some comprehensive high schools had enrollments of a few thousand pupils, offering hundreds of courses on campuses that rivaled many liberal arts colleges in size. Pupils could choose from a variety of electives as well as become involved in an array of extracurricular programs, from traditional academic clubs (e.g., Latin, Spanish, physics) to special interest groups (from the radio club to Future Teachers of America), or ever popular sports teams (usually as fans more than as players).[45] Visitors from European nations were struck both by the numbers of pupils attending secondary schools and by the range of nonacademic programs and activities found in them.

Some pupils engaged in so many extracurricular activities that parents and teachers wondered if anyone had any time to study. Indeed, academic course taking in high school probably declined overall by mid-century, according to some prominent studies completed by the 1950s.[46] The decline was likely most pronounced in the bigger, urban high schools, not in the small schools where differentiation was less likely and specialized programs with specific vocational aims were less popular. High schools remained remarkably diverse. In 1954, there were nearly 24,000 high schools in America, and fifty-five percent of them enrolled fewer than 200 pupils. Less than 100 pupils were found in over 7,000 of the nation's high schools, so separate tracks there were also a pipe dream.[47]

By the 1950s, the public school system was vast, and it remained central to the life of many communities, preparing a growing number of pupils for college (the gateway to the professions and white-collar work) and many more for blue-collar jobs in industry and for the lowest paid, mundane work in the service economy. Then, as now, the major identification of citizens in some communities with their schools was with sports teams, not with their academic programs. As historians David L. Angus and Jeffrey E. Mirel argue, comprehensive high schools never intended to offer high-quality academic instruction to everyone, and vocational or watered-down instruction too often remained the norm for poorer students.[48] In addition, the rise of peer groups as an unintended consequence of age-graded instruction meant that, as social scientists Robert and Helen Lynd found in their classic studies of "Middletown" decades earlier, the high school was filled with cliques, groups, and anti-intellectual impulses befitting an institution that tried to perform so many diverse academic and nonacademic functions.[49]

COLD WAR, CIVIL RIGHTS, AND POLITICS

During the cold war and the civil rights movement, the schools were tugged in opposite directions, asked to strengthen academic excellence but also to ensure social inclusion and greater equality.[50] Rights-consciousness and American prosperity nurtured other groups to demand fairer treatment in the schools, leading to an explosion of programs in special education by the 1970s, demands for more educational access and equity that piggybacked on the black civil rights movement.[51] Women's groups successfully fought for federal legislation to ensure more access for girls to sports programs and other school activities. Activists for language-minority pupils demanded the expansion of more federal spending on bilingual/bicultural education programs. The more schools did and the longer students attended, the more everyone expected and then complained when reality fell short of expectations. Throughout the second half of the century, as before, citizens from across a wide spectrum of society would continue to find fault with the schools and yet turn to them to address grave social and economic ills not centrally of their making. The Great Society's plan to end poverty through education and federal programs was no less utopian than the recent dreamy idea of leaving no child behind.

Combined enrollments of elementary and secondary public school students stood at about twenty-five million at mid-century. The baby boom and explosion of newcomers from distant lands, as well as from Mexico and Latin America, following the revision of the nation's immigration laws in 1965, meant that by the 2000 school year the combined enrollments had risen to an astounding forty-seven million pupils.[52] During the post-World War II era, America also faced cold and hot wars, the decline of its industrial supremacy evident in the rise of the rust belt by the 1970s, and the intensification of international economic competition as European and Asian nations rebuilt their infrastructure and strengthened their educational systems. By the 1980s, Republican leadership questioned the academic quality of public education and endorsed a variety of private school and choice alternatives, and governors, business leaders, and leaders of both major political parties called for higher academic standards and no retreat from the well-seasoned notion that schools could be all things to all people.

From the 1950s through the early 1960s, the federal government was forced to address the hoary problem of its role in education. By law and custom, schools were state established and locally controlled, and the national government (unlike the situation in the rest of the Western world) played a small role in educational policy making or funding. The Russian sputniks forced Republicans, as a cold war measure, to pass the National Defense Education Act (1958) to enhance math and science instruction, leading to a wave of new pedagogical initiatives in those areas and more support for language training, history, and geography on the college level, which advanced learning in subjects deemed vital to the national interest.[53] The civil rights movement, however, was the most important moral force for change in challenging the federal government's largely laissez faire role in shaping school policy. In 1950, about one percent of school budgets came from the federal government, mostly for vocational and a handful of other special programs.[54] In the coming decades, that percentage wavered and never reached ten percent, but its programs often leveraged important changes in program development and educational access for previously underserved populations.[55]

With the striking down of de jure segregation as unconstitutional by the U.S. Supreme Court in 1954 in *Brown v. Board of Education*, citizens and their elected officials were faced with the prospect of dismantling the segregated schools of the South, and the ruling ultimately raised serious issues related to Northern systems, too. As many scholars have shown, the South largely resisted most efforts at integration until the Great Society of Lyndon Baines Johnson's administration, when the Justice Department and newly empowered federal agencies forced local districts to desegregate.[56] By the 1970s, federal and district courts had also upheld or sponsored complex desegregation plans to require major Northern urban areas as well to desegregate, usually through busing, which accelerated white flight to the suburbs, which helped make inner cities the residence of more nonwhite, poorer people. By the 1970s, the U.S. Supreme Court had also rejected demands for equal funding for schools attended by rich and poor children alike and in an equally famous case dealing with Detroit ruled against plans to integrate largely white suburbs with a largely black city system.[57]

The role that schools played in local communities thus remained as complicated and complex as ever. Many parents were deeply distressed when the U.S. Supreme Court banned state-sponsored prayer in the public schools in the early 1960s.[58] The realization that blue-collar jobs in the manufacturing sector were undergoing decline, visibly apparent by the 1970s, also accelerated complaints that the schools were not preparing youth well enough for a changing labor market and growing consumer society, for which goods would largely arrive here from distant shores, produced by cheaper labor. Schools were often blamed for shortcomings in the nation's economy, even though the nation lacked any coherent industrial policy or much urban planning; the magic of market competition became the solution for every imaginable economic and social problem.

In addition, politics played its hand in the quest for racially inclusive schools. Racial integration in the schools stalled with the rise of conservatism, notably in the formerly Democratic South, which increasingly voted Republican. As president in the 1980s, Ronald Reagan cut federal spending on schools, which had accelerated considerably during the Great Society years, which had witnessed the establishment of Head Start, programs in bilingual education, and numerous other initiatives. He also favored more aid for private schools and policies that ensured less racial integration. In his 1980 campaign, Reagan promised to eliminate the federal Department of Education, which had been established by his Democratic predecessor, Jimmy Carter, in 1979.[59] Instead, the department helped sponsor the writing of *A Nation at Risk*, a landmark report that appeared in 1983. One of the most widely quoted educational documents in history, it blamed schools for helping to weaken the economy through its cafeteria-style curriculum on the high school level and low standards of achievement. Ever since the 1980s, governors and presidents of both parties and citizens generally have largely agreed that academic standards are too low and must be raised.[60]

While governor of Arkansas in the 1980s, Bill Clinton was elevated to national prominence as a leader within the Democratic Leadership Council, showing how Southern moderates could alter his party's liberal image in part by sharing the Republican view that the nation needed to raise standards in the schools. As governor he championed teacher testing to weed out the weakest teachers. Clinton's signature legislation as president, America 2000 and Goals 2000, promised among other things to make America a world leader in mathematics and sciences by the end of the twentieth century.[61] That goal was not achieved, but bipartisan cooperation was evident in the twenty-first century with the passage of the No Child Left Behind Act in 2002.[62] The act mandated the regular testing of pupils in a few subjects, though without specifying the same standards per se for every state. The notion that schools are academically mediocre remains a powerful idea embraced by many citizens and elected officials. Democrats such as Clinton endorsed more choice programs within public schools, usually in the form of charter schools, which have more independence and freedom from bureaucratic rules that govern most school systems.

Thousands of charter schools have now formed across the nation. Republicans, in turn, have been more favorable to choice programs outside of public schools—for example, through voucher programs, through which parents receive some portion of public tax monies to opt out of the public system. Voucher proposals are mightily opposed by teachers' unions and have been turned down by voters in several states. But Cleveland, Ohio, and Milwaukee, Wisconsin have voucher plans that have been successfully upheld by the courts.[63]

In the second half of the twentieth century, then, schools faced some mighty winds of change, ranging from the cold war, the civil rights movement, the Great Society, and the Republican counterrevolution to liberalism. From every movement came visible signs of change in the form of new educational programs and initiatives. Cold war fears of military decline elevated the importance of mathematics and science achievement, which received a large boost in the 1950s. The contemporaneous civil rights movement also engaged federal interest. Massive resistance and Southern foot dragging on the matter of desegregation led to the threat of federal prosecution and withdrawal of federal funds to schools that refused to integrate their schools, and ultimately led to court-approved mandatory busing; many schools might have been integrated in name only, as African-American students discovered when they were disproportionately tracked into nonacademic courses of study, but the federal government had played a major role in changing behavior and ending Jim Crow, legally if not in practice.[64] By the early 1970s, Southern systems of education were actually in a formal sense more racially integrated than Northern systems were, something no one in 1954 could have ever imagined. The separation of inner cities (which became poorer and more nonwhite) and suburbs (which became more white and affluent) occurred throughout much of the nation but with greatest intensity in the North and Midwest. This certainly undermined the dream of integration for many citizens.

The civil rights movement obviously had not achieved all of its goals, but it soon fed the desires of other groups to demand their rights, too. Special education programs, buttressed by federal legislation in the 1970s, ensured that children with any number of physical handicaps or learning disabilities could attend schools, which had not been the case before the 1950s. The variety of Great Society programs that aimed to lift achievement among the poor did not achieve their lofty goals to everyone's satisfaction but ensured that there would be a federal presence in efforts at school improvement. The initial Elementary and Secondary Education Act of 1965 has been reauthorized in different forms since its initial passage, including the recent No Child Left Behind legislation. Liberal times have given way to more conservative times, and the focus and intent of programs obviously change, but thanks to the historical evolution of public education over the last fifty years, it is inconceivable that there will not continue to be some important federal role in school policy.

CONCLUSION

While change is certainly a constant factor in history, this chapter has also underscored some of the ways in which traditional practices, ideals, and behaviors also survive over time. It's clear that schools and individual classrooms can be enormously diverse places of learning and socialization. Some inner-city schools are completely nonwhite and suffer from massive underfunding compared to schools in affluent white suburbs. Some schools, even when poorly funded, may nonetheless serve as a bright spot in a child's life: a place to be safe, enjoy a hot meal, and aspire to transcend poverty through hard work and academic achievement. Some suburban schools, despite their relatively favorable advantage in terms of wealth, have mediocre track records of achievement, while others have academic standards that rival some small accredited colleges. The multiple roles that schools play in society is remarkable, a weight borne by few other public institutions. But even when change is apparent, as is so clear in any appraisal of school and society since World War II, schools often retain many familiar features.

For example, numerous scholars who have studied the classroom behavior of teachers and pupils often demonstrate that traditional practices remain common. Compared to their peers in most Western nations, for example, American teachers rely much more heavily on textbooks as the basis for instruction; in areas such as mathematics and science, for example, many teachers are teaching out of field—that is, they were not formally or well educated in the subjects they are hired to teach. In addition, with the emphasis on standardized testing, policies that aim to raise achievement have reinforced didactic teaching practices, which have long been the mainstay of most classrooms. Teaching to the test has been a concern of some educators since the nineteenth century, when the first timed, written, competitive tests were administered to urban children in England and America. Complaints about Gradgrind-like instruction, in which children try to memorize facts or rules they often do not master or understand, has resurfaced in recent years in the wake of the testing requirements of No Child Left Behind legislation.[65]

Long before the national government played such an obvious role in promoting testing, students of educational practice discovered that many classrooms were filled with teachers who talked and lectured most of the time, while pupils were for instructional purposes at least largely passive. Bolts were removed that once attached school desks to the floor, but the new desks—often made of plastic—often remained lined up in a row on carpets or linoleum floors, with teachers mostly talking and pupils mostly listening. Elementary school teachers have smaller class sizes than a half-century ago, and many of their classrooms are brightly decorated and inviting places for children, with small libraries in the corner and tables sometimes replacing individual desks. But it's also the case that testing requirements reinforce the use of workbooks in some form and textbooks generally.

When educational researcher John Goodlad and other scholars studied teaching practices in a variety of schools in the 1970s and 1980s, they discovered that memorization, reliance on textbooks and workbooks, and pupil passivity were widespread in elementary classrooms.[66] Philip Cusick described similar realities in secondary classrooms in his book, *Inside High School.*[67] He noted that many pupils were disengaged and spent considerable time simply listening to teachers, well-schooled in their use of chalk and talk. Boredom

FIGURE 5.2: *Children beside School Bus,* Humboldt County, Nevada. William A. Wilson, photographer. Buckaroos in Paradise Collection (1945–1982), American Memory, Library of Congress. Accessed on October 22, 2008 at http://hdl.loc.gov/loc.afc/afc96ran.46476.

written on their faces, students coped with classroom routine by doodling, day dreaming, and otherwise marking the time. All of this occurred at a time when teacher educators often enjoined future teachers to inspire pupils to inquire, discover, and understand rather than simply memorize facts to be reproduced on competitive exams.

Capturing the diversity of America's public school system over the course of the twentieth century remains challenging, perhaps impossible. From big cities to rural areas, from one coast to the other, public schools often serve different student populations, enjoy different levels of financial and community support, and teach children who face radically different futures. Yet the schools continue despite their many critics to educate around ninety percent of the school-going population below the college level. One thing is certain: Americans expect more from schools than they can possibly deliver. Parents want the very best for their own children, yet many believe in the idea of human equality. No one has explained to teachers how children can be excellent and equal too. Also, schools obviously perform a host of social, economic, and political functions. Rising competition from highly productive Asian nations understandably makes Americans nervous, and low-achieving schools are often held accountable for some the nation's failure to compete well in the international marketplace. Schools have thus been asked to help children succeed in a competitive world economy, develop good citizenship, learn social norms, and behave morally, all admirable, if hard to define, ideals not always practiced in the larger society.

CHAPTER SIX

Life Cycle

KATHERINE JELLISON

MIDDLE-CLASS LIFE CYCLE

In the early twentieth century, members of the urban middle class continued to follow the unique life cycle pattern they had established in the late Victorian era. Men and women married, set up independent households, and shortly thereafter began having children. Use of birth control allowed middle-class women to restrict reproduction to the early years of marriage and to give birth to their last baby well before menopause, thereby reducing average family size and increasing the time and resources devoted to each child. As a result, children in these families were able to remain in school continuously and delay full-time employment until their formal schooling ended. Once they completed their education, most young people then left their birth families to pursue for themselves the emblems of middle-class adulthood: job, marriage, and parenthood. As the century progressed, this life cycle pattern extended beyond the middle class, achieving its widest acceptance in the United States and Western Europe during the quarter century following World War II. By the 1970s, numerous political and cultural developments—including the re-emergence of Western feminism—challenged this family-life script. In the closing decades of the twentieth century, Western society accepted a greater variety of family life cycle choices and practices.

WOMEN'S AND CHILDREN'S LABOR

While the growing middle class of industrialized Europe and North America continued in the early twentieth century to organize family life around the

Victorian concepts of male breadwinner, female homemaker, and an extended period of childhood, rural families and those of the urban working class still necessarily relied on women's and children's labor force participation. In 1907 Germany, 26.4 percent of all women were classified as "economically active." In 1911, 38.7 percent of French women and 25.7 percent of British women were so classified. Urban shop clerks, factory workers, and domestic servants probably comprised the majority of women enumerated in official accounts. Census and survey takers often overlooked seasonal agricultural laborers and urban women who earned money by taking in sewing, laundry, or boarders. In North America, women's labor on the family farm was likewise frequently ignored. But in 1919, a pioneering survey of farm women in the American Midwest revealed their extensive participation in farm production and marketing: eighty-nine percent raised poultry flocks, sixty-seven percent tended gardens, and sixty-six percent manufactured butter.[1]

Rural children were also "economically active" in the early twentieth century, as were many of their counterparts in the urban working class. In 1900, one in six American children between the ages of ten and sixteen was gainfully employed on a full-time basis. After a series of hard-fought campaigns, Progressive Movement activists in the United States and reformers elsewhere in the industrialized West secured legislation that limited or prohibited the employment of young children in mines and factories, but agricultural labor remained largely unregulated. A 1920 report indicated that sixty-one

FIGURE 6.1: *Children Working in Field*. Long after laws prohibited their labor in urban settings, children continued to toil on farms. Photograph by Russell Lee. (Courtesy of FSA Collection, Library of Congress.)

FIGURE 6.2: *Children in School*. Compulsory education laws ensured that Western children spent much of their time in the classroom. Photograph by Philip Bonn. (Courtesy of OWI Collection, Library of Congress.)

percent of working Americans under the age of sixteen were employed in agriculture; eighty-eight percent of those labored on the family farm. And while children under sixteen no longer toiled in settings that enforced child labor laws, their older siblings still worked in large numbers. Boys and girls in their late teens made up a significant portion of the urban industrial labor force and often contributed substantially to their families' support. In the aftermath of the 1911 fire that killed 146 workers at New York's Triangle Shirtwaist Factory, investigators learned how extensively Jewish and Italian immigrant families relied on the wages that their teenage daughters earned in the garment industry. Victims' families faced economic disaster with the loss of daughters who had been "supporting old fathers and mothers, both in [the United States] and abroad; mothering and supporting younger brothers and sisters, [and] sending brothers to high school."[2]

Along with child labor laws, compulsory education statutes helped limit the workforce participation of children under sixteen. By 1920, laws in the industrialized West mandated that children remain in school for eight to ten years. In rural regions, however, such laws were nonexistent or unenforced. In the American South, truancy officials looked the other way when African American youngsters abandoned underfunded, segregated schools to work in the cotton fields. Children in Europe's agrarian periphery—Russia, the

Balkans, Spain, Portugal, Italy, Greece, and Ireland—also frequently spent their days in the farm field rather than the classroom.[3]

DECLINE IN BIRTHRATES

Early twentieth-century child labor practices had a measurable effect on Western birthrates. In agriculturally based communities throughout the West, child labor remained vital to economic survival, and birthrates continued to be higher than those of the urban middle class. Working-class urban families who depended on wage-earning children—particularly when in their late teens—likewise continued to have more offspring than middle-class families did. In the 1920s, for instance, the average working-class family in Britain had 3.05 children, while the typical professional-class family had only 1.69. Although family size remained dependent on factors of location and class, the overall Western birthrate was significantly lower in the early twentieth century than it had been two generations earlier. With the exception of highly rural and staunchly Roman Catholic Ireland, the birthrate declined within all classes and ethnic groups. Between 1875 and 1913, it fell from 51.5 live births per 1,000 population to 43.1 per 1,000 in largely peasant Russia. In largely industrialized England and Wales, the birthrate dropped from 35.4 per 1,000 in 1875 to 24.1 per thousand in 1913. In France, which pioneered intentional family limitation practices in the late eighteenth century, an already low birthrate of 25.9 per 1,000 in 1875 fell to 18.8 per 1,000 in 1913.[4]

The overall decline of the Western birthrate resulted primarily from abstinence and coitus interruptus. The population that most purposefully and successfully limited family size, the urban middle class, also often availed itself of other means. Barrier methods—the condom and the diaphragm—played a role, as did abortion. The passage of strict anti-abortion laws throughout the industrialized West in the middle and late nineteenth century reflected concern that middle-class women were increasingly using the procedure as a form of birth control. Reliance on abortion and even barrier methods required skirting the letter of the law. In the United States, for instance, condom sales were legal only for the prevention of sexually transmitted disease, not the prevention of pregnancy. Nevertheless, women of the urban working class frequently sought the birth control knowledge that middle-class women employed so effectively. Working-class women's desire for reliable birth control information in the 1910s and 1920s resulted from a variety of factors. Child labor and compulsory education laws lessened the reliance on children as wage earners. Increased concerns about urban overcrowding and health conditions also played a role, as did the ideas of female self-determination that filtered into working-class neighborhoods from the American and British suffrage movements. Responding to the needs of working-class women in New York, Margaret Sanger established a Brooklyn birth control clinic in 1916. In Britain, Marie Stopes founded a similar facility in London.[5]

Extension of birth control to a larger portion of the Western population coincided with the devastating impact of World War I on Europe's female-to-male ratio. Of the ten million lives lost in the war, the vast majority were young men of marriageable age. This left their surviving female counterparts without reproductive partners. The 1921 British census revealed 1,209 single women between the ages of twenty-five and twenty-nine for every 1,000 men in the same age group. Ten years later, fifty percent of these women were still single, and long-term statistics indicated that thirty-five percent of them never married during their reproductive years. Similar patterns occurred among the other major combatant nations.[6]

STATE POLICIES ON FAMILY GROWTH AND BIRTH CONTROL

Under these circumstances, several Western nations undertook measures to reverse declining birthrates and prevent so-called national suicide at a time when eugenicists preached the doctrine of genetic control. In the 1920s and 1930s, Germany, France, Italy, Sweden, and the Soviet Union all devised plans to increase national birthrates. The Soviet Union, which had legalized abortion in 1920, now made it illegal again in the mid-1930s. Other new policies in the Soviet Union and elsewhere included medals for prolific mothers, family allowances that increased with the birth of each child, and public housing for large families. At the same time, however, many Western nations began to legalize contraception. By 1940, couples in most states of the United States and in predominantly Protestant Britain, Scandinavia, and the Netherlands could now legally use methods they had once skirted the law to employ. And the Great Depression of the 1930s provided strong economic incentive to put those methods into practice. In the United States, the birthrate fell from 30 births per 1,000 population in 1909–1910 to only 19 between 1936 and 1940, and the average number of births per woman declined from 3.56 in 1900 to 2.1 in 1940. Along with legalizing contraception, Sweden and Norway also eased restrictions on abortion. Sweden, in fact, provides the best example of the increasing popularity of birth control. At a time when their government was both providing incentives for large families and allowing legal access to birth control, most Swedes chose to limit family size. The Swedish birthrate, which had stood at 26 births per 1,000 population between 1901 and 1910, fell to only 15 births per 1,000 between 1931 and 1940. The desire for smaller families, however, reached well beyond Scandinavia and other Protestant nations to Roman Catholic countries as well. In Italy, where Mussolini cooperated with the Vatican and officially banned both contraception and abortion, the birthrate nevertheless fell from 27 per 1,000 between 1926 and 1930 to 23 per 1,000 between 1936 and 1940.[7]

COURTSHIP AND DATING

The accepted route to marriage and reproduction also underwent change in the West at this time. Middle-class courtship, which had continued to follow Victorian conventions during the first two decades of the twentieth century, now took on new characteristics in the interwar years. Whereas Victorian customs had required a young man to call on his sweetheart at home under the watchful eye of the young woman's parents, new technologies and changing notions of proper womanhood began to alter those rules in the 1920s. Increasing access to automobiles and to commercial entertainment sites, such as the movie theaters and amusement parks where urban working-class youth had long congregated, meant that young middle-class couples now moved their courtship away from the girl's front porch or parlor and into arenas beyond direct adult supervision. In the wake of the successful British and American suffrage movements, young women of the 1920s enjoyed a new sense of emancipation as they went on unsupervised outings with their beaux and wore the leg-baring, easily mass-produced, and relatively inexpensive chemise dress inspired by French designer Coco Chanel. These liberated flappers—so named because their unbuckled galoshes flapped when they walked—joined their male partners to create the world of unchaperoned dating.[8]

As parental control over children's courtship practices lapsed, so too did their influence over when and whom their children married. Although this situation might logically have been expected to lower the average marriage age, it did not. In locations where the new courtship patterns first took hold—the United States, the United Kingdom, and northwestern Europe—the long-standing custom of newlyweds establishing their own independent households prevented such developments. Unlike cultures where extended family living arrangements prevailed, the industrialized West expected economic self-sufficiency prior to marriage. Compulsory education requirements that kept young people out of the full-time workforce until their late teens, and the economic chaos of the Great Depression, prevented average marriage ages from falling. In 1930s Britain, for instance, women typically married in their middle twenties and men in their late twenties. In the United States, the average marriage age at the dawn of the Depression was 24.3 for men and 21.3 for women. By 1939, after a decade of economic turmoil, those averages rose to 26.7 for men and 23.3 for women. Such relatively high marriage ages provided a further check on the birthrate throughout the industrialized West.[9]

THE IMPACT OF WORLD WAR II
ON FAMILY LIFE

Western family life trends altered dramatically with the onset of World War II. In Europe, the war placed women, children, and the elderly at equal risk with men of military age and disrupted any semblance of normal family life. Consumer shortages, widespread male and female employment in war manufacturing and the military, and high civilian and military casualty rates affected daily life both in Britain and on the continent. In the Nazi-occupied territories, mass arrests, starvation, forced labor, and the annihilation of entire families in Hitler's death camps took an additional and devastating toll. In the Soviet Union, Stalin's wartime crackdown on suspected enemies of the state also divided and destroyed families as millions faced execution or imprisonment in the gulag.[10]

One of the most obvious changes in wartime family life was the transformation of women's responsibilities. The Soviet Union and Great Britain even drafted women into war service. Women comprised seventy-five percent of the Soviet agricultural labor force and made up a majority of factory workers. Of necessity, conscripted farm and factory laborers often found themselves on the war front providing support services for the Red Army. In addition, thousands of female volunteers served in active combat as pilots, artillery gunners, and tank operators. British women did not participate in combat but provided support services to fighting men, raised the nation's crops, and worked in factories. By 1943, ninety percent of single women between eighteen and forty were in British industry or the military. For married women of the same age, the figure was eighty percent. On the eve of D-Day, 7,120,000 female conscripts and volunteers between the ages of fourteen and fifty-nine had been mobilized for British war service.[11]

Unlike their Allied opponents, the Axis powers did not draft women into war service, but conditions in Germany and Italy similarly prevented women from performing their traditional family duties. In Germany, half a million women worked as support staff for the military. They initially served as clerical staff and telephone operators, but by the end of the war they were aiming searchlights, firing antiaircraft guns, driving trucks and ambulances, nursing the wounded, and participating in fire fights.[12]

Although its impact was less devastating than in Europe, World War II also changed family life and the family life cycle in North America. In Canada and the United States, young men served in the military in large numbers, as did a much smaller number of North American women. More significantly, when men left for military service, women took their places in the civilian workforce. In the United States, female employment grew by more than fifty percent as patriotism and the high wages to be earned in so-called men's jobs drew women into the workforce for the duration. The proportion of all American women who were employed rose from 27.6 percent to 37 percent during the war, and by 1945 women made up over 36 percent of the nation's total civilian workforce. Three-fourths of the nation's new women workers were married; by war's end, one in four American wives was employed. And one-third of these new workers had children under the age of fourteen. With little government support, America's Rosie the Riveters faced some daunting challenges. Federal funding supported a few war industry daycare facilities, but these centers provided care for only ten percent of the children who needed it. Most women had to rely on friends, neighbors, family members, or paid babysitters to fill the gap. Concern about older children centered on the fear that teenagers, lacking maternal supervision during the workday, would fall into bad habits or even break the law. In particular, communities near military bases worried that underage, "khaki-wacky" girls would enter into sexual relationships with servicemen.[13]

The war also had a major impact on the American marriage rate. In the first full year of American participation in the war, higher incomes and the rush to marry before young men left for military service raised the rate from a peacetime 11.9 marriages per 1,000 population to a record 13.2 per 1,000. And this penchant for marriage continued in the postwar era. In 1946, the nation's marriage rate surpassed even its wartime heights and was now double that of any prewar year. Americans focused on marriage and family life as never before. As one young war bride noted, "The idea was to live through the war years, get back with our husbands, have kids and raise a family."[14] And although twenty-five percent of married women remained in the postwar work force, they largely shifted to part-time jobs or lower-paying full-time work that accommodated their household duties and did not challenge the primacy of the male breadwinner. Men also rushed to the comfort of postwar domesticity, heeding advisors who told the returning serviceman that he had "fought for the right to found a family, the privilege of building an enduring home under the folds of freedom's flag."[15]

POSTWAR PROSPERITY AND FAMILY LIFE

The postwar period brought unprecedented prosperity to North America. By the 1950s, the number of American families classified as earning an annual middle-class income—$5,000 after taxes—was growing by more than one million households per year. The booming economy of these years encouraged brides and grooms to establish their new households at very young ages. The era's glorification of married love and its sexual double standard, which sanctioned sexual expression for women only within marriage, contributed to the formation of households by very young couples. In the words of one teenage bride of the era, "I got married in order to have a sex life. I thought that was why everyone got married."[16] As a result of these economic and ideological factors, women's median age at first marriage, which was 21.5 years in 1940, fell to 20.3 years by 1950. For men during this same period, median first-marriage age dropped from 24.3 years to 22.7. In the fifteen years following Pearl Harbor, the percentage of men who married in their early twenties doubled. During this same period, economic prosperity and younger marriages also resulted in a doubling of the fertility rate for women in their early twenties. The postwar baby boom was underway.[17]

In contrast to the rosy scenario that Americans enjoyed, displaced and homeless war survivors throughout Europe spent the early postwar period reconstituting their families, rebuilding their homes, and recovering from their physical and psychological wounds. But after Marshall Plan aid from the United States helped repair the infrastructure and economy of Western Europe, families there began to follow patterns similar to those of North America. By 1960, the worst was over, and from the mid-1960s onward, Western Europeans lived better than they ever had before. New and improved housing stock, medical improvements—including the introduction of antibiotics—and wider access to modern household, communication, and transportation technology all played a role. By every previous European living-standard measure—per capita and disposable income, longevity, health, and education—Western Europeans enjoyed an unprecedented quality of life. As in the United States, greater prosperity now allowed men and women to marry in their early twenties. But unlike the American baby boom, which lasted for eighteen years, the Western European birthrate rose only in the immediate postwar period. From 1950 onward, it continued its century-long decline.[18]

DIFFERENT PATTERNS
IN EASTERN EUROPE

Different patterns prevailed in Eastern Europe, where Soviet hegemony colored many aspects of postwar family life. Compared to Western Europe, postwar reconstruction there was slow, and the results were often inadequate. Housing, consumer goods, and the quality of medical care remained inferior to that of Western Europe. A comparison of East Germany (the German Democratic Republic/GDR) and West Germany (the Federal Republic of Germany/FRG) illustrates some of the major differences between Eastern Bloc and Western Bloc family life. Guaranteed employment and housing—however modest—allowed East Germans to marry at an earlier age than their counterparts in the FRG. In 1960, the average marriage age for East German women was 22.5, and was 23.9 for men; in West Germany, the averages were 23.7 for women and 25.9 for men. The GDR expected women as well as men to participate in the workforce, but this situation did not cause a significant difference between East and West German fertility rates. In 1960, forty-five percent of all East German women were in the labor force, and the average number of births per woman was 2.33. In the FRG, thirty-seven percent of women were employed, and the birthrate was 2.36 per woman. Enjoying a more generous parental support system than in West Germany or in other nations of the Eastern Bloc, East German women continued to increase their workforce participation while maintaining a birthrate comparable to—or even exceeding—that of the FRG. By the end of the 1960s, forty-five percent of West German women aged twenty-five to sixty were in the work force, and the West German fertility rate was 2.01 births per woman. In the GDR, seventy-three percent of women between twenty-five and sixty were employed, and the fertility rate was 2.19 births per woman.[19]

CHANGING ROLES FOR WOMEN

Whether they resided in the Eastern or Western Bloc, postwar families continued to rely primarily on wives and mothers to perform daily domestic tasks. Postwar restoration of normal family patterns meant a return to clearly defined gender roles, even as European and North American women increased their workforce participation. While women, including those of the middle class, increasingly shared breadwinning responsibilities with men, men did not return the favor by taking on a greater share of women's traditional home-making tasks. Even in communist nations and those in Western Europe that provided extensive childcare and maternity benefits, women remained largely defined by their domestic responsibilities. A feminist movement that addressed the politics of housework and women's domestic role was nonexistent in Eastern Europe and did not emerge in North America and Western Europe until the late 1960s and early 1970s.[20]

Following World War I and women's achievement of the right to vote in Britain (1918) and the United States (1920), organized feminism maintained a relatively low profile for the next several decades. By 1970, a number of factors coalesced to bring new attention to women's issues. In the United States, where feminism reemerged with particular strength, the civil rights and anti-war movements of the 1960s provided young women with new language and strategies to identify and challenge existing gender hierarchies. At the same time, older women who had experienced the expanded job opportunities of World War II were tiring of their more constrained postwar circumstances, a frustration voiced in Betty Friedan's 1963 bestseller *The Feminine Mystique*. French writer Simone de Beauvoir influenced Friedan and other American feminists with her book *The Second Sex* (1949), which focused on the social construction of gender roles with its argument that "women are not born but are made."[21]

The re-energized American feminist movement of the 1960s led the way for a reemergence of Western European feminism in the 1970s. Building on and refining her earlier arguments, de Beauvoir became a leading spokeswoman for European feminism, which often aligned itself with Western European socialism. In Europe and America, feminists of the 1970s questioned existing assumptions about male and female relationships, including the notion that women automatically took on primary responsibility for childcare and housework. They also drew attention to the problems of violence against women, sexual assault, the sexual double standard, and continuing prohibitions against certain types of birth control.[22]

THE FEMINIST MOVEMENT
AND THE LIFE CYCLE

The feminist revolution of the 1960s and 1970s had a significant impact on the life cycle of American and Western European families. Feminist movement pressure lowered many of the continuing legal and cultural barriers to women's employment at the same time that the troubled economy of the 1970s caused more families to rely on a second income. In 1950, one-third of U.S. women were employed, and only half of them held full-time jobs. By 1975, nearly half of American women were employed, and more than seventy percent had full-time positions. Nations that sponsored family support services witnessed an even higher increase in female employment. In 1960, thirty percent of Swedish women and thirty-seven percent of Danish women were in the work-force. By 1980, seventy-one percent of women in Sweden and sixty percent of those in Denmark were employed. But even in the United States, which lacked state-sponsored daycare or maternal leave programs, much of the increase in female employment occurred among married women with young children. By the mid-1970s, two in five married mothers of preschool-age children and over half of American wives with school-age children were in the paid labor force.[23]

In the 1970s, the spread of feminist ideology and the increase in women's paid employment began to undermine postwar ideas and practices regarding marriage and family. Increasingly, Americans and Western Europeans viewed female adulthood as a period that combined marriage, motherhood, and a strong workplace identity. Girls still wanted a family when they grew up, but as a Swedish guidance counselor noted, "*Every* girl now thinks in terms of a job."[24] An American sociologist described the new girlhood fantasy: "There is still the prince, but happily-ever-after now includes a career."[25] With paid employment now viewed as a permanent feature of their lives, young women of the 1970s spent more time training for and establishing jobs before they entered marriage. In the United States, women's median age at first marriage rose from 20.3 years in the early 1950s to 21 two decades later. And older brides generally translated into older grooms, as women continued the long-term trend of marrying men who were a few years older than themselves.[26]

The later start in marriage generally translated into a later and abbreviated period of reproduction for Western couples. In 1957, only twenty-nine percent of Americans aged twenty-one to twenty-nine were childless; by 1976, fifty percent of persons in that age range had no children. During this same period, the American birthrate fell from an average three to four births per woman to only two. Along with changes in marriage age, increased access to birth control affected birthrates in both America and Western Europe. Between 1960 and 1973, American women benefited from introduction of the birth control pill and Supreme Court decisions that overturned those state laws still prohibit-ing contraceptive use and first-trimester abortions. By the 1960s and 1970s, abortion had been legal in Scandinavia and most of the Eastern Bloc for a num-ber of years. After the Soviet Union reinstated legal abortion in the mid-1950s, it became the nation's primary means of birth control. But elsewhere in Europe, feminists and other leftists engaged in bitter and lengthy campaigns to change birth control policies. Birth control campaigns were particularly hard-fought in Catholic nations, but between 1968 and 1985, France, Italy, and Spain all amended their laws to allow first contraception and then abortion. By 1990, fertility rates in all three nations were among the lowest in Europe. In these nations and elsewhere in Western Europe, women now typically delayed having their first child until their late twenties.[27]

DIVORCE REFORM

At approximately the same time that birth control reform swept through Western Europe and North America, so did divorce reform. In the United States, a major turning point occurred in 1966, when New York, then the nation's second most populous state, amended its notoriously restrictive statute to include reasons other than adultery as grounds for divorce. Then on New Year's Day 1970, California, the nation's most populous state, became the first to allow divorce on nonadversarial grounds, ending the practice of one spouse assuming guilt or fault for the end of a marriage. Other states quickly followed suit, either implementing "irretrievable breakdown" of a marriage or incompatibility of the spouses as the only grounds for divorce or adding this no-fault option to existing grounds such as adultery, cruelty, or abandonment. By August 1977, only three states continued to practice an adversarial system of divorce in which one party always assumed guilt for the end of the union.[28]

At roughly the same time that American no-fault laws were simplifying the pathway to legal divorce, the nation's Roman Catholic clergy were becoming more generous in granting church annulments to marriages that had ended in civil divorce. As a result, a greater number of Catholics could now end unhappy marriages via divorce but still maintain the option of marrying a new spouse in a Catholic ceremony. Legal reforms in the 1970s, along with nearly simultaneous changes in the attitude of many Roman Catholic clergy, contributed to a skyrocketing divorce rate. And in addition to female employment having an effect on marriage age and birthrate, it also had an impact on the Western divorce rate. Demographers attributed the doubling of America's divorce rate between 1966 and 1976 in part to women's expanded presence in the workplace. Women who earned a wage of their own were simply less reluctant to end unhappy marriages. By the early 1980s, some estimates indicated that one in two U.S. marriages was ending in divorce.[29]

The American divorce revolution of the 1960s and 1970s played a role in dismantling the idea that marriage was a contract in which the husband automatically assumed economic support of the wife. When a marriage ended with neither spouse at fault, the law could no longer require a cruel, adulterous, or otherwise guilty husband to pay his ex-wife alimony. Additionally, the U.S. Supreme Court rendered the concept of alimony ostensibly gender-neutral when it ruled in the late 1970s that women as well as men could be potentially liable for the financial support of an ex-spouse. In practice, however, evolving divorce laws of the 1970s led to a situation in which the typical ex-spouse—whether male or female—was expected to be self-supporting and also contribute to the economic support of any minor children that the marriage had produced.[30]

Divorce reform also occurred in Western Europe and resulted in similar changes in family life. The most dramatic change took place in Italy, where the Roman Catholic Church had long opposed legalizing divorce. When a new law in 1970 allowed divorce under highly controlled circumstances, the church launched a four-year campaign for its repeal that resulted in significant feminist backlash. In a 1974 referendum, 59.3 percent of the electorate voted to retain the law, with women voters noticeably outpacing men in their support. Divorce reform in Italy and elsewhere resulted in an increased divorce rate of fifty percent or more throughout most of Western Europe between 1970 and 1980. In turn, the number of single-parent families rose, as did the number of blended families that resulted from divorce and remarriage. In the early 1980s, the proportion of Western European families headed by a single parent rose to between ten and fifteen percent of all families with dependent children.[31]

THE RISE OF COHABITATION

High divorce rates and other challenges to marriage left young Americans and Western Europeans with what social scientists termed a more neutral attitude toward married life. While a national mental health survey in 1957 indicated that forty-six percent of Americans in the twenty-one to twenty-nine age range held a negative attitude toward persons who did not marry, a follow-up study in 1976 showed that only twenty-two percent of persons in that age group harbored negative feelings toward people who remained single. Analysts noted that this "increased tolerance of people who reject marriage as a way of life" represented the most dramatic difference between responses to the 1957 survey and answers to the 1976 study.[32] In particular, the extremely negative attitude that single women themselves once held toward their unmarried status and failure to conform to the postwar domestic ideal had significantly dissipated by 1976. In summarizing survey results, scholars surmised that young people no longer believed that marriage was a necessary component of well-adjusted adulthood.[33]

One result of this change in attitudes was an increased rate of nonmarital cohabitation in both America and Europe. U.S. Census Bureau statistics indicated that the number of cohabiting couples more than doubled between 1970 and 1979 to reach a total of 1,346,000. The largest increase occurred among childless couples under the age of twenty-five. For members of that population group, the number of couples living together rose from 29,000 in 1970 to 274,000 in 1979—an eightfold increase. By 1975, eighteen percent of twenty- to thirty-year-old men who participated in a national survey reported that they had lived for six months or more with a female partner to whom they were not married. In total, the number of cohabiting couples in America rose forty percent in just the two years between 1977 and 1979. Western Europe followed similar trends. In 1981, forty-five percent of Danish women aged twenty to twenty-four and forty-four percent of Swedish women in that age range lived with nonmarital partners. These living arrangements contributed to a dramatic rise in out-of-wedlock pregnancies throughout the West. By 1989, thirty-six percent of Norwegian births, forty-six percent of Danish births, and fifty-two percent of Swedish births were to unmarried women. In Austria, Finland, France, and Great Britain, approximately one-fourth of births were to single women.[34]

THE GAY AND LESBIAN RIGHTS MOVEMENT

A final way in which the feminist movement of the 1960s and 1970s changed Western family life was the launch of a high-profile gay and lesbian rights movement. With its questioning of traditional gender roles and relationships, feminism provided ideology and language for persons who faced discrimination in same-sex relationships. Most activists identify the movement's starting point as the evening in June 1969 when gay customers began resisting police harassment at New York's Stonewall Inn bar. Forty years later, same-sex marriage would be legal in the American states of Massachusetts, Connecticut, Vermont, Iowa, and New Hampshire and in the Netherlands, Belgium, Spain, Canada, Norway, and South Africa.[35]

As a result of the dramatic changes of the 1970s, the Western family life cycle was significantly altered as the twentieth century drew to a close. The changes for women were particularly striking. By the 1980s, only forty percent of women followed the life sequence of their mothers' generation: work, marriage, childbearing, and homemaking. Many of them were cohabiting and having children out of wedlock. And although most would eventually marry, they no longer assumed they would marry by a particular age or stay married to one person for life. Surveys in the 1960s showed ninety percent of Americans agreeing that there was a best age for marriage, but only forty percent held that viewpoint in the 1980s. By the end of that decade, American women's median age at first marriage had risen to 23.2 years, and the average age of all American brides (first and multiple marriages combined) was 28.6 years. In Western Europe, women's mean age at first marriage ranged from a high of 27 in Switzerland to around 25 in most other nations.[36]

During the last decade of the twentieth century, following the collapse of the Soviet Union, Eastern European families began to follow life cycle patterns that more closely resembled those of Western Europe and North America. The East German experience represents the most dramatic example of change. In the closing years of the old regime, a young woman in the GDR typically completed her formal education at sixteen, began full-time employment at seventeen, married by the time she was twenty-one, and had at least one child by twenty-two. In contrast, at age twenty-two her West German counterpart was just completing her education and would not marry and begin having children for at least another five years. After the fall of the Berlin Wall in 1989 and German reunification the following year, women of the former GDR quickly adopted a similar life script. The average age at first marriage for both women and men in the former GDR jumped by half a decade within three years of unification. And by the late 1990s, women of the former East Germany were giving birth to their first child at an average age of twenty-seven. Delayed marriage and childbirth resulted in part from the loss of jobs, stipends, and childcare support that East Germany's communist regime had once guaranteed. But East German women's conformity to long-established West German patterns also resulted from new opportunities to travel or to enjoy other experiences denied them in the old GDR. Like their Western European counterparts, youth of the former Soviet Bloc often desired a period of personal pleasure and self development before settling down to the responsibilities of marriage and family.[37]

CONCLUSIONS

As the twentieth century came to an end, only a small minority of Western families conformed to the Victorian ideal: a breadwinner and a homemaker who married young and shortly thereafter had children. By 2000, the average age at which people married and became parents had increased significantly.

And throughout the West, women were active and permanent members of the paid labor force regardless of their marital status and whether or not they were mothers. In an age of high divorce rates and an increasingly neutral attitude toward marriage, a growing number of families were organizing themselves outside of marriage. The choice to remain single or to cohabitate with a person of the same or opposite sex had gained greater acceptance. By 2005, even with family-values Republicans controlling their government, less than half of America's households (49.7 percent) contained a legally wed couple. Greater latitude also existed about when—or even whether—individuals or couples reproduced. Parenthood outside of—or prior to—marriage was becoming the norm in much of Western Europe, and it was a growing trend elsewhere. Once children were born, Western parents faced greater uncertainty about when they would leave the nest. High housing costs and the desire for a period of self discovery before settling down caused more young adults to remain in—or return to—their parents' homes. In the century's last decade, the number of young Americans who had completed their education but still resided with their parents was significantly higher (especially among men) than it had been a generation earlier. All these changes made defining the typical Western family life cycle more problematic in 2000 than in 1900. Even middle-class Westerners now tolerated a range of family forms and life-cycle sequences that their Victorian counterparts would have found unthinkable. By 2000, the class that had invented the twentieth-century family ideal rarely followed its precepts.[38]

CHAPTER SEVEN

The State

KRISTE LINDENMEYER
AND JEANINE GRAHAM

Throughout a twentieth century marked by major armed conflicts and substantial political, economic, environmental, and social transformations, the lives of children and their families were threatened, neglected, and destroyed but also variously idealized and supported. Religion, culture, location, timing, and socioeconomic circumstance contributed to the diversity of experiences for children and their families. Ethnicity, gender, and class were also powerful influences. Furthermore, the continued rural-to-urban migration shifting Western societies from agricultural to industrialized economies dramatically expanded the influence of overarching authorities, whether democratic, authoritarian, religious, or autocratic, on family units and the communities where they lived.

Whatever their outward appearance of compliance or cooperation, families were by no means passive in their reactions to changes in their societies and environments. The "one child per family" policy in China is a case in point.[1] From the early twentieth century through today, abhorrent state policies too often contribute to the suffering and destruction of families. Sadly, examples all too easily come to mind: the forced deportation of the kulaks in Soviet Russia as part of the government's massive land collectivization program begun in 1929; Nazi concentration camps that targeted children and their families viewed as contrary to the national ideal defined by the state; the mass destruction and murder of urban elites under the Khmer Rouge in Cambodia in the late 1970s; and the ongoing redistribution of white settler farms in postcolonial Zimbabwe. Yet, without in any way diminishing the trauma of such policies for children and their families in the name of the state, it is possible to say that the twentieth century was also an era when both democratic and authoritarian regimes extended the range of their activities and established, in different guises, a form of welfare state focused on the well-being of families and children. Consequently, around the world, protecting the rights of children is increasingly acknowledged as a responsibility of the state.

Obviously, national comparisons over time are complicated by the environment, politics, and economics that shape priorities underpinning public social welfare policies at various points within national histories. Comparative peace, prosperity, and demographic homogeneity, for example, contribute to the development of public policies directed at families and children. However, policies vary even among the most generous countries, and it is not always easy to clearly identify the reasons for such differences. For instance, in a recent Organization for Economic Co-operation and Development (OECD) survey among European Union (EU) countries, Belgium, Finland, France, and Luxembourg ranked as the most generous for children and families. Austria,

FIGURE 7.1: *Children at Jordon Downs Housing Projects, 1950*. Shades of L.A. Archives/Los Angeles Public Library. http://jpgl.lapl.org/pics04/00001539.jpg. Courtesy of Los Angeles Public Library.

Denmark, Germany, Holland, Sweden, and the United Kingdom were an intermediate group in terms of the level of support provided, while Greece, Ireland, Italy, Portugal, and Spain offered the lowest level of direct financial help to families. Some critics may complain that the survey failed to include other important factors that directly affect the lives of children and their families. When a wider framework is considered, one in which there is a greater concern to balance family and workplace responsibilities—through maternity leave, child-care provisions, flexible working hours, and holiday arrangements, for instance—Scandinavian and Francophone countries provided the greatest level of support, while Mediterranean countries provided the least. Such factors include state-supported maternity leave, child-care provisions, flexible working hours, and holiday arrangements but deemphasize direct payments to parents of young children. With this broader framework in mind, Mediterranean countries provide the least support, while the Scandinavian and Francophone nations are the most generous. On the other hand, a historical comparison examining the nascent welfare states emerging at the very beginning of the twentieth century would focus more on the regulation of child and female labor, forms of health and unemployment insurance offered to male breadwinners and the elderly, and the provision of pensions to widows with dependent children.[2]

The increasing intersection of private lives and public policies occurred during decades of significant transformation in the nature of family life throughout the twentieth century. As a somewhat random sample of post–World War II state enactments suggests, legislation tended to be more a response to social change than a catalyst for it. Paid parental/maternal leave and subsidized child care, long established in Sweden, France, and other Western European nations is now also available in many Eastern European countries. Education for children is now universally viewed as a government responsibility, but there is a wide variance in accessibility. For example, the Indonesian government accepted responsibility for children's education in 1945 and, in 1989, affirmed the right of every Indonesian child to have nine years of elementary education, even though delivery on that commitment continues to be hampered by limited public funding and conservative cultural traditions. Social change is reflected in public policy like Israeli legislation, passed in 1989, aimed at preventing child abuse and protecting vulnerable people within families. Consequently, children's voices are heard in divorce and custody cases, a contrast with long-held religious beliefs that children are the property of fathers. Other such policies directed at families are grounded in cultural rather than solely religious beliefs. For example, the prohibition on mixed-race marriages in South Africa, established in 1949, was removed in the 1996 constitutional reforms of the postapartheid regime. And, in a greater recognition of women's rights, an updated civil code in 2002 addresses gender inequality in Turkey and replaces the traditional notion of the husband as head of the household that linked traditional religious and cultural practices.[3]

Other rights were specifically directed at children. In the 1980s, Scandinavian countries recognized government's responsibility to protect a legal right of every child to have a place in a state-supported childcare nursery. The reform also reflected significant trends altering the nature of family life, especially in Western societies. The increased participation of mothers in the paid workforce, the rise in single-parent families, an awareness of gender inequality and racial discrimination, as well as a decline in formal religious observance are among such trends. In addition, the simpler composition of households as the nuclear family became more common than extended family living arrangements; the growing international recognition, in principle but not always in practice, of fundamental human rights; a rise in divorce and decline in marriage rates; along with the emergence and social acceptance of new forms of family structures (reconstituted or blended families and homosexual or lesbian/gay relationships) are also important trends.[4]

This chapter aims to illustrate the complexity of state–family/child relationships through a detailed study of one country and one central issue. As American social work pioneer Grace Abbott observed in 1938: "The progress of a state may be measured by the extent to which it safeguards the rights of its children." Abbott's perspective was well-informed. In 1912, the United States became the first nation in the world to establish a federal agency (the U.S. Children's Bureau) focused solely on the issues concerning its youngest citizens. Abbott joined the agency in its early years and worked as its chief from 1921 to 1934. She also helped to write the seminal child welfare sections of the 1935 Social Security Act and lobbied tirelessly at the international level for public recognition of children's rights. Throughout the twentieth century, advocates like Abbott gained momentum for the issue of protections children and family in the United States, Scandinavia, and other Western democracies. The United Nations *Declaration of the Rights of the Child* in 1959 and the 1989 UN *Convention on the Rights of the Child* and its 2002 protocols condemning the use of children as prostitutes and soldiers, reflected, at least in principle, the near universal acceptance of the idea that children had distinct rights, most often connected to sustaining strong families through government support. Signatories to the convention acknowledged that "childhood is entitled to special care and assistance" and commit to the ideal that "in all actions concerning children, whether undertaken by public or private social welfare institutions, courts of law, administrative authorities or legislative bodies, the best interests of the child shall be a primary consideration." Yet the United States is still the only UN member nation that has not signed the 1989 convention, a position that seems in stark contrast with the innovation and leadership shown in 1912. Examining the major turning points in the evolution of U.S. policy reveals many of the underlying issues and ambiguities that shape children's relationship to the state, providing a case study that invites comparison with the processes of establishing children's rights in other (predominantly democratic) societies in the twentieth century. In most instances, the promotion of children's rights needs to be viewed within the broader context of policies that focus on family well-being. In this chapter, however, priority is given to the issues arising from state efforts to regulate and shape children and family life.[5]

THE CHILD AND THE STATE
IN EARLY AMERICA

In sixteenth-century England, children held a legal status similar to that of adults. But by the time English colonies were established in North America, childhood had been redefined as a clear period of dependency, similar to other groups not considered fully capable of independence: slaves, married women, American Indians, and the mentally ill. The length and extent of childhood dependency expanded in the years leading up to and during the American Revolution.[6]

From the colonial era to the end of the nineteenth century, the patriarchal family dominated, with male heads of household legally and socially responsible for dependents. Fathers were charged with providing for children's "maintenance and protection ... as a natural duty" and "education suitable to their station in life: a duty pointed out by reason."[7] In general, the state designated colonial children as either legitimate or bastards for purposes of inheritance and as a means of enforcing the integrity of marriage as a tool used to maintain the social and economic status quo. Where slavery existed, poor-law officials classified all enslaved children as bastards. Poverty could also contribute to an altered status for children and parents. Throughout all British colonies, poverty weakened parental custody rights under English Common Law. The legal concept of *parens patriae* recognized the power of the state to intervene in children's lives as the ultimate parent. Prior to the twentieth century, however, courts generally restricted application of that principle to children without family support. State-ordered and state-sanctioned indenture of poor children and orphans, for example, continued from the first colonial settlements through the early twentieth century in England and the United States. In the United States, even after the constitutional elimination of slavery in 1865, racial discrimination worked in conjunction with traditions rooted in English poor laws to create legal avenues for Southern states to indenture black children, even if they were from intact families.[8]

Some laws in the colonial period recognized some rights for children and adolescents but also emphasized the patriarchal family as an ideal that put parents, namely fathers, as the natural guardians responsible for protecting children's rights. Specifically, education was a parental (paternal) responsibility. Young people were educated at home and in apprenticeships. Children from poor and even middle-class households were contracted by parents to apprenticeships recognized by the government.[9]

Even early on, however, some individuals criticized this arrangement as being insufficient for the long-term well-being of society. Puritan minister Cotton Mather urged New Englanders to consider an alternative to indenture as the means of education for children. He called for the establishment of religious schools in order to "Save us from the Mischiefs and Scandals of an Uncultivated Offspring." Mather also argued that "Schools, wherein the Youth may by able Masters be Taught the Things that are necessary to qualify them for future Serviceableness, and have their Manners therewithal well-formed under a Laudable Discipline, and be over and above Well-Catechised in the principles of Religion."[10] Despite Mather's suggestion, few schools were established in North America in the seventeenth or eighteenth centuries, and the state did not assume responsibility for educating children. Parental and state-ordered indenture was a common experience for young Americans.

Besides using forced indenture to support parental and state economic interests, colonial governments also dealt with the care of orphaned and homeless children. Some abandoned children certainly benefited from the state-authorized indenture system since few other alternatives existed for their care. Government attempted to protect indentured children from abuse and exploitation. Colonial Maryland established an orphan court system in 1651 and three decades later appointed special juries to oversee the welfare of orphans under its care. However, in practice, government oversight and intervention on behalf of such children was often too little, too late. Colonial court records note abuse by parents and guardians, but courts rarely checked adult authority.[11] Concerns about indentured children's circumstances and the best ways to care for abandoned children contributed to the creation of the first orphanages in North America. In 1729, the Roman Catholic Ursuline sisters opened an orphan asylum in New Orleans. Nine years later, German Lutherans, influenced by the success of August Hermann Francke's orphanage and religious school in Halle, Germany, established a similar institution in colonial Georgia. After another nine years, the famous Great Awaking minister George Whitefield organized the Bethesda Asylum nearby. Whitefield argued that orphanages were a means of "freeing [indentured] children from slavery" and a way to guarantee that youngsters without parents would have religious instruction.[12] However, most orphanages continued to bind out or indenture children as a way to pay for their support.

After the American Revolution, Charleston, South Carolina hosted the first secular public orphanage, opening its doors in 1790. Children's orphan asylums were also created in Philadelphia and New York City. In 1799, Baltimore established an orphanage for impoverished girls. Eighteenth-century alms houses, or poor houses as they were often called, placed children in the same facilities as adults. The creation of distinct orphan asylums suggested that children were dependents with needs separate from those of adults. Adoption was not a legal option in the colonies and not socially acceptable until after the American Civil War.[13]

Mortality and morbidity rates often reached fifty percent in orphanages. Crowded and poor conditions spread disease even in the most benevolent institutions. Another problem was the fact that orphan asylums almost exclusively served white children, leaving nonwhites with even fewer options for help. Homeless free black children were extremely likely to be forced into slavery. In the United States, a black child inherited the legal status of his or her mother, and homeless children were assumed to be slaves. Fathers were irrelevant under the law. As nineteenth-century civil rights leader and abolitionist Frederick Douglass argued, "Slavery has not use for fathers or families."[14] Sister Elizabeth Lange, founder of the Oblate Sisters of Providence, an order of Roman Catholic nuns of African descent, opened the first orphanage in North America for free black children, in Baltimore, Maryland in 1828, but few other such institutions followed.

The American Revolution heightened appreciation for democratic ideals such as individualism and independence. But, of course, this ideology did not end slavery and in some ways further increased a status of dependency for all children. Fathers retained primary legal authority, but Americans also began to put greater importance on the companionate, republican, nuclear family as representative of the American ideal. The republican model was a more democratic and less patriarchal vision of domestic life, with the nuclear family holding greater autonomy from the state. As Michael Grossberg explains,

"Under the sway of republican theory and culture, the home and the polity displayed some striking similarities. These included a deep aversion to authority and unchecked government activism."[15]

THE STATE AND THE RISE OF
THE AMERICAN MIDDLE-CLASS
CHILDHOOD IDEAL

The nineteenth century's transition from an economy based on agriculture to a more industrialized and urban nation contributed to dramatic changes in the American family and the child's relationship to the state. The first federal census conducted in 1790 revealed that 95 percent of children and adults lived on farms or in villages of less than 2,500 people. In 1920, the census showed that for the first time in U.S. history, a majority of Americans resided in urban areas. Greater family autonomy along with the beginnings of industrialization provided fertile ground for the growth of urban middle-class families and their redefinition of the American childhood ideal. The revised model held nuclear families in highest esteem and called for a protected and dependent childhood from birth through adolescence. The new ideal emphasized children's sentimental value over their potential economic contributions and called for youngsters to spend more time in school than working at chores or for wages.[16]

The glorification of the nuclear family and a protected childhood went hand-in-hand with America's self-identification as a morally superior nation based on Protestant Christian values. The focus on nuclear families contributed to a reduction in the use of bastardy as a legal category for children. Of course some babies were born outside of marriage, but the emphasis on nuclear families as fundamental to republican democracy expanded the definitions of legitimacy. By the beginning of the twentieth century, in the United States, as in Britain and other Western countries, membership in a nuclear family became society's and the state's most important measure of normalcy in a child's life. Within and beyond the United States, however, distinctions between legitimate and illegitimate children continued to be legally significant, particularly when issues of inheritance were at stake as, for instance, in German (1896) and Swiss (1907) civil codes.[17]

The reliance on the nuclear family also paralleled an expansion of school-based education, a significant sphere for the extension of state involvement in children's lives. Schools were a tool for helping parents to educate children and for unifying a diverse nation. The U.S. Land Ordinance of 1785 set aside acreage in townships for schools in the Northwest Territories. Most states and territories, however, did not actually establish public schools until the 1820s common school movement championed by Horace Mann. By the mid-nineteenth century, publicly funded elementary schools were common in American towns and cities. Evangelical Christian theology dominated the curriculum, as evidenced in texts such *McGuffey Readers,* first published in 1836. Catholic churches, responding to the rise of nativism and anti-Catholicism, established parochial schools by the mid-nineteenth century, but few communities offered public or private education beyond grammar school. Boston is credited with opening the nation's first public high school, in 1821, but throughout the nineteenth and early twentieth century only a minority of American adolescents spent any time in school beyond the eighth grade—less than ten percent in 1815 and only twenty percent as late as 1915.[18]

African American children, however, did not generally benefit from public schools at all. In antebellum America, most black children, free and enslaved, were systematically denied access to public schooling, even in states without slavery. In the South, the Civil War and Reconstruction ended slavery and introduced the region's first efforts to establish public schools, for blacks or whites. From 1865 to 1870, the federal government spent $5 million in more than 1,000 Freedmen Bureau schools. The end of Reconstruction ended the Freedman's Bureau experiment and left poor Southern states with little money for, or commitment to, public education. The Supreme Court's 1896 *Plessy v. Ferguson* decision further complicated the situation by condoning state-mandated racial segregation, leading to the creation of an expensive dual education system in Jim Crow states. More significant, the court's 1899 *Cummings v. Richmond Board of Education* ruling specifically extended federal approval of segregation to public education and went further by permitting separate and unequal schools. Overall, in Southern states there was little commitment to public education for whites or blacks well into the twentieth century. In California, segregation restricted Asian students' attendance in public schools, and segregation in Texas also sent children of Mexican heritage to separate schools.[19]

Many American Indian children were also segregated in school. After the Civil War, the federal government enforced the Indian reservation system and began funding day and boarding schools. Some boarding schools were located on reservations, but others were located at a great distance from reservations and, consequently, families. Curriculum in the Indian schools promoted vocational skills and assimilation to white society. Many students found their education useless when they returned to their families or were hindered by prejudice when they tried to assimilate to society outside of reservations and, often, far from the support of their families.[20]

In 1910, President Theodore Roosevelt's commissioner of Indian Education, Francis E. Leupp, criticized the government-run schools as "simple educational almshouses." In 1928, an independent reviewer called government support for Indian children's education "grossly inadequate" and commended the trend to place students in day schools near their homes over boarding schools far from reservation lands.[21]

Midwestern states scored the nineteenth century's highest literacy rates. Community leaders viewed public schools as an effective means for promoting shared values and civilizing the frontier. Good schools attracted parents looking to the western lands as a new opportunity for improving the lives of their children. The promotion of school as the primary work of childhood and part of the pathway to a better life led states in the late nineteenth century to pass compulsory school attendance laws. Despite wide disparities in quality and access, public schools had a broad reach that spread the middle-class childhood ideal to all regions of the United States. As was already the case for youngsters in many parts of northwestern Europe and in Britain and its Dominions (Australia, Canada, Ireland, New Zealand, and white South Africa), attending elementary school became a right of passage for U.S. children. In 1930, ninety-five percent of all Americans under fourteen years of age attended school for at least part of the year.[22]

New state child labor regulations went hand-in-hand with the growth of elementary schools. As the history of indenture and apprenticeship shows, in the colonial and early national period children's work was viewed as an asset to the state. The shift away from an agricultural-based economy, however, encouraged a growing number of young people into wage-labor jobs. Up to the mid-nineteenth century, physical capacity rather than numerical age generally defined when a young person moved from childhood dependency to greater independence and adultlike responsibilities. After 1850, schools and a growing focus on age-based grade levels placed more importance on age than on physical capacity. The first factories in the United States hired workers ten years old and under, but by the Civil War, discipline problems and the availability of cheap adult labor meant that only a minority of factories employed children. Instead, most young people worked in agriculture, either as important economic contributors to their families or as slaves. After the Civil War, many children continued to work in the nation's fields, but a growing proportion also labored for wages in America's mines, streets, and factories. For some adults, the shift suggested exploitation and abuse that ran contrary to the rising middle-class childhood ideal. Consequently, reformers began to call for state regulation of what they called America's child labor problem.[23]

Despite a growing condemnation of child labor in the Progressive Era, from 1870 to 1910 the percentage of children under fourteen years of age working increased from 13.2 to 18.4 percent. Boys were more likely to work for wages than were girls. States in the northeast began to pass laws before the Civil War regulating the employment of children under fourteen years of age, but change was slow. Many families depended on children's meager wages, and Americans tended to resist the regulation of child labor as a threat to parental authority. Comparable attitudes were expressed during similar debates in other industrializing countries. Within the United Kingdom, for example, the regulation of child labor in factories and mines preceded the beginnings of compulsory elementary education passed in 1870. Restrictions on country children working in the agricultural sector, however, proved much harder to enforce. In the Australasian colonies, legislators tried to circumvent parental opposition to compulsory education by setting a minimum age for youth employment above the minimum age for leaving school. Yet even when parents were fined for their children's absenteeism at school, attendance was still erratic, especially when there were younger siblings that needed care. Throughout the nineteenth century, the domestic or external work of older siblings was often vital to the functioning of a working-class household. The combination of compulsory education and child labor laws had structural implications for family life, as the distinction between dependents and (paid) working members became more pronounced, and the prolonged dependence of children contributed to policies designed to ensure that a male breadwinner's wage would be sufficient to support his family.[24]

The growing popularity of the middle-class childhood ideal and the expansion of cities after the Civil War drew new attention to the plight of urban children living in poverty. Children's susceptibility to contagious disease, exploitive labor, and domestic abuse was nothing new. Nevertheless, by the late nineteenth century, many adults in industrializing nation's like the United States feared that modern economic progress was happening at the expense of its children. Critics noted that the increasingly visible social problems of hunger, disease, vice, crime, and despair seemed to hit children the hardest and weakened vulnerable families. In his 1890 book about New York City's tenement neighborhoods, *How the Other Half Lives*, muckraking journalist Jacob Riis wrote, "the problem of the children [and] their number ... in these swarms [is enough to] make one stand aghast."[25] Poverty and dislocation rendered more serious a problem that was regarded, in the United Kingdom and elsewhere, as a potential threat to social order.

The recognition of poverty in the nation's cities encouraged the development of new charities centered on needy children. The Society for the Prevention of Cruelty to Children (SPCC) was established in New York City in 1875. Charles Loring Brace's Children's Aid Society (CAS) became one of the most influential of the new children's charities promoting a solution to the growing number of poor children in urban America. From 1854 to 1930, Brace's CAS worked closely with state authorities to send approximately 200,000 children from New York City to farms in the Midwest and west (as well as a few to Canada and Mexico). The work of the CAS contributed to and resulted from the heightened social focus on the nuclear family as an ideal important to the nation's democratic future. Many of the youngsters under the CAS's care were newcomers to the United States or were the children of immigrant parents. Even though these children were often from Roman Catholic families, Brace's organization promoted "Protestant Christianity and religious conversion."[26]

The creation of juvenile courts in the late nineteenth and early twentieth centuries, within and beyond the United States, also reflected the new philosophy distinguishing children's rights from those of adults. In 1874, Massachusetts created special court procedures for children involved in crimes. Benjamin Barr Lindsey championed the idea of a special children's court in Denver, Colorado in 1899, and California's Miriam Van Waters also became an advocate for juvenile courts. Cook County, Illinois established the first official U.S. juvenile court in 1899, three years after Norway had inaugurated the world's first such system. Other nation's followed, and by 1920, within the U.S. forty of the forty-eight states had adopted something close to the Illinois' juvenile model. Juvenile courts were designated to hear cases involving children accused of crimes as well as those of abused and neglected children. By 1910, some states also created separate family courts to hear domestic welfare cases involving questions concerning custody, abuse, neglect, and illegitimacy. Juvenile courts were based on the idea that young offenders and victims were emotionally immature and should not be in the same courts or under the same procedures as adults. In other words, children received special protections as dependents of the state under the law, but these protections did not include the guarantee of constitutional rights. Adult concerns about antisocial behavior committed by members of the younger generation were nothing new, nor was the idea that children needed state protection from abusive adults. As Anthony Platt argues, however, the rush to establish juvenile courts in the early twentieth century was a recognition of children's dependent status and evidence of a national obsession with preventing and controlling delinquency. The United States was by no means unique in this concern. Larrikinism was a significant youth-related issue in the Australasian colonies at this time, for example, and was viewed as a troublesome symptom of weakening of family bonds and discipline in frontier societies. Within the United States, many adults worried about the acculturation of children, especially adolescents, from immigrant families. The answer seemed to demand a strengthening of *parens patriae* as a right of childhood.[27]

THE CENTURY OF THE CHILD

The new emphasis on protecting children's dependency as a universal right of childhood encouraged a growing chorus of child welfare advocates calling for increased government intervention on behalf of the young. American social reformer and child welfare advocate Florence Kelley was among the loudest voices in this movement. In her 1905 book, *Some Ethical Gains through Legislation,* Kelley argued that *all* children had "a right to childhood" that demanded federal protection.[28]

In 1909, Theodore Roosevelt called the first White House Conference on children's issues. This meeting was the first of similar presidential conferences held each decade throughout the twentieth century. Three major ideas about the relationship of the child and the state came out of the 1909 meeting. First, participants declared that all children had the right to, as much as possible, a "normal homelife," meaning a nuclear family with a father who was the sole breadwinner and a mother who was the family's full-time caretaker. Participants contended that if a child's family failed to meet the ideal, foster care and state support for children of widows or mothers abandoned by their husbands should be provided through mothers' pensions rather than removing children from their homes and placing them in orphanages. Second, the meeting underscored the idea that while all children were dependent on adults, every child had a right to a protected and dependent status protected by the state. Third, conference attendees endorsed a call for the creation of a federal agency mandated to lobby solely on behalf of the nation's youngest citizens.[29]

The White House Conference's report clearly reflected trends within the United States but also pointed to ideas shared by child welfare activists in other industrializing countries where the adverse impact of social and economic change was most evident among vulnerable working-class children. In 1909, Swedish author and social critic Ellen Key declared that a new era had arrived, "the century of the child."[30] In hindsight this claim was overly optimistic, but it showed the important shift, clearly discernible in the developing welfare policies of most Western democracies, toward giving the state a much larger role in the lives of children based on the idea that children had rights distinct from adults. Awareness of changing fertility patterns in the West, lowering the size of middle-class families in particular, also contributed to widespread acceptance of the notion that children were not simply the possessions of their parents but also represented a nation's social capital.

On April 8, 1912, U.S. President William Howard Taft signed the legislation creating the U.S. Children's Bureau. As noted earlier, the U.S. Children's Bureau was the first federal agency in the world mandated to center its attention solely on improving the lives of a nation's youngest citizens. The U.S. Congress authorized the bureau to "investigate and report … upon all matters pertaining to the welfare of children and child life among all classes" of Americans. Some people feared that the Children's Bureau would usurp parental authority. Others worried that the agency was too closely connected to the National Child Labor Committee and the controversial anti-child labor movement. Support for the agency was strong, however, and the bureau's leadership devised a strategy aimed at silencing its critics. Supporters spelled out a broad agenda for the new bureau defined as issues surrounding the "whole child." Women active in progressive reform became the bureau's most vocal supporters, and President Taft appointed a woman, Julia C. Lathrop, as chief, an important step seven years before national female suffrage was ratified in the United States.[31]

The creation of the U.S. Children's Bureau was a significant shift in policy concerning the child and the state. However, the agency's staff and supporters faced significant problems that hindered progress. Limited to investigation and reporting, Congress initially allocated a tiny budget of only $25,640. The bureau's supporters' argument that only a single agency advocating on behalf of the whole child could protect children's best interest was open to criticism from the start. As part of a compromise to gain passage of congressional legislation, supporters agreed to give authority over children's schooling to the already established Bureau of Education. Furthermore, over the next two decades, powerful critics of the bureau such as the American Manufacturers' Association and the American Medical Association gained strength and eventually attracted other influential opponents. Faced with these difficulties, Lathrop devised a plan to increase the Children's Bureau's budget, use women volunteers to build public support for the agency's work, and avoid the controversial issue of child labor by centering on curbing the nation's high infant mortality rate. It was difficult for even the bureau's staunchest political opponents to argue against efforts designed to save babies' lives.

In 1915, the U.S. Children's Bureau sponsored the first federal infant mortality study, conducted in Johnstown, Pennsylvania. Many Americans were surprised to learn that results suggested an extrapolated U.S. infant mortality rate of 131 deaths per 1,000 live births. This ranked the largest industrial and economic power in the world an embarrassing twelfth out of twenty comparable nations. Furthermore, the Johnstown study showed that the level of a father's earnings was the leading indicator pointing to a child's chances for survival or early death. The link between poverty and high infant mortality seems obvious today, but this was new information at the time that challenged traditional views about the causes of high children's death rates among poor families.[32]

Lathrop and her staff called for local and state governments to improve public sanitation, offer infant and child health education for mothers, and require birth certificates. They also suggested that mandatory birth certificates would help authorities identify newborns in need of public health services. Such efforts fed into the idea that children, no matter their families' circumstances, had a right to life and protection that was a government responsibility. These were concepts already embedded in British and French laws protecting infants passed prior to World War I.[33]

In 1921, the U.S. Congress took another important step in expanding government authority on behalf of children by passing the Sheppard-Towner Maternity and Infancy Act. This seminal legislation provided federal funds, matched by the individual states, for state-run programs designed to reduce infant and maternal mortality rates as well as to improve children's overall health. Sheppard-Towner programs focused on educating mothers in the best practices of high-quality health care and promoted diagnostic clinics run by physicians. At the time, the United States was part of a growing international trend. Similar initiatives were already in place in other nations, both with and without government support. For example, Egypt's Centres for Motherhood and Childcare began in 1912,[34] and the Royal New Zealand Plunket Society was founded in 1907 "to help the mothers and save the babies."[35] Both organizations were initially dependent on voluntary and charitable assistance. Funded with government money, Sheppard-Towner was also partly staffed by volunteers. Popular with the public, the program faced strong opposition from the American Medical Association and insurance companies that labeled it socialized medicine. In the midst of a more conservative political climate by the mid-1920s, Congress allowed Sheppard-Towner to expire in 1929. Although short lived, Sheppard-Towner contributed to the dramatic reduction in the American infant mortality rate to 68 deaths per 1,000 live births by 1930. The experiment also underscored the idea that the federal and state government could have a positive influence on the lives of children.[36]

The U.S. Children's Bureau's early work linking a father's income and infant mortality also suggested a tie between poverty and exploitive child labor. Like anti-child labor advocates in many industrialized countries, by the early twentieth century reformers in the United States had some success regulating the employment of children under fourteen through the passage of state laws. But also as in other nations, American parents, employers, and young workers found ways to thwart such laws. For the U.S. Children's Bureau and its supporters, promoting mandatory birth certificates was a way to decrease infant mortality and provide verification of a child's age that could be used to enforce child labor regulations. Passage of the United States' first federal child labor law, the Keating-Owen Act in 1916, moved the anti-child labor debate in the United States from the state to the federal level. The law regulated child labor by barring the sale goods of goods produced by children under fourteen from interstate commerce. Though the legislation was celebrated as a victory for anti-child labor advocates, the U.S. Supreme Court declared it unconstitutional in its 1918 *Hammer v. Dagenhart* decision and denounced a similar act in the 1922 *Bailey v. Drexel Furniture Company* ruling. In response, advocates achieved passage of a constitutional amendment barring child labor, but the amendment was never ratified by the necessary number of states.[37]

The onset of the Great Depression in 1929 was marked around the world. In the United States, it encouraged a growing number of adults to agree that children's wage labor should be regulated in order to open jobs for adults. The reaction by the public, press, and government officials to a strike by young garment workers in Pennsylvania in 1933 revealed the seedbed for this reformist atmosphere. Americans had generally ignored a strike by young factory workers in the same region in 1903, but in 1933 newspapers dubbed the work stoppage "The Baby Strike." A public outcry arose in support of the strikers. Adolescents aged fourteen, fifteen, and sixteen comprised forty percent of the region's mill workers. Mandatory school attendance laws in Pennsylvania provided provisions for teens to quit school if they had a job. Despite the legal loophole, Pennsylvania's governor Gifford Pinchot (R) called the young workers' employment "exploitive" and held "sweatshop" hearings where adolescent strikers testified about poor conditions in the factories. The press provided sympathetic coverage for the strikers, and government officials condemned factory owners. The next year the state legislature ended provisions for the employment of anyone under sixteen years of age. President Franklin Roosevelt joined the chorus condemning child labor, and in 1938, the U.S. Congress passed the Fair Labor Standards Act (FLSA). The act included a variety of protections for adult workers and prohibited the employment of children under sixteen. It also regulated wage work among sixteen- and seventeen-year-olds and outlawed the employment of older teens in certain industries. The FLSA set the federal standards for regulation of child labor in the United States, and the nation's Supreme Court upheld the law in 1943. Rooted in the nineteenth century's arguments against child labor, the FLSA did not protect all children from exploitive labor. Most obvious was the exemption for agricultural labor similar to the rules in earlier English factory acts and in New Zealand's measures of the 1930s that did not regulate against children working within a family enterprise. Still, the FLSA was important New Deal legislation that ended most forms of exploitive child labor in the United States and underscored a government policy prescribing household chores and school as the only proper work of childhood.[38]

The 1935 Social Security Act (SSA) also pointed to an important shift in federal responsibility for children as part of the New Deal in the United States. The economic crisis of the Great Depression expanded the number of youngsters in America's orphanages, and homelessness increased for both children and adults. The SSA included programs designed to provide a safety net for children and their families. The SSA's Aid to Dependent Children (ADC, renamed Aid to Families with Dependent Children in 1960) program was similar to state-run and state-funded mothers' pensions established earlier to provide "worthy" mothers with small stipends for children living in families without a male breadwinner. The federal origins and funding for ADC in the New Deal universalized the program at minimum levels in all states. For the first time, the federal government filled the economic role of fathers for children in families without a male breadwinner and mandated that mothers receiving stipends for their children stay out of the paid labor force. The SSA also provided survivor's benefits for children, health care and stipends to support disabled youngsters, and funding for an infant and maternity child health program for mothers and babies in poor families known as Title V. The SSA programs did not end poverty and glaringly did not include national health insurance. Another weakness was the fact that ADC required states to provide matching funds, and distribution of monies for needy children was done by local authorities who too often upheld discriminatory racial and ethnic practices consistent with the status quo. In addition, initially ADC was not available to children born out of wedlock or for those with divorced parents. Rules changed by the 1960s, but, as was not uncommon in other welfare regimes providing targeted assistance to single parents, morality judgments about recipients and the label of *welfare* rather than *entitlement* contributed to ADC's unevenness and rising unpopularity. In contrast, the more universal forms of family allowances that became state policy in France, for example, or the so-called family salary adopted in Sweden during the interwar period, engendered greater public support within those countries. Nevertheless, the SSA's child welfare programs were key components in the shift introducing the federal responsibility for protecting children's right to dependency from birth through age seventeen.[39]

Other New Deal programs that touched children's lives were more temporary but contributed to the promotion of the middle-class childhood ideal for all young Americans. For example, the 1933 launch of the Civilian Conservation Corps (CCC) provided federally funded employment for males sixteen through twenty-three years of age. The CCC also introduced many recruits to middle-class standards of behavior and gave some boys the opportunity to earn a high school diploma. President Roosevelt's executive order creating the National Youth Administration (NYA) took the idea further by paying teens and young people in their early twenties stipends to stay in school full time and remain at home with their families. Millions of young Americans participated in the CCC and NYA programs. One consequence was that in 1937, a majority of seventeen-year-olds graduated from high school for the first time in American history. Staying in school lengthened childhood dependency through high school graduation for most white American youth, but the effect was disproportionately less for African American pupils.[40]

President Herbert Hoover had sponsored a White House Conference in 1930 on children's issues that released a *Children's Charter* listing nineteen rights of childhood. The charter was mostly viewed as expressing romanticized sentimentalities because the Hoover Administration did not initiate any programs to encourage its application. Franklin Roosevelt's New Deal did not end poverty among children, but it clearly established an important federal role in protecting American children's welfare.[41]

The entrance of the United States into World War II continued the federal government's reach into the lives of young Americans. However, some results in efforts to achieve the middle-class childhood ideal were steps backward rather than steps forward. For example, Roosevelt's Executive Order 9066 in February 1942 forced children of Japanese American descent, the vast majority of whom were U.S. citizens, to move to isolated government relocation centers. Some children and their families stayed in these centers for the duration of the war. Another negative consequence was the fact that government-ordered rationing of building materials virtually ended the construction of new schools and recreational facilities. In 1943, with the virtual end of unemployment, the federal government discontinued work-relief agencies like the WPA, and also the NYA and CCC. Further, the need for workers for America's defense effort led to the relaxation of many hard-won child labor regulations. The military also attracted sixteen- and seventeen-year-old boys who lied about their age. Consequently, there was a short decline in graduation rates that ended immediately following the war. On the other hand, some children's programs benefited from the nation's focus on the war effort. In late 1942, many of the WPA's day nurseries were brought under the Lanham Act as part of the federal government's goal to attract married women, even those with children, into the workplace. Another program expanded the SSA's Title V as the Emergency Maternal and Infant Care Program (EMIC). Congress responded to concerns about low morale in the military among enlisted men with pregnant wives and newborns in need of quality health care. From 1943 through 1949, one in every seven births in the United States benefited from EMIC funding. Upon demobilization, Congress ended support for both the Lanham nurseries and the EMIC, but the barrier to federal responsibility for children's welfare had been broken in the New Deal and war years.[42] After the war, a reorganization of the federal government reordered responsibility for administering federal child welfare policies. As a symbol of its diminished status, in 1946 the Children's Bureau lost "U.S." as part of its name and was transferred from the Department of Labor to a lower level ranking within the new Federal Security Agency. In 1953, the agency moved to the new Department of Health, Education, and Welfare, an even larger and more complex bureaucracy. As part of the restructuring, the government's child health programs went to the Public Health Service, and child labor regulation enforcement stayed in the Department of Labor. The Children's Bureau was functionally reduced to a low-level clearinghouse. This new circumstance ended the experiment begun in 1912 giving children's issues a single voice in the federal government.[43]

THE POSTWAR YEARS AND BEYOND

Although the single voice experiment was over, the federal child–state relationship continued to expand in the late twentieth century. It also reflected a national ambivalence about the role of government in protecting children's dependency. Similar to the situation in several other countries also debating how best to expand assistance to children and families, Americans seemed to collectively agree that children had a right to a protected childhood but disagreed about how best to achieve that goal. Another complication was the onset of the cold war and a reinvigoration of the independent nuclear family as an icon of American identity. By the 1950s, a more inclusive application of ADC (renamed Aid to Families with Dependent Children in 1960) was strongly criticized as a welfare program for lazy mothers that encouraged women to have children outside of marriage. Some cold war rhetoric suggested that the program was immoral, socialistic, and communist. A few child welfare efforts, however, did achieve congressional approval as part of President Lyndon Johnson's Great Society programs. An outstanding example was Head Start for early childhood education directed at children from poor families and Job Corps' vocational training for disadvantaged teens. As evidence of changing attitudes about family life, Congress expanded Social Security programs for children but for the first time required parents of a child over six receiving benefits to register for job training. In another reversal of past attitudes, the 1978 Indian Child Welfare Act discouraged sending American Indian children to boarding schools far from their families and gave tribal courts authority over child welfare on reservations.[44]

Public schools and juvenile courts also experienced many changes after World War II. In its 1954 decision, *Brown v. Board of Education, Topeka, Kansas,* the U.S. Supreme Court ended legal school segregation but did not bring equality to public school education. In another important case, the court ruled in *In re Gault* (1967), that juvenile courts must provide young offenders with the same procedural rights guaranteed to adults. However, in 1971, the court ruled in McKeiver v. Pennsylvania that juveniles did not have the constitutional right to jury trials although the court did not prohibit them. While these rulings were a clear recognition of children's rights guaranteed under the U.S. Constitution, ambivalence continued, and other legal actions enacted in the 1980s allowed for teenage offenders in juvenile courts to be tried and punished as adults.[45]

A similar ambivalence is evident in Supreme Court rulings regarding young American's right to free speech, gender equality, and social welfare granted to poor families. In 1969 the U.S. Supreme Court's decision in *Tinker v. Des Moines Independent Community School District* protected students' right to free speech. However, later court decisions curbed those rights in public schools. Other issues gained protections such as gender equality in education and athletics in Title IX, enacted in 1972. The 1990 Americans with Disabilities Act required more equal access to public facilities and services for children and adults. About the same time, aid for poor children was shifted in 1996 when Congress replaced Aid to Families with Dependent Children with the Temporary Assistance to Needy Families (TANF) program. TANF expanded funding for child care in poor families but also put new requirements on needy parents to work or attend job training. In 1997, Congress expanded health care for children in needy families through the State Children's Health Insurance Program (SCHIP), but in 2008, President George W. Bush vetoed plans to further expand the initiative. In 2009, Congress revisited the question, and President Barack Obama signed the expanded SCHIP into law. Access to affordable health care remains one of the most significant challenges for Americans and their children.[46]

During the late twentieth-century, social and demographic changes in the United States, Europe, and Scandinavia, complicated the relationship of the child and the family to the state. How children, families, and governments responded to these changes obviously varied from country to country in character, intensity, and scope. However, no country, including the United States, could escape or ignore these changes. Expectations of long-term employment and a lasting marriage had been basic tenets of social policy toward the family since the early twentieth century.[47] Mirroring trends in many Western societies, U.S. divorce rates doubled from the 1960s through the 1970s and contributed to higher poverty rates among children. Incidences of single parenthood as a result of children being born outside marriage also increased, and many of these children lived in poverty. The frequency of adoption increased, especially a rise in international adoptions, but neither Congress nor the United Nations responded with protections for children adopted across national boundaries. Similar to general trends around the world, the overall well-being of most young people improved in the late twentieth century, but great inequalities remained. For example, the U.S. infant mortality rate continued to rank poorly compared to other nations. In the late twentieth century, some American cities had rates comparable to developing nations ranked among the world's most needy. Many American public schools continued to struggle and the 2002 No Child Left Behind Act failed to promote higher quality education among America's children.

As Steven Mintz argues, "During the late twentieth century there was a widespread impression that children's well-being was declining precipitously and that many of society's worst problems could be attributed to the young." Furthermore, surveys showed that "adults believed that young people accounted for 40 percent of the nation's violent crime, three times the actual rate." The same misperceptions were true about what adults identified as an epidemic of teenage pregnancy when, in reality, the teen pregnancy rate was lower than it had been at any time in American history.[48]

CONCLUSION

Since the early twentieth century, the United States, like many Western nations, has focused on defining the parameters of children's rights within the context of a middle-class childhood ideal. The United Nations' adoption of the 1948 *Universal Declaration of Human Rights* did not specifically mention children, but the recognition of a need for special protections for the world's children as a right is evident in the United Nations' passage of the *Convention on the Rights of the Child* in 1959. It took another thirty-plus years for the document to gain acceptance. In 2009, it is somewhat ironic that the United States, the first nation in the world to establish a federal bureau solely focused on advocating for the interests of children, is the only member nation that has not signed the *Convention on the Rights of the Child*. The history of Americans' struggle to define the relationship of the child and the state reveals the triumph of the American middle-class childhood ideal as an important framework in the *Convention on the Rights of the Child*.[49] But the United States' reluctance to sign the document is also evidence of a continuing ambivalence about how governments can best protect children's right to dependency within a political and cultural world dominated by adults. This is an especially complex issue in the United States, where throughout the nation's history Americans celebrated the idea of independence and self-reliance. Another question is whether those core values, also embraced by other countries, can reflect the increasing diversity of family life and the mixing of different cultural groups in a world that continues to grow smaller each day. Formulating acceptable and effective state policies for family and child welfare seems more straightforward in more homogeneous countries like Japan, but even there, demographics are changing.

Federal–state tensions within the U.S. political system are a complicating factor in the evolution of national policies defining children's rights and assisting families. Many of the issues discussed in this chapter are also contentious in Western democracies operating within other constitutional frameworks. The vexed question of parental authority vis-à-vis state intervention, noted in relation to the creation of the U.S. Children's Bureau, has been and continues to be at the center of debate about policies addressing children and families. Disagreement over programs about sex education in public schools or pupil access to contraception is just one example in which viewpoints are polarized in even the most liberal-minded nations. Twentieth-century debates over the abolition of corporal punishment in schools and the prohibition of physical discipline within the home are others.[50] Nordic countries were the first to enact such protection, continuing a century-long preeminence in initiating child-centered policies with an emphasis on children's rights. Corporal punishment in schools, for instance, ceased in Sweden in the late 1940s and was abolished in Norway in 1969. It was still used as a form of discipline in English state schools until 1987. Nordic governments also took the lead in establishing the child's right to be protected from physical punishment by parents or caregivers. Legislation in Norway (1972), Sweden (1980), Finland (1983) and Denmark (1985) set a precedent later followed by Austria in 1989. Despite its long-established tradition of state intervention on behalf of children, New Zealand took until 2007 before repealing section 59 of the 1961 Crimes Act, which had hitherto provided abusive parents with a spurious legal defense of exercising "reasonable punishment" when beating their children. Norway was also the first state to establish an official ombudsman for children (1982), setting a precedent followed in Australia, New Zealand, Britain, and Northern Ireland and contributing to the later formation of the European Network of Ombudsmen for Children in 1997.[51]

Political considerations and vested interests may help or hinder the pace at which children's rights are secured, but underpinning the varied experiences of children within Western democratic regimes are a series of ongoing debates concerning the limitations of state intervention in families in the best interests of the child. Cultural and socioeconomic differences exacerbate the problem, especially among cultural minority groups seeking employment and opportunity, generally for the sake of their children, across international boundaries. The high incidence of domestic violence, poverty, overcrowding, unskilled employment, substance abuse, low educational attainment, and poor child health statistics among Pacific Island communities within New Zealand, for instance, highlights the complexity of the problems that state welfare policies endeavor to address. Similarly, the increased rate of intercountry migration within the European Union since the breakup of the USSR and the situation of migrant workers and their families, separated by legal circumstance and economic necessity, are just two of the many factors that complicate the relationship between states, families, and children in the early twentieth century.[52]

When establishing national welfare systems concerning children and families, reformers commonly investigated what was happening in other countries, with a view to adopting or adapting strategies that might be applicable to their own society's needs. U.S. initiatives, for instance, had a strong influence on the evolution of child welfare policies in New Zealand prior to World War II. The larrikin problem evident in many growing Western cities in the late nineteenth century, for example, had both Australian and New Zealand officials closely scrutinizing U.S. practices and facilities. During 1909, industrial school visitor William Reece toured England, Germany, and the United States to view procedures for dealing with juvenile offenders. His report urged the establishment of children's courts in accordance with the U.S. model And when the New Zealand Education Department began to advocate boarding out (or foster care for) children instead of committing them to institutions, its annual report for 1909 included considerable detail from the 1909 White House Conference, at which foster care was deemed preferable for children dependent upon the state for their care. A visit to the United States and Canada in 1925 by New

Zealand's first Superintendent of Child Welfare, John Beck, confirmed his preference for this unit to be, administratively, part of a much larger and more centralized agency dealing with the whole spectrum of social welfare.[53]

Moreover, given the late nineteenth-century interconnectedness of the British imperial and American worlds, shared concerns led to common policy developments, particularly in relation to youngsters identified as neglected or delinquent. Ideas of child protection and child saving prompted religious and other voluntary agencies to focus on new strategies for the promotion of children's well-being. Hence, an English National Society for the Prevention of Cruelty to Children emerged in 1889, addressing concerns similar to those of the SPCC, established in the United States in 1875. The first Canadian Children's Aid Society (CAS), founded in Ontario in 1891, was followed only two years later by Ontario's first child welfare legislation, designed to better protect children and to prevent their being subjected to cruelty. Here, as in other democratic societies, cooperation between voluntary and state sectors would be long-standing: the Canadian CAS and the provincial government authorities worked effectively together throughout much of the twentieth century.[54]

FIGURE 7.2: *Crowded Playground Slide, 1950*. Shades of L.A. Archives/Los Angeles Public Library. http://jpgl.lapl.org/pics43/00041433.jpg. Courtesy of Los Angeles Public Library.

The fact that several of the most significant advances in promoting children's rights occurred in the United States during the 1930s and 1940s suggests that federal intervention was more acceptable in a time of obvious national difficulty. Democracies with a much stronger tradition of state involvement—in housing, health, education, income support, and public works, for instance—generally implemented a more comprehensive range of child-centered measures throughout the century with, usually, less opposition or controversy. Moving beyond recognition to the implementation of children's rights in the second half of the twentieth century was a process made more problematic when the legacy of past inequalities, for indigenous peoples and racial minorities, was (and is) still being addressed and when generational differences found (and find) overt expression in changing codes of morality and sexuality and new patterns of personal relationships. The twentieth century witnessed the power of the state to transform children's lives being exercised in brutal, destructive, and authoritarian ways by totalitarian or dictatorial regimes, both religious and secular. There were, and continue to be, many instances where the capacity of a state to intervene on behalf of its children has been limited only by the unwillingness of its leaders to do so. Nevertheless, many constructive and successful partnerships forged throughout the century on behalf of young people—involving state agencies, nongovernmental organizations, local authorities, community groups, volunteer or charitable societies, schools, institutions, families, and dedicated individuals—reflect a widely shared commitment to the principles of the 1989 charter of children's rights. Something of Ellen Key's vision may have been realized after all. The onset of the recent economic crisis suggests that like the 1930s, it is time to try new models for advancing opportunities for the world's youngest citizens.

CHAPTER EIGHT

Faith and Religion

JON PAHL

Within the history of Christianity—to take one crucial case—both collaboration with and resistance to nationalist civil religions have marked the history of young people during the twentieth century. Tracking these patterns of resistance and collaboration can shed light on historical contingencies in discrete contexts and on how young people shaped their own religious experiences under social constructions. We will examine closely two case studies—of Christian youth in Nazi Germany between 1933 and 1945, and of Christian youth in the United States from 1930 to the present. In a concluding section, we will explore briefly broader global patterns of how Christian young people, and other young people of faith, engaged religion with political and social issues.

SACRIFICES FOR ONE GERMANY

Historians have often noted, obliquely, that the Nazi Party and its Hitler Jugend (HJ) manifested more than a little affinity with religious patterns of behavior. Hitler Youth were part of a movement dedicated to a "dogmatic, quasi-mystical doctrine" and a "political creed," suggested Peter D. Stachura.[1] German youth under the Nazi regime were, according to H. W. Koch, devotees of a "myth of obedience" and "myth of self-sacrifice and unquestioning loyalty."[2] Members of the movement were subjected to, in the words of Michael H. Kater, a "catechism of beliefs" in which an older youth served as a "spiritual mentor" to a younger, and in which all youth were caught up in "comradeship, harmony, and sacrifice under the authority of a strong and omniscient leader."[3] Most pointedly, Rolf Giesen suggests that "the Nazis were looking for martyrs to turn their movement into a semi-religious order with the quality of a death cult that prepares others to die for the cause."[4] The Hitler Youth was the religious training ground for this Nazi civil religion of death and sacrifice.

During the Weimar Republic, manifold youth organizations—Wandervogel, or hiking clubs, and Bündische Jugend, or youth associations—competed for the loyalty of German young people. Some were overtly political—ranging across communist, centrist, and right-wing ideologies. Some were overtly religious—either Protestant or Catholic. Most were explicitly neither. Walter Laqueur, among the first historians to trace aspects of German youth history, located the origins of a distinctly romantic movement of and for youth in Germany to the late nineteenth century, although many of the male groups took on increasingly paramilitary trappings after World War I. According to Laqueur, though, "the experience of personal integration into a charismatic group was the emotional basis" of membership in one of these independent—that is, nondenominationally affiliated—societies.[5] Among religious societies, however, and especially among Protestants—who had united into an evangelical national church in 1871—loyalties not only were based on local charismatic leaders but were reinforced according to doctrinal and ecclesiastical purity in a church increasingly defined along nationalist lines. In the Hitler Youth, the charismatic and emotional quality of the secular German youth societies came together with the ideological and national contours of the Protestant religious groups.

The process was uneven across regions and organizations, but Protestant youth generally shared the Nazis' antipathy to Weimar democracy and supposed decadence, and shared their anti-Semitism. That is not to say that the Protestant youth movements were integrated into the Hitler Youth with complete harmony; repression, threats, and violence were also involved.[6] And yet across institutional arrangements and community sensibilities, and even more in patterns of discourse and practice, the Hitler Youth adapted, incorporated, or twisted—to use Doris L. Bergen's metaphor—the diffuse doctrines and rituals of Protestant Christianity. Such borrowings and adaptations made the Hitler Youth movement seem spiritually new, intense, and modern to participants, especially in contrast to the lax and staid faith of their elders, yet the process also lent the Nazi youth groups a comfortable and reassuring continuity.[7] Hitler Youth slogans, films, uniforms, songs, rituals, and communal sensibilities developed and intensified patterns that made participation in the HJ not only possible but attractive to many Protestant young people. The state church gave way to the state *as* church, and youth were indoctrinated and habituated accordingly.

As in so many arenas across Germany, 1933 was the pivotal year for youth. In early 1932 the Hitler Youth had been outlawed by the Weimar government, along with other uniformed branches of the Nazi party, but this actually led to growth in HJ membership.[8] Economic depression coupled with enduring shame over the German loss in World War I had triggered fears about future prospects among youth and their parents.[9] Many Germans across generations began in response to side with nationalist movements like the Nazis, who promised a way out of the Weimar instability and a way toward a renewed German *Volk*. In July 1932 the Nazis won the largest number of seats in the Reichstag elections, and in January, 1933 Adolf Hitler was elected *Reichschancellor*. Melita Maschmann, who was fifteen at the time, wrote later about watching the parades through Berlin to celebrate the führer's victory. She remembered "groups of girls and boys scarcely older than [myself] among them." And she identified with "the crashing tread of the feet, the somber pomp of the red and black flags, the flickering light from the torches on the faces and the songs with melodies that were at once aggressive and sentimental." She identified, in short, with the marching Hitler Youth. Such identification made her realize that in this new Germany "boys and girls in the marching columns did count. Like the adults, they carried banners on which the names of their dead were written."[10] To identify with the sacrifices of soldiers from World War I, and to develop a corresponding will to sacrifice one's self on behalf of Germany and the führer, constituted the ecstatic communal sensibility that marked the civil religion of the Hitler Youth from 1933 until its end.

In the summer of 1933, Baldur von Schirach was appointed *Reichsjugend-führer*, responsible directly to Hitler. He quickly moved to unite all German youth movements and to foster the identification with Hitler and willing-ness to sacrifice oneself that marked the movement's secular spirituality. In December 1933, he persuaded the Protestant *Reichsbischof* (another position appointed by Hitler), Ludwig Müller, to sign an agreement incorporating all of the Protestant youth societies into the HJ. Very limited resistance came from local youth leaders.[11] The Protestant youth societies had been right-leaning politically for decades, and most of them had already been leaking members into the HJ.[12] Catholic youth groups were spared organizational incorporation into the Hitler Youth by the concordat signed between the Vati-can and Hitler in July 1933. Yet many Catholic youth joined the HJ on the local level, and parameters for those Catholic youth groups that continued to meet were severely circumscribed by new laws. As the regime established itself, Catholic resistance largely evaporated. Theodore S. Hamerow summarizes the developments succinctly: "The Catholic hierarchy moved from distrust to collaboration."[13] Across religions, joining the Hitler Youth generally moved from a voluntary option, to an enthusiastic prospect, to an all-but-mandatory obligation. Membership increases were steady and dramatic: from 18,000 in 1930, to 2 million in 1933, to 5.4 million, or nearly sixty percent of German youth in 1936. That same year saw a law passed mandating that "the entire German youth within the territory of the Reich is coordinated in the Hitler Youth." This was fanciful, but it allowed for the prohibition of any other groups and for the persecution of dissenters. And by 1939, after another law mandated that "all adolescents from age 10 to 18 are obligated to put in service in the Hitler Youth," membership reached 8 million, or 98.1 percent of the targeted group.[14]

FIGURE 8.1: *Hitler Youth Recruiting Poster, c. 1941*. The print reads: "Youth serve the Führer. All ten-year olds in the HJ." Photo Credit: Library of Congress Prints and Photograph Division, Digital ID ppmsca. 18609. http://en.wikipedia.org/wiki/Image:Hitler_jugend.jpg. Public domain in the United States.

The religious contours of the Hitler Youth for women, the Bund Deutscher Mädel (BDM), mirrored those across the broader HJ movement, with distinctive emphases on women's sacrificial duties to marry and mate. Upon joining, women had to purchase uniforms to be worn at all times—a dark blue skirt, white blouse, and black kerchief with a knotted tie of leather strips. The men wore brown shirts and black shorts. Such uniform sacred garb, which characterized the ethos of the entire Nazi regime, was matched by sacred times for BDM members on Wednesday evenings and Saturday afternoons, and sacred places—HJ club houses, which were festooned with Nazi flags and photos of Hitler. At these clubs, local groups would meet to organize sporting events, film nights, or camping expeditions, hear speeches by older youth leaders, and sing. HJ songbooks were variants on Protestant hymnbooks. The BDM songbook, for instance, *Wir Mädel Singen*, mirrored ecclesiastical hymnals by beginning with Advent and Christmas songs, moving through the New Year down to the führer's birthday, on April 20—which became the HJ's major spring festival to rival Easter. National hymns like "Deutschland, Heiliges Wort" ("Germany, Holy Word") appeared near the back of the book.[15] These ritual patterns of sacred garb, times, space, and song undermined the authority of both church and family in the lives of youth. "Führer worship was at the center" of all HJ activities, Michael H. Kater concludes, yet "most Hitler Youths in the fold loved its program of activities and did feel looked after, knowing that they would graduate to become bearers of the new Reich."[16]

Schirach, who fancied himself a poet, constantly articulated how the HJ sought to submerge the identities of individual youths into an identity with Hitler. One of Schirach's poetic efforts, titled simply "Hitler," captured the mystical mentality concisely: "In many thousands you follow behind me," the poem began, "And you are I, and I am you."[17] To follow Hitler and Schirach into the HJ meant, preeminently, to sacrifice. The official Hitler Youth song, "Die Fahnenlied," also written by Schirach, made the point clear in its refrain:

Our flag flutters before us
Our flag represents the new era
And our flag leads us to eternity!
Yes, our flag means more to us than death.[18]

The civil religion of the Hitler Youth compressed the identities of German youth into the one identity with the führer, symbolized by the swastika, and displaced the natural desire for life into a willingness to sacrifice unto death, with the promise of resurrection in the collective German *Volk*.

Such notions of sacrifice and salvation were, of course, classical tropes in Christian theology. Christ had sacrificed himself to save humanity, and Christians were called to sacrifice themselves out of gratitude to God. Nowhere where these notions of sacrifice more vividly articulated and translated into support for the Hitler Youth than in Nazi propaganda films. Two films in particular from this crucial period reveal the communal sensibility of sacrifice that was developing. The first, *Hitlerjunge Quex*, or Hitler Youth Quex, premiered on September 11, 1933. Its subtitle gave away the plot: "A Film about Youth's Spirit of Sacrifice."[19] It depicted a fictionalized version of the life and death of Herbert Norkus, a teenaged Hitler Youth member murdered by communists while distributing tracts in Berlin in early 1932.[20] The young Quex—which translates as "quicksilver"—represented the active energy of Hitler Youth and their willingness to be martyred. After a long struggle against his parents, notably his communist father, Quex eventually moves out of his family home to live in a Hitler Youth Hostel.[21] There he is quickly absorbed into the movement. When he receives his uniform, he belongs; his allegiance has shifted from his family to the HJ. When he dies, his blood spills on a flag, in which he is literally wrapped. The film ends with the strains of "Die Fahnenlied" and a scene filled with columns of marching Hitler Youth. It opened to rave reviews in Munich, where thousands of Hitler Youth lined the streets leading to the cinema, and where Hitler himself attended the showing. The film was eventually viewed by over twenty million Germans, and was shown at Hitler Youth film hours until as late as 1942.[22]

The second film was Leni Riefenstahl's 1934 *Triumph des Willens* (*Triumph of the Will*), her justly (in)famous documentary of the Nazi Party Congress in Nuremberg from that year. Riefenstahl had been raised, nominally, as Lutheran. She inherited the diffuse notions of Christian identity familiar to many Protestants in Germany. She thus easily transferred her loyalties from a transcendent God to a transcendent führer and encouraged the same through her considerable art. Two scenes are crucial for our purposes. The first is Riefenstahl's coverage of the Reich Labor Service Review. This group was a Nazi organization of young German workers into which many Hitler Youth would graduate after turning 18, and it was the foundation for the massive expansion of the German Army once Hitler broke the Treaty of Versailles and Germany's remilitarization began in 1935. In Riefenstahl's scene, a mass of thousands of uniformed laborers, bearing shovels, stand in rank and file on the grounds of the Nuremberg stadium. The camera cuts from one close-up of an individual worker to another, and then out to smaller groups as they repeat, in unison, a litany: "Here we stand. We are ready to carry Germany into a new era. Germany!" As "Germany" is uttered,

Riefenstahl cuts abruptly to a close-up of Hitler. Later in the same scene, this identification is made explicit as the chorus of workers intones: "One People. One Führer. One Reich. Germany!"

What follows next is a liturgy of workers in which the theme of the sacrifice of youth—and their potential resurrection—is articulated. Alternating shots of a single flag bearer and a long line of flag bearers, Riefenstahl gradually shows the young men lowering the swastikas to the ground, as a narrator intones the sites of famous battles from World War I: "Langemarck ... Tannenberg ... Verdun." But as the flags hang limply on the ground, the narrator's voice rises and he proclaims: "Comrades [who have died before us]!" The flags spring to attention. "You are not dead! You live in Germany!"[23] This ritual of sacrifice and resurrection incorporated Christian motifs into Nazi civil religion. For Protestants across Germany, especially, a theology of the cross, centered on Jesus' death and resurrection, had been the crucial articulation of Christianity on which the faith stood, or fell, ever since Luther made his famous stand before Catholic inquisitors. Such a doctrinal certainty had been communicated to Protestant youth through catechism programs that were widespread across the country's congregations and youth groups. These motifs were now twisted to Nazi purposes.

The other scene of religious significance to youth in *Triumph of the Will* is, naturally, Riefenstahl's coverage of the Hitler Youth Rally.[24] The Nuremberg Stadium is again shown packed with people, with rows of young men in uniform lined up on the field. Boys as young as ten stand on tiptoes to see Hitler as he arrives in the stadium. Baldur von Schirach speaks first, as Riefenstahl's edits cut from close-ups of the speaker, to pans of the young people, to close-ups of Hitler, to close-ups of the youth—again reinforcing the identification of the young masses with the führer. "Just as you," Schirach addresses Hitler, "demonstrate the highest self-sacrifice for this nation, so does this youth desire to be selfless. Because you embody the concept of faithfulness for us, therefore we wish to be faithful." "Faith," again, was the chief virtue in Protestant spirituality, now incarnated in Hitler and his youth. Hitler's own speech, which followed directly after Schirach's, explicitly evoked sacrifice for Germany as the path to eternal life: "You must learn sacrifice," the Führer preached. "Whatever we create today, whatever we do, will all pass away. But in Germany you will live on, and when we can no longer hold the flag ... you must hold it firmly in your fists." The scene ended with the crowd singing together the HJ song, "Die Fahnenlied."

Now, all of this religious rhetoric and ritual indoctrination was not only designed to cultivate members of the Nazi Party and the HJ. It was also targeted at the scapegoating of Jews, and eventually fueled the genocide of the Final Solution. The "one Germany" intended by the HJ and institutionalized in its mandatory membership after 1939, could be mobilized into solidarity against not only a common enemy without in military battle, but toward the so-called purification of Germany by the sacrifice of scapegoats within.[25] Thus *The Nazi Primer: Official Handbook for Schooling the Hitler Youth*, articulated on "historical" and "scientific" grounds that in the early years of the Nazi regime, "daily sacrifice of blood and goods" by the party faithful led to "the severest process of selection" in which the most qualified had gained ascent to leadership. "Today the process of selection must take place along other lines," the *Handbook* went on, namely along the lines of race. "So for us fostering race is one and the same thing as a defensive warfare against mind and blood contamination by the Jews. ... The first opposition measures of the National Socialists must, therefore, aim to remove the Jews from the cultural and economic life of our folk."[26] Anti-Semitism in Nazi Germany had many roots and causes beyond Christian theology and Christian youth groups. But it found a willing reservoir and little resistance among those baptized Christian young people who joined the Hitler Youth and who were indoctrinated into the civil religion of sacrifice for "one people, one Führer, one Reich—Germany."[27]

THE AMBIVALENCE OF CHRISTIAN YOUTH MINISTRIES IN MODERN U.S. HISTORY

In the early 1930s, Lutheran young people in the United States were treated to a debate, of sorts, about the Nazi regime among their leaders. Rev. Walter A. Maier, longtime editor of the *Walther League Messenger*, published a series of articles extolling how "Hitler Shows the Way," assessing "The Credit Side of the Hitler Ledger," and approving of the appearance of "The Spade Brigade" for youth across Germany. According to Maier, Hitler was "cleaning up" the "decadence" of Weimar Germany. Reports of atrocities against Jews were "propaganda." By 1937, another Lutheran youth leader, O. P. Kretzmann, who was stunned by the rise of the führer and who, along with some other Lutherans, thought Hitler was a "blood-thirsty monster," started an alternative publication of his own for Lutheran youth, *The Cresset*. After the Night of Broken Glass in November, 1938, when Nazis destroyed Jewish worship places and businesses, Kretzmann's column in *The Cresset* simply asserted that "Anti-Semitism is Anti-Christian." Between Maier's embrace of the Nazis and Kretzmann's critique ran an ambivalence toward nationalism and civil religion—in Germany and elsewhere—that would mark not only Lutheran but most Christian youth ministries in the modern United States.[28]

The civil religion of the United States emerged in the twentieth-century as a hybrid of Judeo-Christian discourses and practices with national symbols and rituals.[29] "One nation under God" has expressed itself in parades, national holidays like Flag Day and Memorial Day, ritual songs like 'The Star Spangled Banner," and efforts to prohibit flag burning with a constitutional amendment, among other initiatives.[30] Not surprisingly, some Christian youth ministries have been more benevolently disposed than others to this blending of traditional religions with patriotism. A rough spectrum of allegiance ranges from African American resistance, through mainline Protestant and Catholic ambivalence, to Evangelical embrace. Across traditions, however, since roughly the Vietnam era, critiques of American violence and injustice have increased, along with interfaith activism on behalf of social policies and practices that challenged the American civil religion. At the same time, however, many of the national Christian youth groups that articulated these challenges have fallen apart. The Christian youth ministries that have flourished, notably among evangelicals, have largely remained wedded to a custodial merger of Christianity and the American way.[31] The 2006 film *Jesus Camp* documents one such blending of Christianity and American nationalism among evangelical youth leaders and young people.

African American Christian youth ministries have been consistently critical, for obvious reasons, of any innocent version of American civil religion.[32] Absent any unified national denomination, however, various African American Baptists, Methodists, and other Christian youth were organized into groups whose strength depended largely on the charisma and clout of a local congregation. Bethel African Methodist Episcopal Church in Baltimore is a good example. During the Great Depression, Bethel was the headquarters for the City-Wide Young People's Forum, which organized youth into pickets and boycotts against state-sanctioned racism and segregation. Two Maryland lynchings in 1932 and 1933 especially mobilized Baltimore's African American youth, who met on Sundays at local congregations to read scripture, hear sermons, sing gospel songs and spirituals, and organize economically, politically, and socially. Such activism increased in the civil rights movement, notably during a March for Baltimore in 1964, led by a young Dick Gregory.[33] After civil rights legislation ended official segregation, Bethel's youth ministry program focused on developing rites of passage programs that challenged dominant rites for youth of sex, drugs, and rock and roll. Music, social justice (including prison outreach), and college preparation and scholarship programs were among the opportunities that Bethel's youth both developed and took advantage of in the last decades of the twentieth century.[34] Similar youth ministries have existed in African American congregations across the United States. Trinity United Church of Christ in Chicago is one that has been closely studied.[35] The congregation has applied a "kinship model" for youth ministry that "centers on intergenerational, communal worship, and the empowerment of adolescents who can critique mainstream culture from a theological, African-American stance."[36] Trinity's young people have preached on Youth Sundays, joined step (dance) teams, have had their academic accomplishments celebrated from the pulpit, and have otherwise organized and agitated to live out the congregation's motto as a place that is "Unashamedly Black, Unapologetically Christian."

Mainline Protestant youth ministries—of whom Lutherans can serve as a perhaps not entirely typical example—have been both supportive of American nationalism and critical of it.[37] During World War II, U.S. Lutheran youth— many of whom were ethnically German—both served in the U.S. armed forces and supported the efforts against Germany and Japan at home. During the cold war, Lutheran loyalties were less clear, and by the 1960s and especially during Vietnam a significant number of Lutheran young people were engaged with Lutheran Peace Fellowship and in protests against the war.[38] This supposedly anti-American activism triggered the ire of Lutheran patriots and contributed to the demise of the major national youth organizations for Lutherans—the Walther League and the Luther League of America. These schisms among youth groups in the 1960s and 1970s were often highly contentious and fore-shadowed the evolution of the roughly ten million Lutherans in the United States into two major denominations in the last half of the twentieth century: the conservative Lutheran Church—Missouri Synod (LCMS) and the more liberal Evangelical Lutheran Church in America (ELCA). These two national denominations have since 1975 largely left youth ministry to local congregations, with the exception of sponsoring national gatherings that pull together congregational groups once every few years, and a few other joint initiatives such as camps and faith-based programs like the Lutheran Volunteer Corps. Still, among those youth in the ELCA, programs focused on racial and economic justice, environmental activism, antimilitarism, international and interfaith dialogues, and training in nonviolence have become normative. In the LCMS, more traditional catechism programs, Bible studies, missionary projects, and education in keeping with so-called family values have prevailed.[39] Similar ambivalence toward the American civil religion—critical of it, but also embracing it—has developed among young people across youth ministries from historically mainline Protestant groups. A rough continuum from liberal to conservative has emerged among them, with the youth ministries and young people of historic peace churches (Quakers and Mennonites) on one end and conservative Methodist and Presbyterian youth programs on the other, with Episcopalians, Disciples of Christ, Lutherans, American Baptists, and other groups ranged in between.[40]

The histories of Roman Catholic youth ministries and the experiences of Catholic youth in modern America reveal a similarly ambivalent trajectory. On the one hand, Catholic youth in the early and mid-twentieth century were crucial in fostering support for the liberalizing reforms of Vatican II.[41] They had been cultivated in groups like the Catholic Youth Organization (CYO) and the Young Christian Workers (YCW).[42] These Catholic youth ministries combined vernacular (and often coeducational) social and study programs with occasional agitation on behalf of labor and civil rights, along with other activities for youth such as sporting events, camping, and educational opportunities.[43] Activism never dominated the Catholic movements, but programs were tailored to everyday interests of young people, such as sexuality and marriage, workplace ethics, and proper holiday celebrations for Christians. After Vatican II, however, and especially during the cold war and Vietnam Conflict, mainstream Catholic youth ministries muted any critiques of American nationalism and largely concentrated on finding avenues for young people to enter the middle classes. They succeeded wildly in doing so, but in the process groups such as the YCW no longer seemed necessary and folded, just as young Latinos (from predominantly Catholic countries) were immigrating to the United States and joining the workforce in record numbers.[44] As with Protestants, most Catholic young people in the early twenty-first century were engaged, if at all, in local youth groups whose dynamic varied from parish to parish, depending on the charisma and interests of the priest or lay leaders.[45] Catholic parochial schools and colleges continued to play a relatively steady role in inculcating Catholic values, rather than merely those associated with the American civil religion. But even the widely touted Catholic educational system was by the twenty-first century less focused on classical Catholic dogma, sacramentalism, or social teachings, and less reserved for Catholic students, than it had been in the past.[46] Catholic social teachings against the death penalty and on behalf of peace, for instance, tended to get obscured in youth ministries and education by dissonance with American feminism, on the one hand, and by the pedophilia scandal that rocked parishes across the United States, on the other. Such dissonance was evident also in intensified Catholic activism on behalf of the antiabortion movement, which coincided precisely with the family values that often merged Christianity and American nationalism, but also was represented as a critique of the secular values that some Catholics felt excluded them from full participation in civil society.[47]

Many Protestant evangelicals joined Catholic youth and youth leaders in this effort to extend Christian custodial responsibility for the American civil religion.[48] Evangelical Protestant youth were among the first to mobilize through the nineteenth-century Young Men's and Young Women's Christian Associations.[49] By the twenty-first century, however, these organizations had largely accommodated themselves to the secular spirituality of the market, with a dash of patriotism and philanthropy occasionally evident, depending on local circumstances.[50] More durably Christian, but often no less patriotic, were evangelical youth movements such as Youth for Christ (YFC). In the early years of YFC, during the 1940s, when led by Billy Graham, the group's members evidenced a tension between Christian separatism and patriotic

FIGURE 8.2: *Billy Graham, Evangelist and Founder of Youth for Christ, April 11, 1966.* Photo credit: Public domain. U.S. News and World. Released to Library of Congress, Prints and Photographs Division, Digital ID ppmsc.03261.   http://commons.wikimedia. org/wiki/Image:Billy_Graham_bw_photo,_ April_11,_1966.jpg.

commitment to the causes of the American nation.[51] Over time, the Christian elements were largely reduced in YFC to personal witnessing and morality, personal prayer and Bible study, and participation in large revivalist rallies held in stadiums across the country.[52] Patriotism, on the other hand, came to be unquestioned, as Graham's own evolution into the so-called pastor to the Presidents might suggest.[53] Almost nothing culturally critical appears in the YFC publications until well after the Vietnam Conflict.[54] By then, therapeutic relational evangelism had replaced the large YFC rallies, and local YFC offices worked with youth from local congregations to hold praise worship and Bible studies, along with educational events.[55] Some activism was directed at secular humanism and the teaching of evolution in local schools, but a therapeutic ethos and pop-culture style of enthusiastic Christian contemporary worship dominated the experiences of most YFC members.[56]

Jesus Camp, the 2006 film by Heidi Ewing and Rachel Grady, documents one of these trajectories among groups akin to YFC. Set in Missouri and North Dakota, *Jesus Camp* focuses on the experiences and voices of a group of young people. The youth are filmed at home (where their parents support their religious passions), at church (where they participate in Christian worship and activism that can only be described as militant), and at the Youth on Fire camp at Devil's Lake, North Dakota, a summer camp run by evangelical pastor Becky Fischer. In the crucial scene for our purposes, an Australian colleague of Pastor Fischer is preaching to the young people who are attending camp.[57] The setting is a rustic assembly hall. "Who's ready for some fun tonight?" he asks in a typical beginning for a youth sermon. But then he goes on: "You're not going to be the same person you came [*sic*] after this camp. You're going to be radical, you're going to be on fire. How many of you want to be those who would give up their lives for Jesus?" The children cheer; some raise their hands. The preacher then picks up a hammer, which he identifies as his "big Holy Ghost Hammer." "We're going to break some things … here tonight. We're going to break the power of the enemy in government." He then picks up a porcelain coffee cup, which he proclaims represents those "enemies" who took God out of schools. "God wants to put godly, righteous people in government," he says. The children cheer again. He then invites them, one by one, to come up and smash a cup placed on a table with the hammer, as they say "We break the power of the devil in this government." The sounds of smashing porcelain cups repeat themselves on the sound track. '"Fire in the world; in the world!" shouts nine-year-old Rachel. "Jesus! Jesus!" shouts eleven-year-old Levi, swaying from side to side. Many children begin to cry. The camera eventually focuses in on a close-up of a third child, Tory, who is red-faced, sobbing.

She takes the microphone, at the encouragement of Pastor Fischer. "Pray it out," Fischer exhorts her. "Lord," the child begins, "I just pray for change over our nation. ... I proclaim the Lion of Judah," Tory shouts, holding her little fist in the air, as the music crescendos, and the crowd claps. Words from Pastor Fischer conclude the scene, as the young people reenact a military drama set to Christian rock music, also seen earlier in the film: "Take these prophecies and do what the Apostle Paul said, and make war with them," Fischer shouts as the children march. "This means war! This means war! This means war! Are you a part of it, or not?"

Now, it would be misleading to suggest that *Jesus Camp* represented the only kind of experience open to young people in twenty-first-century American evangelicalism, much less in Christian youth ministries at large. Among evangelicals, there are also significant youth ministry movements, and individuals, who have been informed by programs associated with groups like Sojourners, building on an earlier legacy of countercultural evangelical activism.[58] Sojourners, led since the Vietnam era by Jim Wallis, takes the Bible-centered spirituality of evangelicalism, turns it away from therapeutic personal morality, and turns it toward critique of the American civil religion and its economic inequities and militarism.[59] Evangelical young people have participated in several initiatives that successfully focused attention on social justice issues, such as World Vision's Thirty Hour Famine, and the Souper Bowl of Caring, both of which are fundraisers and awareness campaigns for world hunger relief. Increasingly, evangelical youth are also engaging in environmental and interfaith activism, and in global efforts at peacemaking, although these are more controversial than the poverty-reduction programs.[60]

Nevertheless, the best one can say about modern Christian youth ministry in the United States is that over the decades, millions of young Americans have been informed by, and have often embraced, an ambivalent legacy of relationship with the American civil religion and with American nationalism.[61] Some youth, especially out of African American youth ministries, have emerged as activist critics and have transformed the society. Some, especially among evangelicals, have been Christian true believers in the American way, willing to sacrifice themselves on behalf of their faith.

GLOBAL DEVELOPMENTS

The history of religious youth active in peacemaking and critical of civil religions begins in India. A young lawyer who had lived for a while in apartheid South Africa, where he read the arguments in favor of nonviolence by Leo

Tolstoy, began to develop in 1914 what he called *satyagraha* and *ahimsa*—soul or truth force and nonviolent resistance.[62] Mohandas Gandhi mobilized the Indian masses, including many young people, to engage in protests, marches, and boycotts against the British Empire. That Empire had suppressed Hindu practice and sought to supplant it with a civil religion/Christian hybrid. Gandhi's movement, which was by no means only a youth movement, could not have been accomplished without young people and was undeniably built on a traditional spiritual foundation, rather than in collaboration with a state or civil religion. It successfully mobilized Hindu spiritual practices and discourses, along with openness to interfaith dialogue and collaboration, *against* the British Empire's civil religion and state apparatus. The fact that the world's most populous democracy has since threatened to develop its own civil religion of Hindu nationalism does not negate what Gandhi and multitudes of young Indians accomplished between 1930 and 1948.[63]

Observing Gandhi's movement from afar, young people of faith across many traditions and regions have been motivated to imitate his methods.[64] Across northern Europe, even prior to World War II, but especially afterward, young Christians became increasingly active in the ecumenical movement to unite Christians across denominational and national lines. Young German theologian Dietrich Bonhoeffer, who died at the hands of the Nazis, was among the early leaders, but Suzanne de Dietrich, Tracy Strong, and Madeleine Barot were also influential.[65] Youth or young adults were pivotal in the 1948 founding of the World Council of Churches (WCC), headquartered in Geneva, and have participated with varying degrees of representation ever since. From 2000 to 2010 the WCC has focused on overcoming violence, in conjunction with all of the living Nobel Peace Prize Winners and the United Nations.[66]

Such engagement with nonviolence on the part of Christian youth across northern Europe bore particular fruit in Latin America, Poland, and elsewhere. In Latin America, liberation theology, which was a potent blend of Marxism and Christianity in opposition to imperialist or colonial and neo-colonial ideologies, mobilized what Jose Miguez Bonino called the "younger generation" of Latin America theologians in the 1960s and 1970s. Since then, the explosion of Pentecostalism in Latin America has turned Christian youth inward to spiritual experience, and away from revolutionary praxis.[67] Yet many young people within Pentecostalism and among mainstream Protestant and Roman Catholic communities still seek to craft a Christianity that contributes to more just, inclusive, and democratic cultures, in contrast to the civil religions associated with either Spanish colonialism or neoliberal development.

FIGURE 8.3: *Gandhi at Dandi, Gujarat,*
April 5, 1930. Gandhi is picking salt on the
beach at the end of the Salt March, accompanied by youth. Photo credit: Public domain.
http://commons.wikimedia.org/wiki/
Image:Salt_March.jpg.

In Poland, a Catholic youth movement, called Oaza ("Oasis"), was a catalyst among the many movements that led to Solidarity, the intellectual-workers
organization that overthrew the communist regime.[68] Led initially in 1954 by
Fr. Franciszek Blachnicki, but inspired as it grew by the example of Cardinal
Karyl Wojtyła, who became Pope John Paul II in 1978, these fifteen-day summer camps into the Polish mountains began as training for altar boys—which
was understood as an internal church matter by the communist state. The state,
which had outlawed the CYA in 1956, of course ran its own summer camps
and planned vacations and excursions for youth, which were explicitly designed
to deter church attendance and foster loyalty to the communist regime and
its antireligious civil religion. Gradually, Oaza was transformed from a program for altar boys to a program for all Catholic youth to a program for
Catholic families. As the retreats increased in numbers of participants in the
late 1970s, the state moved to curtail them, including exiling Fr. Blachnicki

to Germany (where he died in 1987). The concerns of state officials were shared by some conservative Catholics in Poland starting in 1975, when Oaza began collaboration with U.S. evangelical and Pentecostal youth ministries, such as Campus Crusade for Christ, and when members began to talk about a "Polish theology of liberation."[69] By 1979, when Pope John Paul II made a nine-day visit to Poland, where he spoke to thirteen million people, this theology of liberation—as a nonviolent, ecumenical, democratic movement for workers' and human rights—was on its way to becoming a common language of solidarity across church and society.[70] It was born in Oaza but had ripple effects across the Soviet bloc.[71] It was thus no coincidence when the Pope celebrated World Youth Day in 1991 at Jasna Góra, the Shrine of Our Lady of Częstochowa—one of the centers of the Oaza movement. Fr. Blachnicki had become, to some, "Poland's 'Gandhi,'" while in his lifetime the communist regime had called him "a Polish Ayatollah."[72]

As the reference to the Ayatollah Khomeini and the student-led Iranian Revolution might suggest, not all of the stories of religious youth resisting secular regimes can be plotted easily on a romantic grid of liberation. Some young believers have taken the passion of faith and turned it into martyrdom through suicide bombings and other acts of terrorism. Yet for each one of them, hundreds if not millions of religious youth have participated in nonviolent democratic movements over the past several decades in what constitutes, all told, a rather impressive historical development. In South Africa, the antiapartheid movement, led by Archbishop Desmond Tutu, Nelson Mandela, and a group called the Kairos Theologians, had developed a South African liberation theology that channeled the energy of youth who had been burning townships toward the truth and reconciliation that overthrew apartheid and reconstructed South Africa.[73] As profiled in part in the 2004 documentary *Seeds*, Israeli and Palestinian youth met together at various peace camps since 1993 in efforts to foster interfaith dialogue and mutual understanding. Out of Turkey, the Gülen Movement has built, since the mid-1990s, hundreds of schools for Muslim youth, based on the ethic of love and tolerance associated with the movement's founder, M. Fethullah Gülen.[74] And in Burma, socially engaged Buddhist monks in 2007 joined with students to protest a ruthless military regime and its savage civil religion. In each of these cases, the contingencies of discrete cultures lent the interaction of religious traditions with civil religions and nationalism a different cast, and a different outcome. But the tension was consistent, with religious youth and youth leaders remaining critical agents in determining historical developments.

CHAPTER NINE

Health and Science

DOUG IMIG AND FRANCES WRIGHT

Across the twentieth century, there have been significant improvements in the health of the world's children, yet significant problems and inequities remain. A child born in one of the twenty-four most developed nations, for example, could look forward to a life expectancy of over seventy years. Meanwhile, in fifty-one countries, children can expect less than fifty years of healthy life, and in at least three countries—Malawi, Niger, and Sierra Leone—a newborn faces a life-expectancy of less than thirty years As these figures suggest, inequality at the dawn of the twenty-first century remains a significant predictor of health outcomes. Differences in health outcomes are much more than simply a personal tragedy and cause for family concern. A 1998 study found that the best model for predicting a nation's failure looks to levels of infant mortality, low openness to trade, and a low level of democracy.[1]

As early as the last half of the nineteenth century, demographers noted the correlates of childhood morbidity and mortality. In 1908, Edward Bunnell Phelps documented infant mortality rates across European nations.

As Phelps suggests, infant mortality rates varied widely before the turn of the twentieth century. Notably as well, in four of these nations, infant mortality rates were actually on the rise. Phelps noted the concentration of infant mortality among the children of the poor, suggesting that high rates of infant mortality followed from poor economic circumstances rather than from a lack of parenting skills among the poor.[2]

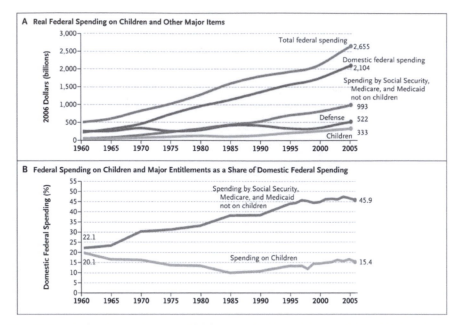

FIGURE 9.1: *Federal Spending on Children in the United States, 1960–2005.* Adapted from Carraso Steurle, and Reynolds 2007. Estimates and projections in Panel A were developed with the use of the budget of the U.S. government, fiscal year 2008, and the Congressional Budget Office. Tax expenditures for children are included in spending on children and domestic federal spending for this exercise. Dollars are adjusted for inflation (Iglehart 2007: 75).

Today, nearly 11,000,000 children younger than five years of age die each year worldwide. As the map that opens this chapter indicates, the distribution of those deaths tracks closely—but imperfectly—with the level of impoverishment of a nation. Six countries account for fifty percent of worldwide deaths in children younger than five years, and forty-two countries account for ninety percent of childhood deaths.[3] Almost all of the nearly 11,000,000 children who will die this year are poor.

Many studies have examined the relationship between poverty and child mortality in the developed world in order to explain why inequities in health outcomes persist in spite of well-established health care and sanitation systems. Lee Rainwater and Timothy Smeeding's comprehensive analysis of income inequities, system inputs, and life outcomes in the developed world shows that many Western nations—including the United States—have rates of child poverty far higher than we would predict based on their resources. In spite of the massive reductions in the infant and child mortality rates in the United States

Table 9.1: A Comparison of the Infant Mortality in the Principal Countries of Europe in the Last Twenty-five Years with the Earlier Periods Named in Bertillon's Table and the Decrease or Increase and Relative Rank in the Case of Each of the Countries.

	Infant Mortality in Periods Named		Deaths per 1,000 Births, 1881–1905	Decrease or Increase	Rank in Order of Lowest Infant Mortality	
	Period of Observa-tion	Deaths per 1,000 Births			Early Period	Later Period
Ireland	1865–83	95.9	99	3.1*	1	2
Norway	1866–82	104.9	94	10.9	2	1
Scotland	1865–81	122.0	123	1.0*	3	4
Sweden	1866–82	131.9	104	27.9	4	3
Denmark	1870–82	137.5	132	5.5	5	5
Belgium	1867–83	148.2	158	9.8*	6	9
England and Wales	1866–82	149.2	146	3.2	7	7
Finland	1878–80	164.9	144	20.9	8	6
France	1875–82	166.2	160	6.2	9	10
The Netherlands	1878–81	193.2	162	31.2	10	11
Switzerland	1869–80	195.2	153	42.2	11	8
Prussia	1874–82	207.8	202	5.8	12	13
Italy	1872–83	209.7	175	34.7	13	12
Romania	1875–82	250.0	203	47.0	14	14
Austria	1866–83	255.3	223	32.3	15	15
Russia in Europe	1867–78	266.8	268	1.2*	16	16
Averages		174.9	159.1	15.8		

*Increase.

in the last century, impoverished American children have infant mortality rates comparable to third-world countries.[4]

Today the leading causes of infant and child deaths worldwide are pneumonia (nineteen percent), diarrhea (eighteen percent), malaria (eight percent), neonatal pneumonia or sepsis (ten percent), preterm delivery (ten percent), and asphyxia at birth (eight percent). Behind all of these conditions is undernutrition and poverty. Excluding neonatal causes, the five leading worldwide causes of death in children today are pneumonia, diarrheal diseases, malaria, measles, and HIV/AIDS.[5]

Much of the improvement in worldwide health is due to improved sanitation, safer water, and the development of antibiotics and sulfa drugs. As a result of these improvements, infant mortality rates worldwide have improved dramatically. In East Asia, for example, they have dropped from 175 per 1,000 in 1950 to 52 per 1,000 in 1995. Other successes include the development of effective vaccines that have nearly eradicated smallpox and polio. Worldwide, however, 1,100,000,000 people still lack clean water and 2,600,000,000 lack a basic toilet. At the macro-level, improved access to basic sanitation has improved, but there are critical disparities. By 2002, 93 percent of the population in the Americas had access to clean and safe drinking water; virtually 100 percent of North Americans, 83 percent of Central Americans, and—within that region—only 75 percent of Guatemalans had access to a safe water supply.[6]

According to the World Health Organization (WHO), children in families in absolute poverty (subsisting on less than one dollar per day) were five times more likely to die between birth and five years of age, and two and a half times more likely to die between fifteen and fifty-nine than were their nonpoor peers. Historically, wealth led to child health. Undernutrition likely is responsible for 2,200,000 deaths among children younger than five, and vitamin deficiencies are responsible for another 1,000,000 infant and child deaths worldwide each year. Effective public health campaigns supporting breastfeeding practices and better access to nutritious weaning foods are likely to be keys to better rates of survival for the world's poor children.[7]

Today, however, trends in population health track less directly with overall levels of income growth than they respond to than other factors, such as access to health technology. Most recent gains in child health result from technological advances rather than income growth. Technological advances include the development of oral rehydration therapy (against diarrhea) and the development and dissemination of pharmaceuticals.[8]

Even the wealthiest regions have marked disparities in child health. Within Europe, WHO officials note a widening east–west gap in children's health. "Despite overall improvement, children's health in the European Region shows large differences ... both within and between countries. Social inequalities are increasing in all countries, and ... poverty is the greatest threat to children's health, regardless of a country's level of development."[9]

A CENTURY OF CHILDREN'S HEALTH IN AMERICA

Of all the changes that have transformed American childhood, "perhaps none has been more significant than the dramatic reduction in the likelihood of death, disease, or physical incapacitation" among children). At the turn of the twentieth century, nearly twenty-five percent of all children in the United States failed to survive the first five years of life, and close to a third failed to make it to ten. Paralleling trends worldwide, the improvement in the life expectancy of American children was initially driven by improving nutrition, living, and educational standards, and by improvements in sanitation. Over the last decades of the century, improvements in child health and survival have increasingly been the consequence of technology and developments in scientific medicine.[10]

As the twentieth century began, about six percent of all children failed to survive the first month of life. Another seven percent failed to make it to their first birthday, falling—most likely—to gastrointestinal disorders that claimed tens of thousands of babies each year, especially during the hot summer months. Another seven percent of all children aged one through four died before the end of their second year, falling to infectious respiratory diseases. Traditional infectious childhood diseases—measles, whooping cough, scarlet fever, and diphtheria—together accounted for twenty-three percent of all young child deaths. During the first two decades of the twentieth century, 250,000 American infants died each year before their first birthday. "In the poorest families, one child in six died within a year of birth."[11]

City living was particularly dangerous to the health and survival of children at the turn of the century. By 1900, New England, with its concentration of industrial towns and high population density, had become the least healthy section of the country for children. A child in the Midwest had a thirty percent better chance of surviving than did a child in New England. Meanwhile, there were significant health disparities among racial groups. African American children were twice as likely to die before age five as were white children. Moreover, childhood was frequently marred by significant illness, leaving children blind or deaf from infection or accident. Children were commonly stunted or crippled by rickets, scoliosis, tuberculosis, diphtheria, or scarlet fever. As the twentieth century dawned, poliomyelitis would come to replace diphtheria as "the most terrifying childhood scourge."[12]

Today, less than one percent of American children fail to reach age one, and of those who see their first birthday, less than one percent fail to reach age twenty. While the last few decades have seen the resurgence of tuberculosis and the appearance of AIDS, "infectious disease in general is no longer the handmaiden of death."[13]

Between the 1880s and the 1920s, infant mortality rates began to fall dramatically, particularly in America's large cities. By 1915 the rate in New York had dropped to ten percent. Similar declines occurred in other large cities, driven largely by improvements in the milk supply. "The summer diarrheal epidemics that had plagued American urban infants since the eighteenth century had all but disappeared by the 1920s."[14]

As is true around the world, the improved health of young Americans over the twentieth century closely corresponded with the socioeconomic status of their families. Socioeconomic status remains the best predictor of whether a pregnant woman will receive early prenatal care, or that newborns will be vaccinated. Race also remains a significant determinant of child health. At the end of the twentieth century, infant mortality among black children was two and a half times higher than for whites, and among Native Americans it was two and a third times higher.[15]

The chief causes of death among children have also changed over the century. There was a dramatic drop in the number and proportion of child deaths caused by infectious disease, and a corresponding increase in the proportion (though not the number) of child deaths from chronic and degenerative diseases and from external causes, including accidents, injuries, homicide, and suicide. This pattern is markedly different from the situation in the developing world, where most infant deaths occur today.

WHAT ACCOUNTS FOR THE CHANGE IN THE HEALTH OF AMERICAN CHILDREN OVER THE CENTURY?

Behind the dramatic improvement in American children's health over the twentieth century were a "wide array of socioeconomic ... behavioral, political, and technological and scientific developments." These included declining fertility and better nutrition and housing, leading to a reduction of disease and death. Additionally, improvements in the water supply, sewer systems, and effective waste removal contributed to health improvements. A third key factor was the work of public health officials and their allies in social work and medicine in combating the transmission of disease, and in educating the public in the basics of preventive, infant, and child hygiene.[16]

During the first decades of the twentieth century, increased attention was paid to the children of the poor. Social and political changes supported and shaped these developments, including increasing governmental support for medical and public health services, the increasing urbanization of the American population, waves of immigration from southern and eastern Europe, and the internal migration of African Americans from the South into the large cities of the North. The age distribution of Americans also was profoundly different.

At the turn of the twentieth century, children constituted almost half of the U.S. population (forty-six percent in 1890), while the elderly accounted for less than four percent. Today, children account for roughly twenty-five percent of the U.S. population, and the aged (those over sixty-five) account for more than twelve percent of the population.[17] Despite our aging population, children continue to constitute the largest group in poverty.

By the late nineteenth century, private charities were offering maternal and infant health care through so-called friendly visits, pure-milk stations, and child health clinics. Alarmed by overcrowding, and high rates of crime and disease, social reformers initiated calls for progressive reform. At milk stations, clean milk and well-child exams were offered to poor children.[18]

The fight to secure a safe milk supply was one of the first major nationwide public campaigns on behalf of children's health and well-being in America, and in key respects it was the campaign that built the networks and developed the strategic arsenal that would be employed over the next few decades in the American fight for children's health and well-being, leading to the Children's Bureau, the Owen-Keating (child labor) Act, the Sheppard-Towner (child and maternal health) Act, and key aspects of the Social Security Act concerning children's health.

THE SAFE MILK CAMPAIGN

As early as the 1890s, Nathan Straus had demonstrated the importance of milk safety to infant health. Straus was able to demonstrate that safe milk reduced the likelihood that children would contract diarrheal diseases. In fact, he was able to "cut the death rate in half for children at the Randall Island Infant Asylum in New York City" by feeding the foundlings only pasteurized milk.[19]

The result was a growing fund of knowledge, and a growing national consensus around a number of aspects of infant mortality: First, diarrheal diseases were the principal cause of infant mortality. Second, nutrition and safe feeding practices were the best way to reduce the risk of infant mortality. Third, in most circumstances breast-milk was the best food for infants. And fourth, the safety of the milk supply was a public health concern.[20] (Campaigns to champion breast-feeding as a mother's "protection against trouble" were launched across the century precisely because this fund of knowledge about how to fight infant mortality was shared by medical professionals but had not been diffused to the general public. There was significantly less unified under-standing of how to prevent infant mortality among individuals from different social and economic backgrounds.)

Straus's findings led to the establishment of milk depots and local regulatory reforms. The milk sanitation movement sought both to improve milk safety and to raise the caloric intake of poor mothers and infants. In Memphis, Tennessee, Memory McCord started the Cynthia Milk Fund in 1914 after encountering a starving mother who had stopped lactating, carrying what "appeared to be the skeleton of a child."[21]

Begun as a volunteer effort, the Cynthia Milk Fund bought quarts of milk for the poor. Soon, the fund partnered with the Board of Health to organize milk meetings and distribution centers offering education in scientifically based parenting practice. These meetings provided a forum where low-income women were instructed in nutrition, hygiene, and the value of milk as a food source.

As the fund grew, it established a clinic at General Hospital where babies receiving milk from the fund received routine check-ups from public health nurses. Nutrition classes were offered at the clinics, and visiting nurses made house calls to check on the condition of each child fed under the fund. Eventually, the fund established a coupon system—anticipating the food stamp program that followed.[22]

Women's clubs stood at the organizational core of the milk safety movement. The Los Angeles effort, for example, was spearheaded by the Friday Morning Club. Like the concurrent City Beautiful movement, the milk sanitation movement was a bi-racial though not integrated effort: white and black women's clubs assumed responsibility for the municipal housekeeping of their individual neighborhoods.[23]

Infant mortality represented a critical challenge to municipal housekeeping. As S. C. Kingsley, a prominent child welfare advocate in Chicago, observed: "visit those homes in the portions of your city where the white hearse goes most often, and you will find the weakest places in your municipal housekeeping." In Chicago, the Women's Auxiliary Board of Provident Hospital directed the Provident infant feeding program, which provided "free pure milk to babies in poor black neighborhoods."[24]

The municipal efforts of local women's clubs, in turn, were woven together by national women's magazines and by national child health and women's organizations. At the national level, the milk safety campaign was spearheaded by two groups—the American Child Hygiene Association and the Child Health Organization—and these organizations, in turn, followed international developments carefully, participated in international conferences (e.g., the 1907 Second International Conference on School Hygiene held in London, England), and followed the effects of starvation on European children during and following World War I. American Child Health Association president Herbert Hoover recalled: "my vivid experience with millions of children in Europe naturally turned my mind to examine our own house."[25]

The American Child Health Association also directed a widely publicized national survey in 1925 on the health of children in cities across the country. The 1925 survey exposed the uneven American municipal commitment to public health when it came to the well-being of children. Among key findings of the survey were the following:

- 431 cities had no full-time health official,
- half of the cities in the survey failed to keep reliable child birth/mortality records,
- vaccinations were not required in 37 cities,
- pasteurization of the milk supply was required in only 8 cities (47 cities pasteurized less than half of the milk supplied), and
- 21 cities offered no health instruction.

Meanwhile, the average American child brushed his or her teeth five days out of seven, and two in five children drank "one or more cups of coffee a day."[26] The milk safety movement found another champion in the mass-circulation women's magazines that dominated the era. These magazines spread news of the work of municipal clubs and informed club women of the findings of the national campaign. In both May and June of 1910, for example, *Good House-keeping* published articles on the "Victory Won by [Portland's] Housewives" in the pure milk war, and offered a strategic primer on "What Any Women's Club Can Do in Reforming the Milk Supply."[27]

Despite the epidemiological evidence, and the support of club women, national women's magazines, and national organizations, pasteurization and milk safety standards provoked suspicion from producers and business groups who opposed regulation of their industries and the costs that improved milk safety imposed on farmers and dairies (variously including cement floors in cow barns, tuberculosis tests of livestock, and pasteurization). But reformers ultimately prevailed. Their efforts were aided immeasurably by a 1913 U.S. Supreme Court ruling that city health officials had the right to regulate milk suppliers whether or not the milk was produced within city limits.[28]

The safe milk campaign reformers' successes were far-reaching—resulting in a rapid drop in infant illness and death. Coupled with the development of effective vaccines for smallpox and diphtheria, diarrheal diseases were no longer the chief cause of infant mortality in the United States. The Standard Milk

Ordinance drafted by the American Child Health Association (ACHA) was adopted by 247 communities, and 183 additional cities enacted some version of the standard ordinance—versions that the ACHA often considered watered down.[29] The implications for children's health were profound: between 1900 and 1930, the infant mortality rate declined by seventy percent in the United States.

To the progressives, the negative consequences of unregulated urbanization, poverty, hunger, disease, and despair seemed to hit children the hardest. In the words of journalist Jacob Riis: "nothing is now better understood than that in the rescue of children is the key to the problem of city poverty." Activists argued that increasing the income of breadwinners would better meet the needs of families and children, as would providing widows with aid so they could provide maternal love to their children rather than placing them in institutions.[30]

Activists at the turn of the century also argued about where to place responsibility for poor child health and well-being: was the problem poor parents or poor parenting? Early in the century, many physicians argued that "insufficient family income rather than laziness or ignorance led mothers to stop breastfeeding." But even then, "most reformers ... shifted the blame for infant deaths ... to mothers" and attributed "a lack of education, inadequate diet, and faulty child-rearing practices" to "defects in intelligence and moral character."[31] This debate continues today.

The subsequent history of child health in America is characterized by an ongoing debate as to whether the health needs of poor children constitute a medical or social problem, and whether such needs are a suitable matter for government intervention.[32]

In 1912, Congress established the U.S. Children's Bureau to "investigate and report ... upon all matters pertaining to the welfare of children and child life among all classes of our people." As its first official act, the bureau began to collect birth certificate data in order to track infant mortality rates. The bureau used "data to embarrass Americans into action." As the bureau argued: "the mere business of being a baby in the United States must be classified as an extra-hazardous occupation." In its first years, the Children's Bureau saw a reduction in infant mortality rates from 131 per 1,000 live births to 85.8 between 1913 and 1920.[33]

INFANT AND MATERNAL HEALTH:
THE SHEPPARD-TOWNER ACT

In anticipation of the women's vote, political support grew in the teens for so-called women's issues. In this environment, Congress passed the

Sheppard-Towner Maternity and Infancy Act in 1921. Sheppard-Towner offered a national education and diagnostic program designed to reduce infant and maternal mortality and improve children's health. Sheppard-Towner increased the number of rural clinics providing maternal, infant, and child care and health instruction.

Coalitions and networks built through the campaign for safe milk raised general public awareness of the problem of infant mortality and linked child well-being to safe milk and living conditions. The Sheppard-Towner campaign imported the organizational network and tactical repertoire developed by the earlier movement.[34]

Sheppard-Towner provided federal matching funds to states that established prenatal health care programs for expectant mothers, and it supported nurse home visiting programs for lactating mothers and their infants. Echoing the tension within the child health movement over where to lay responsibility for child health, Sheppard-Towner evolved from a health bill to a health education and outreach program.

The first version of the bill provided for "medical and nursing care at home or at a hospital when necessary."[35] The final version dropped all language concerning the provision of health care, and instead provided for *public education* efforts undertaken by public health nurses and community volunteers, and for nurses to make home visits to pregnant women to instruct them in prenatal care and child rearing techniques. The bill that ultimately emerged was a product of fear, according to William Frederick Bigelow, editor of *Good Housekeeping* magazine, chiefly the fear of socialized medicine: "The ghost that scared the whole United States Senate was ... the whole nation asking Uncle Sam to hurry up and send a doctor."[36]

Both Sheppard-Towner and the safe milk movement had roots in European programs. The American milk depot was modeled on the French *goutes de lait*. and Sheppard-Towner took inspiration from European public health nursing programs. Historian Rima Apple also found deep roots of the Sheppard-Towner clinics in private health clinics that operated across the United States early in the twentieth century that were sponsored by both white and African American women's organizations.[37]

The Children's Bureau built alliances with the General Federation of Women's Clubs, the Congress of Mothers, and Parent Teacher Associations to raise support for the new federal program. These women's groups, in turn, took the prenatal and maternal care message to their local communities and sponsored programs such as Baby Week. To "address the constructive side of infant care" and reach "not only individual parents but communities," the bureau worked with local groups to sponsor "meetings, exhibits, ... flags distributed by Boy Scouts or other organizations to every house where there is a baby; processions, plays, tableaus, school children's essays and more." Individual women's clubs also lobbied their national, state, and local officials through letter writing campaigns.[38]

Sheppard-Towner supporters partnered with major women's magazines to publish educational articles and run petition drives that would reach women across the country. Magazines including *Good Housekeeping*, and *The Ladies' Home Journal* wrote on the importance of prenatal care and parental education.

The child savers well understood that suffrage was a critical weapon in their arsenal. William Frederick Bigelow, editor of *Good Housekeeping*, argued in February of 1920 that "politicians are expecting to wait with this bill [Sheppard-Towner] until the women of the country make an issue of it ... For the sake of every mother to be and every child unborn, women should take their ballots in their hands and hold them up for every man in Congress to see." In the same issue, Anne Martin argued: "Our enfranchisement [as women] has been urged not only because it is just, but because of weapon of the vote will arm us more effectively to protect women and children, to improve the race ... the greatest woman's issue and the most needed conversation measure is immediate governmental action for the protection of maternal and infant life and health."[39] Martin was convinced that concerted action by newly enfranchised female voters would carry the day: "Only four million women could vote in 1916 ... yet we succeeded in making the national woman suffrage amendment a political issue in the last presidential election ... With four times as many women voters in 1920, we can surely make an equally good fight for the lives of the mothers and babies of this country."[40]

The Social Security Act (SSA) contained several streams of funding for children. Title IV provided funds to states for the Aid to Dependent Children program, and Title V echoed the public health programs of the Sheppard-Towner Act.[41] The SSA also illustrates the enduring political silence of children in American politics. In spite of the fact that the number of children receiving relief in the 1930s was seven times the number of persons over age sixty five receiving such aid, the vast majority of social security provisions went to support the aged in American society.

According to historian Janet Golden, the most important change in the provision of child health over the twentieth century was the medicalization of diagnosis, treatment, and management. Whereas parents in earlier eras would

have consulted friends, relatives, or domestic medical manuals, at the beginning of the twentieth century, it was increasingly the general practitioner who
called at the home of the sick child. "By the end of the century it would most
likely be a pediatrician, seen in an office visit or, in the case of an emergency,
at the hospital."[42] By the end of the century, very sick children—rich and
poor—would most likely be treated in hospitals.

Advances in medical science and technology advanced the cultural authority of pediatrics as the best way to care for children's health. Births moved
from home to hospital over the century, and the care of newborns became
increasingly sophisticated. Technologies such as incubators helped preserve
the lives of premature infants. Improvements in surgery benefited children,
and old diseases of childhood such as tuberculosis and diphtheria began to
be conquered with new medicines and preventive measures that followed the
development of germ theory.[43]

Pediatrics itself is largely a product of the twentieth century. On the eve
of World War I, there were fewer than 900 doctors identified as pediatri-
cians in the United States. Twenty years later there were close to 4,000.[44]
By mid-century, pediatrics had become a regular part of the medical school
curriculum, and, in 1941, the American Pediatric Society was born.

During the late 1940s and early 1950s, polio was the leading cause of
paralysis and other crippling conditions among American youth. Franklin D. Roosevelt helped to establish the National Foundation for Infantile
Paralysis, which began the March of Dimes campaign to raise money for
research into polio. With the creation of the Salk vaccine for polio, followed by the development of the Sabin vaccine, polio was brought under
control. The development of the polio vaccines proved not only a triumph
in the conquest of the disease but also an important contribution to the
development of virology more generally.[45]

Part of the legacy of the American civil rights movements of the 1950s
and 1960s was an increasing awareness of the inequity in access to medical
care. In 1963, Congressed passed the Maternal and Child Health and Mental
Retardation Planning Amendments to the SSA, which expanded federal funding for child health programs, and established the National Institute of Child
Health and Human Development within the National Institutes of Health.
Critical War on Poverty programs benefiting children include Medicaid (title
XIX of the SSA). Medicaid is the major federal health insurance program for
children today. "Yet access to that program often is thwarted by extensive
paperwork ... low reimbursement rates, and regulations at odds with the
provision of needed services."[46]

The War on Poverty also saw the creation of the federal WIC program (The Special Supplemental Feeding Program for Women, Infants and Children). WIC grew out of two pilot programs undertaken in Memphis, Tennessee and Baltimore, Maryland. The Memphis program gave away iron-rich supplements to poor mothers and established supplemental food programs for low-income families. Children in the program were followed in longitudinal research studies. The findings from these studies, in turn, indicated that the program reduced anemia and infant mortality. Echoing the trajectory of earlier movements for children's health, the program elicited national media interest. The program was featured in an article in *Redbook* magazine titled "How to Save Babies for Two Dimes a Day," which praised the success of the program in bolstering the growth of impoverished infants.[47] In its current greatly expanded format, the WIC program continues to support the nutritional needs of low-income mothers and infants today.

LOOKING FORWARD: CHILDREN'S HEALTH IN THE TWENTY-FIRST CENTURY

In the first years of the twenty-first century, children face a number of new concerns, including rising rates of asthma and diabetes. We also have a much greater understanding of childhood mental health today. Growing recognition of children's mental health concerns, including schizophrenia and learning disabilities, prompted the development of new fields of scientific and medical study, and the development of child guidance clinics and school psychologists' offices.[48]

One constant over the last century concerns health care disparities—particularly disparities in the health of children from different races and social classes. The State Children's Health Insurance Program (SCHIP) is designed to target uninsured children in families not eligible for Medicaid under previous standards.[49] Unlike Medicaid, SCHIP is not an entitlement program but instead depends on state funding levels, underscoring the American reluctance to recognize a right to health care even for children. We still have large numbers of children going without any form of insurance.

As of 2006, sixty percent of Americans were covered by private insurance, twenty-six percent were publicly insured, and sixteen percent were uninsured. Meanwhile, sixty percent of children under eighteen were privately insured, twenty-eight percent were publicly insured, and twelve percent were uninsured. In contrast, forty percent of low-income children are privately insured, forty-three percent are publicly insured, and seventeen percent lack

insurance altogether. Families in poverty are even more reliant on Medicaid, with seventeen percent of their children covered under private insurance,
sixty-one percent on public insurance, and twenty-two percent uninsured.
Medicaid has become increasingly important to families in poverty over the
last several decades as fluctuations in the economy have caused more and
more employers to stop providing families with health insurance.[50]

Uninsured low-income children were four times more likely than their
insured peers to lack a primary care physician or a usual source of medical
care. They were also nearly four times more likely to delay needed medical
care. In addition, nearly one in three uninsured low-income families were
unsure whether they could obtain needed medical care for their children,
as compared to one in ten low-income families on public health insurance
and one in thirteen low-income families on private health insurance.[51] While
providing children with health insurance is not a cure-all for children's health
problems, helping create better access to care through insurance is clearly tied
to improved health outcomes for all children.

In spite of a reduction of over ninety percent in infant mortality rates over
the century, and a near ninety-nine-percent reduction in the maternal mortality rate in the same period, there are persistent inequalities in health outcomes
for women and children of different races. While black mothers were twice as
likely as white mothers to die in child birth at the turn of the last century, they
are now three times as likely as white mothers to die in childbirth. Black infants

FIGURE 9.2: *HIV Kids, Cambodia.* Courtesy of the Sharing Foundation.
Accessed on October 22, 2008, at http://www.flickr.com/photos/cambodia
4kidsorg/417675498.

also have persistently higher rates of infant mortality, low birth weights, and preterm deliveries.[52]

Moreover, seeing a doctor and obtaining needed medical services in the United States continues to be governed to a large degree by a family's ability to pay. Many who could not afford a doctor in the first half of the twentieth century would hope for charity care from hospitals and clinics. At present, government payment schemes such as Medicaid and the SCHIP aid families and children who lack medical insurance. Still, access to these programs is uneven and limited. All too often, poor and low-income children in America receive medical treatment only when they become seriously ill and go to a hospital emergency room. Today, across the developed and developing world, poverty remains the greatest threat to children's health.[53]

CHAPTER TEN

World Contexts

JEANINE GRAHAM

In February 2007, Aboriginal Australians received, at last, a federal government apology for the policies that had caused so much distress and hardship to the children and families of the so-called Stolen Generations. Newly elected Labor prime minister, Kevin Rudd, publicly acknowledged how devastating the ideologically driven scheme had been for the mixed race children forcibly separated from their Aboriginal mothers and the indigenous communities to which they belonged. The assimilationist system of breeding out aboriginal traits and raising the children to be white operated throughout the continent between 1910 and 1970. It was no clandestine policy. Removals were officially sanctioned, records were detailed, and intentions were clear. The adverse consequences were life-long. Yet not until the "Bringing Them Home" report was tabled in parliament in 1997 could the personal testimonies heard by the national commission of inquiry into the separation of Aboriginal and Torres Strait Islander children from their families enter into the public domain for most white Australians. The scale and impact of the scheme at last become apparent to a dominant population with a long tradition of indifference and disdain for Aboriginal people and their culture.[1]

Of course, Australia was not unique in applying discriminatory policies toward its indigenous people. Nor were such attitudes peculiar to the twentieth century. But what gave this tragedy added poignancy was the belief, firmly and genuinely held by many officials and their contemporaries, that the separation policy was unquestionably in the best interests of every child involved.[2]

The anguished pleadings of Aboriginal parents and elders were disregarded. The voices of the children were not heard. Only in a postwar era of decolonization, when fundamental assumptions of cultural superiority were being questioned and undermined, was the inhumanity of the policy recognized and its framework dismantled.

When viewed within a twentieth-century world context, this particular example of social engineering was but one of many experiments and developments that destroyed child and family life. Certainly there were many natural disasters—earthquakes, floods, fires, tsunamis, storms, and drought—in which children were victims of environmental forces beyond human control. The spontaneous destruction wrought in those circumstances bears little comparison with the consequences of manipulative policies deliberately devised and applied by adults against children. The extermination of 1.5 million Jewish children in the Holocaust; and the abduction of young people to serve as child soldiers, laborers, or sex slaves are two obvious examples.

The past century held, and delivered, so much promise for the world's children, through health and welfare initiatives, improved access to public education, and greater understanding of young people's physiological and psychological needs. Both within and between nation states, there were innumerable policies and proposals intended to improve the quality of young lives. As other chapters and studies have shown, many initiatives achieved good results, such as the decline worldwide of infant and early child mortality.[3] In circumstances where assistance was needed, at local, state, and international levels, volunteers and paid workers made child and family well-being their primary focus. Successful partnerships with local communities had a transforming effect on the lives of even the most geographically isolated of children, as Sherpa tributes to mountaineer and humanitarian Sir Edmund Hillary revealed.[4] The fact that the Convention on the Rights of the Child (UNCRC) was passed unanimously by the United Nations Assembly in 1989 and subsequently ratified by 191 of 193 member states was both a remarkable achievement by those involved in the drafting and negotiating processes and a reflection of widely agreed-on beliefs about what constitutes the ideal experiences of late twentieth-century children—despite a predictable discrepancy between ideal and reality concerning individual government implementation of the convention's 54 principles, especially in countries where military expenditure consumes a disproportionate share of the annual budget.[5] Recognizing these positive accomplishments provides a complementary and essential perspective on a century where horror and hope seem to have been in constant juxtaposition.

Ideology and armed aggression have been powerful influences on young people's lives throughout the modern age, as have consumerism, technology, disease, music, cultural marginalization, food, friends, personal belief systems, idealism, family love and support, or violence, abuse, and neglect. In this chapter, which emphasizes some of the more negative features of the twentieth-century world context for children, youth, and their families, the many advantages of growing up in this era are little explored. Millions of children never experienced them. The continuing contradiction between a near-universal international agreement on the principle of children's rights and the extensive denial, disregard, and dismissal of such rights in practice stems largely from political upheavals, factionalism, corruption, prejudice, and poverty. The everyday experiences of Brazilian street children, who are supported by a multitude of official and nongovernmental agencies yet subjected to violence and mistreatment by the police force, symbolize that situation. So too does the statelessness of Lhotshampas children and youth, effectively trapped in refugee camps in southeastern Nepal by seventeen years of inconclusive repatriation negotiations with Bhutan.[6]

IDEOLOGY

Efforts by adults to instill particular codes of behavior and value systems in the young have been an integral part of parenting and community life. Religious organizations and educational institutions, too, have long perceived the advantages of such training from an early age. Youth movements that sought to provide life skills as well as promote ideals of tolerance, cooperation, and service also flourished in the twentieth century—as international participation in the Boy Scout and Girl Guide movements reflects—while countless sporting, cultural, and leisure associations provided an outlet for youth socializing as well as socialization. A significant innovation of the twentieth century, however, was the deliberate targeting and indoctrination of children and young people by a number of powerful political movements, each with the express goal of fostering closer relationships with the state at the expense of loyalty to the family. From the earliest stages of the Bolshevik revolution, for instance, the energies and idealism of young people supportive of the cause were harnessed through the Communist Youth Leagues (Komsomols). In the new Soviet regime, their role in building a new socialist society was also reinforced through educational and health initiatives. The rapid expansion of primary and secondary schools and the spread of kindergartens and nursery schools and the efforts to reduce child mortality through the provision of health clinics and prenatal care: such measures were an integral part of a political ideology that envisaged the role of the state as central in the shaping of children's lives. Young Pioneer organizations provided a variety of activities for children, nine- to fourteen-year-olds especially, after which they graduated to membership in the more overtly political Komsomols. The prominent role of youth in the early economic experiments, such as the first Five Year Plan (1928–1932), reflected a degree of success in the regime's aspirations for molding the attitudes of the younger generation—but the importance of family ties remained. Outward conformity to state ideals was no guarantee of inner conviction, as Eastern Bloc authorities discovered in the postwar era, in the 1960s especially and subsequently in the late 1980s.[7]

Chinese communism after 1949 involved a similar ideologically driven network for youth, through the Little Red Soldiers, Young Pioneers, and Communist Youth Leagues. In this Asian context, too, improving child health and access to education were state priorities, the outcomes of which could be measured in tangible form by the reduction in infant mortality rates and the growing percentage of children and youth enrolled in formal education. Yet, as in the Soviet bloc, the intensive endeavors to inculcate loyalty to the state ahead of family values and (in China) Confucian beliefs, could not be sustained. The impact on individuals varied widely, as an analysis of "purist," "rebellious," "pragmatic," and "conforming" political activists has shown.[8] Nevertheless, as the book *Mao's Last Dancer* reveals, a youthful process of indoctrination, questioning, disillusionment, and rejection was not an easy path to follow, especially when the welfare of family members could be put at risk by one individual's dissent.[9]

More openly militaristic and racist state-sponsored youth organizations flourished in Germany and Italy in the interwar years, contributing to the intergenerational mistrust, dissension, and fear that could develop within families when parental views differed from those of their indoctrinated youth. Under Mussolini's regime (1922–1945), the Balilla (for boys) and Piccole Italiene (for girls) provided a range of youth-oriented activities and propaganda, all designed to promote a sense of national loyalty that would be more powerful than religious or family influences. Significantly, the Catholic Action youth organization continued throughout the 1930s, with a membership rivaling that of the fascist youth movements. In Nazi Germany, Hitler Youth and the League of German Maidens espoused ideologies that emphasized obedience and service to the state, attitudes that would also be expressed in Franco's Spain. Racial hatred against ethnic minorities was an integral part of such nationalist rhetoric. Because access to education, employment, and leisure activities was facilitated by membership in these youth groups, to remain outside was to become a target for discrimination and suspicion. Despite the defeat and discrediting of the Nazi regime in World War II, its ideological legacy remained in the paramilitarism and racist slogans of various neofascist groups that tended to attract unemployed or underemployed anti-immigrant youth in Western Europe and North America. By contrast, the popular Finnish Civil Guard for Boys (later Soldier Boys) and its sister organization, Little Lottas (renamed Lotta Girls), operated successfully as a nationalistic and voluntary defense movement on the Finnish home front during World War II without aspiring to any wider influence.[10]

Political ideologies also influenced youth attitudes in other contexts, perhaps the most pervasive of which, in the twentieth century, were to be found in societies where cultural difference was synonymous with ideas of racial inferiority and superiority, though, as the educational patterns of aristocratic Indian children demonstrate, caste could be a complicating factor.[11] Yet notions of cultural supremacy, so integral to the extension and retention of imperial rule, were also embedded in the social and political structures of countries that were critical of colonialism. Postwar decolonization in Africa and the Pacific was followed by the heady rhetoric of the black civil rights movement in the United States: for minority youth on all continents, it was time to challenge openly the hegemony of white authority and, in the process, to assert a sense of pride in one's identity. Where that control was deeply ingrained in the power structures of the country, as with apartheid in South Africa and segregation in the Southern United States, both civil protest and police reaction generated verbal and physical violence against youth. The U.S. Supreme Court decision, in May 1954, ruling that segregated schools were inherently unequal, could only be implemented by African American children who could survive the antagonism of their fellow students, as at Little Rock, Arkansas in 1957.[12] Family support in such circumstances was crucial. South African police opened fire on the 15,000 black schoolchildren and youths who gathered at Soweto, in June 1976, to demonstrate against the enforced use of Afrikaans as the medium of instruction. Twenty-five were killed and many were wounded.[13] In other societies, however, where a long history of interracial cooperation was a mitigating factor preventing formal legislative discrimination, Martin Luther King's inspirational "I Have a Dream" speech, resonated with indigenous youth. In New Zealand, for example, a predominantly university-educated group, Nga Tamatoa, adapted Black Power slogans and philosophy to an antipodean situation, sometimes affronting their own elders as well as Pakeha (non-Maoris) in their assertion of indigenous rights and identity. At the preschool level, local community grassroots initiatives led to the establishment of *kohanga reo* (language nests), a model subsequently adopted by other First Nations people. The late twentieth-century renaissance of Maori language, artistry, writing, performing arts, and design all stemmed from foundations laid in the protests of this period, as did government endeavors to redress the injustices of nineteenth-century colonialism, land legislation especially, which deprived many tribes of economic resources for decades. In stark contrast with the situation for youth a century earlier, to identify as Maori became a matter of pride.[14] Yet low educational attainment, for young males especially; overcrowded housing; poor health statistics; and disproportionately high rates of family violence, alcohol, drug, and welfare dependency, criminal offending, and unemployment continue to reflect the long-term legacy of socioeconomic advantage experienced by many indigenous families within and beyond Pacific Rim countries.

Where youthful idealism and political ideology were interpreted as outright opposition to an authoritarian regime, the outcomes were sometimes disastrous for young demonstrators, as the fate of Chinese students protesting at various times in Beijing's Tiananmen Square has shown. In 1976, they were forcibly dispersed, with many casualties; in the winter of 1986, their calls for democracy and more freedom of control over their own lives met with official resistance, though not armed violence. In the spring of 1989, however, the Chinese party leadership reacted forcefully against the seven-week student occupation of the square. Brought in from outlying China, young recruits of the People's Liberation Army were ordered to fire indiscriminately on students their own age. Hundreds were killed in the massacre that followed, on June 4 1989, in a violent reprisal that journalists and television crews reported to the world. Student leaders and demonstrators were arrested, and those accused of supporting a movement for democracy were persecuted. Dissidents were sentenced to execution or incarceration. The gulf between the party and a young educated elite widened dramatically in the wake of the party's action against unarmed and peaceful youth. The phenomenon of large-scale student protest, evident in Prague, Paris, London, Berlin, and the United States during the late 1960s and early 1970s, for example, declined, but the passion for change did not, as was readily apparent in youth responses to the collapse of the Berlin Wall (November 1989) and other political transformations throughout Eastern Europe.[15]

Both political and religious movements transcended national boundaries, but consumerism and youth cultures became far more pervasive ideologies in the modern world context, affecting—and connecting—young people on a global scale. Music, fashion, and technology were crucial elements in the development of youth cultures, as mid-century Beatlemania and the ubiquitous denim jeans demonstrated.[16] Food, language (text messaging included), celebrity idols, friendships, peer groups, and social rituals were also key factors. Film, radio, television, mobile phones, personal computers, and the Internet enabled successive generations to develop an awareness of their own and other cultures, even if individual or group autonomy might be circumscribed by religion, regime, class, gender, ethnicity, or family income. Despite Taliban restrictions on their physical and educational freedom, for instance, young women in Herat watched smuggled American and Hindi videos, preferring the latter since "the Indian ones always had good endings where the oppressed person finally wins out," though "everyone wanted *Titanic* hairstyles and clothes" and "all the girls fell in love with Leonardo di Caprio. Even the men wanted the same floppy hair as him with their Taliban beards."[17] There were risks inherent in this growing interconnectedness—text message bullying, predatory pedophiles, the insidious promotion of drugs, alcohol, cigarettes, sex, and fast food—but many late twentieth-century youth were able to grow up with a significant appreciation of cultural, linguistic, and environmental diversity, well beyond that of previous generations. Others experienced poverty, disease, and oppression, and could focus only on their own survival.

CHILDREN AND WAR

Throughout the modern era, armed conflict affected young people's lives in diverse ways, from organized evacuations to urgent flight; from active military participation to involvement in civilian resistance; and from psychological or physical trauma because of direct exposure to bombing, rape, and genocide to the personal tragedy of losing family and identity. The intensity of the impact varied between regions and states, depending on the nature and duration of each conflict and the context in which it was (or is) being fought. The children of Israel and Palestine have never grown up in peace. Nor have the youth of Timor Leste. Those in Northern Ireland now have a chance to do so. Kurdish children do not. Poverty and disease were exacerbated by armed aggression. Starvation or malnutrition has been a natural corollary of conflict-related famine, on the African continent particularly, as demonstrated by the Biafran tragedy during the Nigerian civil war (1967–1970) and the continuing disaster of Darfur. In the second half of the twentieth century, humanitarian interventions could contribute to some amelioration of conditions for children but only in the short term where internal power struggles have persisted, as in Afghanistan, Somalia, and Iraq. With the intensification of sectarian violence—a constant occurrence on the

Indian subcontinent after 1947 and becoming incessant in other regions where religious hatred was, and is, fomented for political ends, as with the concept of jihad—young suicide bombers and their youthful victims all pay a high price for the fanaticism and ambition of their elders.

The last two decades of the twentieth century saw more young lives disrupted and devastated by armed conflict and its consequences than at any other period in the modern era. An estimated 150 million children were killed in international or civil wars since the 1970s, and an equal number were maimed or disabled by severe injury.[18] Conflicts in Central and Latin America, Africa, Asia, and the Middle East were all characterized by high civilian population death rates in which children and women were affected in far greater numbers they had been during earlier wars when the boundaries between civilian and military spheres were more consistently observed. The efforts of international agencies—such as the Red Cross and Red Crescent, Save the Children, United Nations International Children's Emergency Fund (UNICEF), and United Nations High Commission for Refugees (UNHCR)—to afford protection or relief were, and are, constantly hampered by unpredictable or indiscriminate attacks on refugee camps, hospitals, and convoys of supplies and against aid workers themselves.

The vulnerability of youth to exploitation in times of armed conflict has also become acute in recent decades. Despite strong international condemnation of child trafficking and the use of child soldiers, thousands of children in Central and Latin America and in postcolonial African states were at risk of one or both of these situations, partly because of the conflict-related breakdown of family and community connections and the prevailing poverty among the civilian population but primarily because of the callousness of those who abducted or recruited them. Child soldiers were widely deployed in some of the African continent's more recent civil wars—in Sierra Leone, Angola, and the Democratic Republic of Congo (DRC), for instance. Gunpoint abductions by the rebel Lord's Resistance Army (LRA) in northern Uganda—some 8,000 children between 1994 and 1998—led to the closure of most schools in the region by 2002.[19] Exposed to intimidation, torture, and rape, youth could be terrorized into a fighting role, one for which modern light weaponry posed no logistical problem.[20] The violence of their war-related activities has rendered more difficult the problems associated with any subsequent attempts to rehabilitate former child soldiers into civilian society, particularly when the age of abduction interrupted traditional initiation processes, as is apparent among the Tchokwè in Angola.[21] Late twentieth-century conflicts in Ethiopia, Mozambique, Liberia, Myanmar, Cambodia, and Sri Lanka have all involved child soldiers. In Central America's civil wars of the 1970s and 1980s, both children and youth demonstrated some agency in their decision to join guerilla forces: the prospect of regular food and an illusory sense of security could be among the motivations. In both El Salvador and Guatemala, however, soldiers under fifteen years of age were more likely to have been coerced into government forces, a contrast with the underage volunteering that occurred in European and Allied armies during World War I. The abduction of children to work as child labor has continued in areas riven by warfare, such as Angola, Uganda, Rwanda, Mozambique, and Burundi. The emotional and material consequences for families have been profound.[22]

Children, youth, and their parents were prisoners of war, literally and figuratively, throughout the century. British confinement of Boer women and children in southern Africa in 1901–1902; the Jewish children of the ghettos in

FIGURE 10.1: *Holocaust Survivor.* Six-year-old war orphan with Buchenwald badge on his sleeve waits for his name to be called at roll call at Buchenwald camp, Germany, for departure to Switzerland. Pfc. G. A. Haynia, photographer. Record Group 111: Records of the Office of the Chief Signal Officer (111-SC-208199), United States National Archives.

World War II; the incarceration of young Iranian soldiers in Iraqi prisoner-of-war camps in the late 1980s: the deliberate or indirect maltreatment (by neglect or indifference) of young people in conditions of armed combat was not the sole preserve of any one national or ethnic group.[23] Periods of internment also had long-term consequences for the youth involved. More than 120,000 Japanese American youngsters and their relatives, deemed to be a potential threat to national security, spent much of World War II in guarded internment camps, surrounded by barbed wire. Traditional roles and relationships altered as a consequence, as those born in the United States (Nisei) came to exert more influence in their communities than the older generation born abroad (Issei).[24]

While the actual experiences of conflict, displacement, dispossession, and loss were immediate, even children far removed from a theater of war could feel affected personally. In World War I, for instance, school children in all of the British dominions were well socialized into upholding the Allied war effort. Their fundraising, community activities, and education reflected support for the distant conflict in which relatives and friends were involved. Decades later, many of their descendants made pilgrimages to World War I sites of memory—young Australians and New Zealanders to Gallipoli, for instance—while the sons and daughters of World War II veterans accompanied parents to former battle zones and began to understand some of the character traits of an ex-serviceman.[25] Memoirs and oral histories often reflected child adjustment to the physical and psychological consequences of a parent's involvement in war. Writer David Ballantyne's semi-autobiographical novel, *The Cunninghams* (1950), depicted a returned soldier whose post-World War I temper deteriorated apace with his physical health. As the family struggled to make ends meet on a basic war pension, the relationship between an invalid father and his eldest son became increasingly fraught.[26] Such experiences would have been widespread amongst the families of both the Allied forces and the Axis powers. William Tuttle's analysis of the recollections of men and women whose fathers served for the United States in World War II demonstrates the manifold ways in which family relationships were affected.[27] Parental tensions, authoritarianism, alcoholism, drug dependency, and other signs of posttraumatic stress disorder would have affected the children of Vietnam veterans, too. And for youngsters brought up in countries where intensive military conflicts had taken place, there was the additional postwar hazard of dormant land mines, as in Afghanistan, Cambodia, and Angola, and cluster bombs, as in southern Lebanon, where more than one-third of the civilian casualties since late 2006 have been children. Children and youth exposed to nuclear radiation, whether in wartime, as in the Japanese cities of Hiroshima and Nagasaki in August 1945,

FIGURE 10.2: *Children's Peace Monument in Hiroshima.*
Inspired by Sadako Sasaki. Used by permission of Seki-
cho, photographer. Accessed on 10/22/08 at http://common.
wikimedia.org/wiki/image: Sadako Memorial.

or as the consequence of a peacetime accident, such as the Chernobyl explosion
in the Ukraine in April 1986, endured permanent health repercussions. Paternal
exposure to chemical weapons (such as Agent Orange in Vietnam) led to serious
medical problems for soldiers and civilians alike, with genetic and other disorders manifesting themselves in the children of those exposed.[28] Those growing
up in contaminated war zones also contend with the health hazards that are
associated with soil and water pollution, deforestation, and ongoing poverty.

For the surviving twentieth-century children born from sexual liaisons, con-
sensual or forced, between local women and men of an occupying or terrorizing
force, the impact of war was lifelong. The physical appearance of such children,

as with the so-called Brown Babies born in 1940s Britain to African American soldier fathers, made them conspicuous among their peers and rendered them likely to experience bullying and discrimination during and well beyond their formative years. The offspring of Norwegian mothers and German soldiers were similarly treated. Other occupying forces during and after World War II left a similar legacy—for example, German fathers and French mothers in occupied France, Japanese fathers and Korean (1940–1945) or Chinese (1945–1950) mothers, French fathers and Algerian mothers (1954–1962), and American fathers and British (1941–1945) or West German (1945–1956) mothers. The ravages of the Red Army on their route west through Hungary, Romania, Slovakia, and Yugoslavia were at their most intense in Soviet-occupied Germany: some 150,000–200,000 so-called Russian babes were born in that zone alone during 1945–1946. This "human flotsam of war," to use Tony Judt's evocative phrase, also included thousands of orphaned, abandoned, homeless, or disfigured children: more than 49,000 in Czechoslovakia, 60,000 in the Netherlands, over 200,000 in Poland, and possibly as many as 300,000 in Yugoslavia at the end of World War II. Later conflicts had similar consequences. An estimated 100,000 children were fathered by American soldiers posted to Vietnam and neighboring Asian countries in the period of 1965–1975.[29] Abortion and maternal death rates may have been obscure, but the social stigma of being a single mother was not. For children born to collaborators or parents who had been active in a later-discredited political regime, the personal legacy could be one of feeling tainted by a sense of guilt by association. German children, for example, have acknowledged being heavily burdened by revelations of a parent's involvement with, or sympathy for, the Nazi creed.[30] Rape as a deliberate strategy of conflict has yet to be constituted a war crime, but its recent application in the brutal policy of ethnic cleansing in Bosnia, Herzegovina, and Croatia (1991–1994) and Rwanda (1994) was widely condemned. Girls and women violently abused in such circumstances then confronted an ethical dilemma if they became pregnant. Children forced to witness such atrocities were themselves traumatized, as were the adults unable to shield them.[31]

MIGRATION

Ideology and war also influenced the migration of children with or without their families, another constant phenomenon in the twentieth century. Many movements were voluntary, legal, and carefully planned as parents sought better economic and educational opportunities for their children, often at considerable sacrifice for their own careers and at great emotional cost for grandparents and extended family left behind. The substantial increase in the numbers of South Korean families migrating overseas during the 1970s and 1980s is one example. Other migrations were illegal, as with unofficial migrants entering the United States across the Mexican border. And some voyages were hazardous, especially when sealed trucking containers or unseaworthy boats were the means of transport adopted by people smugglers. Political considerations continued to be a motivation for migration, exemplified by the exodus of Hungarian refugees after the uprising of 1956 and the emigration of white South African and Zimbabwean families in recent decades. Philosophical ideals about child saving in an era before state welfare lay behind the placing out of thousands of poor urban children, sent on so-called orphan trains from the eastern states to be fostered by rural families in the farming states of the American Midwest between 1854 and 1932, and also the migration, sponsored by voluntary child care charities such as Thomas Barnardo's and the National Children's Home, of some 2,500 British boys and girls to Australia between 1920 and 1965. Nearly 300 Maltese children were placed by Catholic authorities in orphanages in Western Australia during the 1950s.[32] A strong imperialistic impulse underpinned the vision of the Fairbridge Society, founded in 1909, which sent nearly 3,000 unaccompanied juveniles from the United Kingdom to farm schools in Australia, Canada, and Rhodesia between 1913 and 1960.[33] The official French government policy of moving 1,600 at-risk children from Reunion Island (in Indian Ocean) to metropolitan France between 1963 and 1982, also had mixed outcomes in terms of identity, achievement, and acceptance for the youngsters involved.[34]

In the first half of the century, groups of civilian populations were displaced primarily through war, persecution, famine, or civil unrest. Some of these movements were short-term; others became permanent. Spanish children were evacuated to Britain, Belgium, Denmark, France, Norway, and Sweden during the Spanish Civil War; British children were sent from cities to rural areas and to the United States and the Dominions (Canada, South Africa, Australia, and New Zealand) during World War II; and 734 orphaned Polish children were invited to New Zealand in 1944 for the remainder of the war, few of whom chose subsequently to return to their homeland.[35] Children from the Karelian isthmus were evacuated to western Finland during the Soviet–Finnish conflicts of 1939–1944. Most eventually lost their Karelian homes and had to settle in other parts of southern Finland.[36] Greek children in the northern province of Thrace became enmeshed in the ideological conflict between opposing sides in the Greek Civil War (1946–1949): the establishment of some 50 so-called Childtowns under Greek royal patronage had both a humanitarian and an anticommunist impulse. Although estimates remain contested, it appears that far more Greek children were expatriated to live in Bulgaria, Yugoslavia, and other Soviet Bloc countries, particularly after March 1948.[37] In later decades of the twentieth century, life in a refugee camp became an increasingly common experience for large numbers of families or their remaining members. After World War II, with the succession of political conflicts and upheavals in India and Pakistan, Vietnam, Laos, Cambodia, and Afghanistan, for example, there were significant population movements within and beyond national boundaries. The comprehensive UN report in 1996 that explored the impact of armed conflict on children outlined the rapid growth in the number of refugees and internally displaced people between the early 1980s and the mid-1990s. At least half of the estimated 57 million individuals affected were children. Child-headed family groups were becoming more common.[38]

The scale of these end-of-century migrations dwarfed the forced population movements of earlier decades, in and beyond Europe, before and after the world wars. Many of the effects on children would have been similar for both groups, especially the sense of loss, the abrupt isolation from a familiar cultural and community context, and the constant feelings of fear or insecurity. The situation would have been no better for adults desperate to provide food and protection for their families yet unable to do so. Homes, material possessions, status, language, culture, and a sense of hope for the future were all casualties of such upheavals. Family units could not always survive the strain. Fleeing from one dangerous situation invariably led to a host of new ones. Vietnamese boat people were at the mercy of pirates as well as the weather. Cambodians endeavoring to escape the regime of the Khmer Rouge braved land mines, snipers, border patrols, minimal food supplies, and disease in their attempts to reach safety in Thailand. But there and elsewhere, overcrowded refugee camps were no refuge from illness or assault. Children separated from their families, often through the violent death of a remaining parent or sibling, were particularly at risk of exploitation, abduction, starvation, or infectious diseases. Their vulnerability was further increased by a lack of documentation or any identifying material. In the Great Lakes region of Africa, an impressive tracing program, established by the close cooperation of humanitarian agencies, reunited 33,000 of 100,000 unaccompanied children between 1994 and 1996.[39] Such a success rate highlighted both the scale of the task and the experience such organizations have gathered over years of dealing with the costs to children of incessant armed conflict. Child asylum seekers present additional difficulties.[40]

Internal migrations have also been a feature of the twentieth century, with multiple repercussions for both rural and urban communities. Connections

FIGURE 10.3: *Day Care in Quito, Ecuador.* Three-year-old Miguelito waves goodbye to group of volunteers in Quito, Ecuador. Courtesy of Caitlin Fry, Photographer.

were not necessarily severed—studies of street children in Vietnam, for example, highlighted the ongoing interaction between urban youngsters and their rural families—though the links might have been weakened in ways that led to cultural loss.[41] The rapid urbanization of rural populations to cities had major social and economic consequences for children, because one form of poverty was often replaced by another, as in many Latin American urban centers.[42] The pace and scale of internal migration sometimes found government and city planners unprepared, as was the case with Maori urbanization after World War II. Overcrowding, budget problems, ready access to alcohol, the strangeness of city ways, and the adjustment from a communal to a more individualistic lifestyle made the transition particularly difficult for many rural Maori, as was also the experience of Pasifika migrants whose families emigrated from Pacific Island states to New Zealand in the 1960s.[43] Removed from the extended family support that was so long a characteristic of their kin groups, Maori and Pacific children grew up in urban contexts where neither their language nor culture were appropriately supported. Alcohol-fuelled domestic violence was commonly an added burden. Intergenerational tensions increased. The financial constraints of city living made it difficult for many unskilled and low-paid workers to return to their home communities for funerals (*tangihanga*), gatherings (*hui*), or *marae* working bees (for repairs and maintenance of the meeting house and grounds). Such absences contributed to feelings of shame, awkwardness, and embarrassment among adults whose children therefore missed out on opportunities to interact with relatives and elders or to learn the culture and the language that underpinned their ethnicity. Gang membership frequently offered disaffected youth an alternative, often criminal, substitute identity.[44] Many Aboriginal Australians had similar difficulties of being outwardly indigenous yet knowing little or nothing of their distinctive cultural heritage. Yet urbanization also enabled more First Nations children to have access to higher education and sporting careers, and the emergence of well-qualified and articulate young leaders was a crucial element in

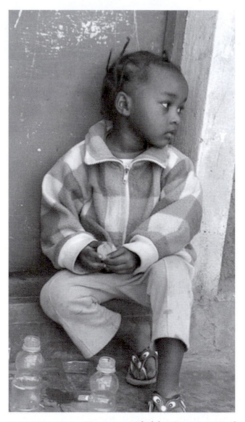

FIGURE 10.4: *Kenyan Child*. Courtesy of Nathaniel Dillon, photographer. Accessed on October 22, 2008, at http://www.flickr.com/photos/ctc-kenya/2713452549.

the success of indigenous peoples' protest movements, in both Australasia and North America in the later decades of the century.

CONCLUSION

Alongside the disruptive impacts of armed aggression and ideology, there emerged a related influence in the modern world, one that was most immediately expressed through humanitarian relief efforts, increasingly embedded in international convention and national legislation, and reflected in a recognition of the civil rights of the young. By 1989, the child as citizen was no longer a contested ideal internationally. How that notion was expressed, fostered, or compromised throughout successive decades varied markedly within countries and communities, as multiple perspectives and policies on the issue of child labor continue to reveal.[45]

Cultural differences are a continuing point of difference in any worldwide recognition of youth citizenship. A Western emphasis on childhood autonomy and individual rights contrasts with traditions of collective responsibility that apply more generally in the global south. Hence the 1990 African Charter on the Rights and Welfare of the Child promulgated by the Organization of African Unity also stressed responsibilities, both of the child and his or her community, while the Vietnamese National Law for Children (August 1991) required youth to show love, respect, piety, and politeness toward their family elders, affection for younger siblings, and solidarity with friends.[46] Societies in which religious or other cultural strictures, such as gender, caste, or ethnicity, determine the nature of childhoods could also prove resistant to change, as in the highlands region of Papua New Guinea and North Yemen.[47] Where there has been an active state or community commitment to public education, however, the transformation in children's lives in the latter decades of the twentieth century has sometimes been quite dramatic, as in Saudi Arabia since 1960.[48] Yet there are marked national and regional disparities in meeting the UNCRC objectives. Poverty and political upheavals have long been major obstacles to children's education, just as poverty remains the most fundamental reason for adults to be economically dependent on the earnings of their offspring. Children's rights seem far more likely to be violated than upheld in such circumstances.

These differences and difficulties did not prevent the growth of a far greater international acknowledgement of children and youth as world citizens. By the end of the twentieth century, there were Commissioners for Children established in several different countries (Wales, Canada, Northern Ireland, and New Zealand, for example) and a European Network of Ombudsmen for

Children (ENOC). The views of children were being heard in a much wider range of forums, from youth parliaments to divorce proceedings where issues of custody and access had to be decided. Researchers began to ask more questions and develop new methodologies as they sought a greater understanding of young people's agency and experiences in the past, and of the societal contexts in which children, youth, and their families operated. That expanding knowledge and awareness of both past and contemporary conditions has exposed the consequences of ongoing and preventable inequalities, well illustrated in the expanding epidemic of child obesity in the developed world, set against malnutrition and starvation in countries ravaged by conflict and environmental destruction. Countries committed to a quality public education program may acknowledge the importance of such an investment for their young but do not always deliver on the vision: the innovative One Laptop Per Child (OLPC) project, which aimed to bring reliable computer technology to school pupils in the African continent and other poor regions of the world, struggles in the face of commercial competition and national agendas. In contrast, the Indian Hole-in-the-Wall Information and Communication Technology (ICT) project, a source of inspiration for the novel behind the Oscar-winning film *Slumdog Millionaire*, continues to expand on the Indian subcontinent and has been established successfully in Uganda.[49] The move toward providing greater protection for children, through defining and acknowledging their rights, may have grown out of war, but the issues that organizations such as UNICEF, UNHCR, and the World Health Organization (WHO) have addressed reflect the continuing and far-reaching effects of conflict on youth, even when some formal peace has been brokered. Malnutrition, lack of educational opportunity, psychological trauma, physical disability, HIV/AIDS: given the contemporary scale of need, on the African continent especially, only a minority of end-of-century children so afflicted will be able to reach their potential as adults. The modern age opened a virtual world of possibilities for young people equipped to access them: conflict, poverty, and disease impair the chances of too many to do so.

NOTES

Introduction

1. Kennedy 1970; Mintz and Kellogg 1988.
2. Key 1909; Zelizer 1985.
3. Lasch 1977; Mintz and Kellogg 1998.
4. Hawes 1971.
5. Chudacoff 1989; Hall 1904.
6. United Nations 1989.
7. United Nations 2000a: 33.
8. United Nations 2005: 133.
9. United Nations 2000a: 14.
10. Lopez and Mathers 2006.
11. United Nations 2000b: 24, 47, 87, 98–99, 111–117.
12. United Nations 2005: 12.
13. Ahmad, Lopez, and Inoue 2000: 589–603.
14. Morgan 2003: 589.
15. Lee 2003: 168.
16. Chesnais 2001: 259.
17. Wilson 2001: 65.
18. Lee 2003: 174.
19. Morgan and King 2001: 11.
20. Folbre 1994: 89.
21. United Nations 1999: 52.
22. United Nations 2002: 108–111.
23. Chesnais 2001: 258.
24. Chesnais 2001: 258–259.
25. Morgan and King 2001: 3–20.
26. von Feilitzen and Carlsson 2002: 9, 13.

27. Cited in Muscari 2002: 285.
28. von Feilitzen and Carlsson 2002: 16–17, 247.
29. United Nations Development Program 2001.
30. United Nations 2000b: 14.
31. United Nations 2005: 2–4.
32. United Nations 1989; Verhellen 2000.
33. United Nations 2005: 10.

Chapter 1

1. Carroll 1906: 24–25.
2. We are thankful to the University of Bedfordshire for the support and resources that were provided to us during the research and writing stages of this project. Special thanks go to Steve Kendall, BA, MA (Lit), for his feedback on the final draft.
3. Halsey 1995; More 2006; Therborn 2004; Hawes and Nybakken 2001: 209–323.
4. Smelser 1982: 59.
5. Tosh 1999.
6. Anderson and Zinsser 2000; French and Poska 2007; Graves 1994.
7. Abbott 2003; Mintz and Kellogg 1988.
8. Abbott 2003: 22–83; Anderson and Zinsser 2000: 197–226.
9. Haue 2004; Hendrick 2003: 130–131; Lowe 2005; Reese 2005.
10. Ham 2004; Mohan 2005.
11. Hair 1982; Macura, Eggers, and Frejka 1999.
12. Halsey 1995; Hendrick 2003; Lindenmeyer 1997.
13. Abbott 2003: 117–145; Fink 2005; Hendrick 2003; Therborn 2004: 181–203.
14. Hobsbawn 1995: 3. See also Abbott 2003.
15. Fraser 2003; West 1996.
16. Ham 2004; Mohan 2005.
17. Finch 1989; Sealander 2003.
18. Fraser 2003.
19. Bock and Thane 1991; Tosh 1999; Grayzel 1999; Mintz and Kellogg 1988.
20. Kamerman and Kahn 1997; Kaufmann et al., 2002; Wilson 2005; Bailey 1988.
21. Probert 2004; Wilson 2005; Riley 1991.
22. Fraser 2003; Hendrick 2003: 145–160; Mason 1994.
23. Finch 1990; Wilson 2005; Mason 1994.
24. Wintermute and Andanaes 2001; Therborn 2004: 223–225.
25. Abbott 2003; Fink 2005.
26. Halsey 1995; Hendrick 2003; Riley 2001.
27. Fletcher 1988: 40.
28. Addison 2005; Grayzel 1999; Gullace 2002; Tuttle 1993; Ericsson and Simonson 2005.
29. Addison 2005.
30. Ministry of Information 2007; Tuttle 1993; Mintz 2004: 254–274.
31. Anderson and Zinsser 2000: 308–332; Abbott 2003: 59–83; Hartmann 1982.
32. Addison 2005; Grayzel 1999.
33. Townsend 1979: 33.

34. Haue 2004; Hendrick 2003: 130–131.
35. Lowe 2005; Watson 2007.
36. Welshman 2005; Meckel 2004.
37. Brown 2006; Wolffe 2007.
38. Panayi 2007; Webster 2005.
39. Fink 2005; Wilson 2005; Anderson and Zinsser 2000.
40. More 2006; Therborn 2004.
41. Addison 2005; Panayi 2007; Webster 2005.
42. Halsey 1995; Panayi 2007; Webster 2005.
43. Key 1909.
44. Croall 1998.
45. Kamerman and Kahn 1997; Kaufman et al., 2002.
46. Abbott 2003; More 2006.
47. Hair 1982; Macura, Eggers, and Frejka 1995; Thane 2005.
48. Westermarck 1901: 32.
49. Abbott 2003; Fink 2005; Hendrick 2003: 234–254; Mintz and Kellogg 1988.
50. Linton 1959: 52.
51. Carroll 1906: 13, 21.

Chapter 2

1. Satterthwaite 2005: 1.
2. Satterthwaite 2005: 3.
3. Sutherland 1997: 222.
4. Abrams 1998.
5. Bagnell 1980; Parr 1980; Blackburn 1993.
6. Holt 1992.
7. Berlanstein 1978–1979.
8. Meese 2005.
9. Adams 1995; Buti 2002; Miller 1996.
10. S. Carter 1997.
11. Public Broadcasting System 2010.
12. Bancroft 2005.
13. Mintz 2004: 205.
14. James 2001: 2.
15. Johnson 1989.
16. McKillop 1979.
17. Wassong 2008.
18. Cavallo 1981.
19. Tillotson 2000, 2002.
20. Cupers 2008: 174.
21. Hall 1904.
22. Comacchio 2006: 190.
23. Wall 2005.
24. Tennant 2002.

25. Girl Scouts of the USA 2010.
26. Comacchio 2006: 198.
27. Miller 2007: 15.
28. Strong-Boag 1988.
29. Lewis 1996.
30. U.S. Department of Agriculture 2010.
31. Budiwski 2010.
32. Weiner 2001.
33. Springhall 1998.
34. Wegs 1989: 6.
35. Sutherland 1997.
36. Gillis 1997; Goode 1963.
37. Gillis 1997: 10.
38. Gordon 1994; Kunzel 1993; Strong-Boag 2006.
39. Strong-Boag 2006: 6–7.
40. Hegar 1999: 23.
41. Moran 1988: 74–78.
42. Lawrence 1996; Lewis 1970.
43. Ewen 1985.
44. Iacovetta 1992.
45. Strong-Boag 2006.
46. Little 1998: 132.
47. Greeff, Waterhouse, and Brocklesby 1999: 36.
48. Davin 1996.
49. Chupik 2006; Liebenberg 1994; Strong-Boag 2007.
50. Chupik and Wright 2006: 77.
51. Botsford-Fraser 2006; Clarke 2004–2005; Summerhayes-Cariou 2006.
52. Beito 2000: 63.
53. Beito 2000: 86.
54. Goldstein 1996: 12; J. Gordon 2002; Slonim 1983.
55. Saunders 1994.
56. Barnes 1979; Graham 1999.
57. Sandler 2006.
58. Greenspoon and Heathorn 2006: 93.
59. Greenspoon and Heathorn 2006: 106.
60. Van Krieken 1991; Myers 2006; Sangster 2002.
61. Cliché 2007, Dalley 1994: 175.
62. Mennill and Strong-Boag 2008.
63. Gordon 1988.
64. Jackson 2002.
65. Sutherland 1997: xiii.
66. Graff 1997: 269.
67. Sutherland 1997: 227.
68. McKim 2002: 88.
69. May 1985: 117.
70. Gleason 1999b: 130.

71. Graham 1994.
72. Peate 1970: 124–125; Gleason 1999a.
73. Lewis 1996: 114.
74. Lewis 1996: 105.
75. Lewis 1996: 105, 210, 151, 194.
76. Howell 1998.
77. Bell and Lim 2005: 629.
78. Pomerantz, Currie, and Kelly, 2004.
79. Gleason 2001.
80. Hall 1995.
81. Chan 2006: 4.
82. Bruser Maynard 1964: 74.
83. Jiwani 2006; Little 2001.
84. Digital History 2010.
85. Historylearningsite.co.uk 2010.
86. Bhabha 2004.
87. Lambert 1990: 17.
88. Maracle 1995: 20.
89. Haig Brown 1988: 98.
90. Obama 2004: 80.
91. Strong-Boag, 1988: 27.
92. Currie 1999.
93. Early 2001.
94. Enfants Entraide 2010.

Chapter 3

1. Boydston 1990; Ross 1993.
2. Ewen 1985.
3. Yans-MacLaughlin 1977.
4. Ewen 1985.
5. Jones 1985.
6. Quoted in Burds 1998: 29.
7. Simonton 1998.
8. Kessler-Harris 1982; Tentler 1979.
9. May 1982; Kessler-Harris 1982.
10. Canning 1996.
11. Davies 1982; Kessler-Harris 1982; Kwolek-Folland 1994.
12. Morantz-Sanchez 1985; Reverby 1987.
13. Simonton 1998.
14. Gullace 2002.
15. Hausen 1987.
16. Davis 2000.
17. Vicinus 1985; Woollacott 2001.
18. Rappaport 2000; Peiss 1998; Sanders 2006.
19. Roberts 1994, 2002; Engelstein 1992.

20. Guenther 2004.
21. de Grazia 1996: 345.
22. Yans-MacLaughlin 1977; Ewen 1985.
23. Zelizer 1985.
24. Ewen 1985.
25. Moehling 2005.
26. Odem 1995.
27. Jacobson 2004.
28. Hilton 2000: 168.
29. Jacobson 2004; Lynd and Lynd 1929: 142 n20.
30. Mintz and Kellogg 1988; Scharf 1980; Cohen 1990.
31. Cohen 1990: 248.
32. Elder 1974; May 1988.
33. Scharf 1980; Ryan 1983; Kessler-Harris 1982.
34. Gluck 1987.
35. Anderson 1981; Hartmann 1982; May 1988.
36. Jacobson 2004.
37. Duis 1996; Westbrook 1993.
38. de Grazia 1992.
39. Bock and Thane 1991.
40. Graves 1994.
41. Vernon 2007; Dawson 2007.
42. Grossman 1995.
43. Bock 1984.
44. Koonz 1987.
45. Quoted in Goldman 1993: 1.
46. Goldman 1993.
47. Goldman 1993: 228.
48. Goldman 1993: 327.
49. Simonton 1998: 186.
50. Anonymous 2005.
51. Quoted in Pulju 2006: 73.
52. May 1988.
53. Coontz 1992.
54. French and Poska 2007: 534–536.
55. May 1988; Wandersee 1981.
56. Cited in Mintz and Kellogg 1988: 190.
57. Cook 2004; Schrum 1998; Spigel 1998.
58. Cited in Hardyment 1995: 73.
59. Moeller 1993.
60. E. Carter 1997.
61. Lasch 1979.
62. Coontz 1992.
63. Hochschild 1989.
64. Stack 1987; Coontz 1992.

65. Schor 2004; Linn 2004; *Merchants of Cool* 2001.
66. Davis and Sensenbrenner, 2000: 68; Chin 2001.
67. Talbot 2001.
68. Stearns 2003.
69. Seiter 1993.
70. Cross 1997.

Chapter 4

 1. Riney-Kehrberg 2005: 38–43; West 1989: 73–98.
 2. *Nebraska Farmer* June 12, 1912: 613.
 3. Riney-Kehrberg 2005: 43–45; West 1989: 73–98.
 4. *Nebraska Farmer* June 19, 1912.
 5. *Nebraska Farmer* 1912–1916.
 6. Riney-Kehrberg 2005: 126–157; West 1989: 101–118.
 7. Babb 1994: 8.
 8. Babb 1994: 122.
 9. Babb 1994: 170.
10. Babb 1994: 171.
11. Heywood 2007: 169.
12. Hendrick 1997: 83.
13. Tian-Shanskaia 1993: 42.
14. Hull 1915: 78.
15. Shears 1971: 181.
16. Shears 1971: 200.
17. Roosevelt 1901: 155–157.
18. Bederman 1995: 77–120.
19. MacLeod 1983: 32, 52, 227.
20. Baden-Powell 2004: 20.
21. Baden-Powell 2004: 21.
22. Hendrick 1997: 83.
23. Mergen 1975: 412–413.
24. Gaster 1995: 11.
25. Gaster 1995: 14.
26. Gaster 1995: 1–31.
27. Gaster 1995: 23.
28. Pyle 2002: 308.
29. Pyle 1993: 152.
30. Jackson 1985: 137.
31. Chudacoff 2007: 108–109.
32. Chudacoff 2007: 73, 108–109.
33. Chudacoff 2007: 114.
34. Packard 1983: 65–66.
35. Hendrick 1997: 83.
36. Heywood 2007: 187–189.

37. Nasaw 1985: 11.
38. Chudacoff 2007: 115.
39. Hendrick 1997: 88.
40. Downs 2002: 15–20.
41. Downs 2002: 37.
42. Downs 2002: 290–295.
43. Manning 1989.
44. Van Slyck 2006: 4.
45. Paris 2001: 52.
46. Paris 2001: 48.
47. Miller 2007: 130–131.
48. Armitage 2007: 4.
49. Armitage 2007: 2.
50. Armitage 2007: 1–4.
51. Kirschenbaum 2002: 284.
52. Enssle 1987: 486–490.
53. Redding 2004b: 66–68.
54. Riney-Kehrberg 1994: 32, 33, 42, 104–105.
55. Kotlowitz 1992 : 3–6, 9, 30–31.
56. Hendrick 1997: 84.
57. Jackson 1985: 279, 280.
58. Hendrick 1997: 84.
59. Pyle 2002: 311–312.
60. Pyle 2002: 310.
61. Pyle 2002: 318–319.
62. Chudacoff 2007: 184.

Chapter 5

1. Maynes 1985: 117–151; Easterlin 1981: 6–8; Easterlin 2000: 18–20; Anderson-Levitt 2005: 991–992; National Center for Educational Statistics 2000: 75–81; United Nations Development Program 2000: 194–197.
2. Heidenheimer 1973: 316.
3. Goldin 2001: 267.
4. Goldin 2001: 269–273; United Nations Development Program 2000: 194–197; National Center for Educational Statistics 2000: 78–80.
5. Messerli 1972.
6. Reese 1995: 182.
7. Reese 1995.
8. Archdeacon 1983: 113.
9. Reese 1986; Tyack 1974.
10. Reese 1995: 119.
11. Reese 1995: 119.
12. Anderson 1988; Clotfelter 2004.
13. Anderson 1988.

14. Kaestle 1983.
15. Tyack 1974.
16. Reese 1995.
17. Tyack 1974.
18. Hays 1964; Wiebe 1967.
19. Tyack 1974.
20. Kliebard 2004.
21. Otto 1934: 149–150.
22. Tyack 1974.
23. Brookes 2004.
24. Minton 1988.
25. Bagley 1925; Tyack 1974; Reese 1995.
26. Reese 1995: 209.
27. Larson 1998.
28. Reese 2005: 228.
29. Cottrol, Diamond, and Ware 2003.
30. Anderson 1988; Reese 1995.
31. Cremin 1961.
32. Kliebard 1999.
33. Kaestle 1983.
34. Cuban 1993.
35. Zilversmith 1993.
36. Kliebard 2004: 51–75.
37. Dewey 1938.
38. Reese 1995: 233, 266.
39. Counts 1930: 129.
40. Angus and Mirel 1999.
41. Koos 1926: 35; Tildsley 1936: 3–6.
42. Anderson 1988.
43. Tyack 1974; Reese 1995.
44. Angus and Mirel 1999.
45. Hines 1998.
46. Latimer 1958.
47. Keller 1960: 241.
48. Angus and Mirel 1999.
49. Lynd and Lynd 1929; Lynd and Lynd 1937; Hines 1998: 99–120.
50. Spring 1976.
51. Reese 1995: 281–285.
52. *Digest of Educational Statistics* 2001: Table 37.
53. Spring 1976; Rudolph 2002.
54. Reese 2005: 241.
55. Kirst 1995: 49.
56. Cottrol, Diamon, and Ware 2003.
57. Sracic 2006; Reese 2005.
58. Reese 2007: 116.

59. Reese 2001: 216.
60. Reese 2005.
61. Ravitch and Vinovskis 1995.
62. Hess and Finn 2004.
63. Reese 2007: 111–112.
64. Clotfelter 2004.
65. Reese 1986.
66. Goodlad 1984.
67. Cusick 1973.

Chapter 6

1. European statistics are based on Bairoch 1968: 27–34. Statistics on Midwestern farm women derive from Ward 1920: 10–11.
2. Sealander 2003: 138; Riney-Kehrberg 2005: 16; Glenn 1990: 83. Even today, child labor laws exempt work on family farms from standards that apply in other settings. For instance, minimum employment age is fourteen in agriculture but sixteen in other sectors of the economy. Minimum age for hazardous labor is sixteen in agriculture but eighteen in all other sectors. See Child Labor Coalition 2008.
3. Anderson and Zinsser 2000: 285; Margo 1990: 18–32.
4. Anderson and Zinsser 2000: 286.
5. Anderson and Zinsser 2000: 286; L. Gordon 2002: 26–32, 156–157.
6. Cable 2007.
7. Harriman 1995: 307–309.
8. Bailey 1988: 13–20; Brumberg 1997: 101–102.
9. Abbott 2003: 44; Bailey 1988: 42.
10. Anderson and Zinsser 2000: 215, 308–313; Miner forthcoming.
11. Miner forthcoming; Ministry of Information 2007: 13.
12. Anderson and Zinsser 2000: 309.
13. Hartmann 1982: 21, 59; May 1988: 59, 68–69, 74.
14. Tuttle 1993: 27.
15. Droke 1945: 68. See also Bailey 1988: 41–42; U.S. Bureau of the Census 1943: 27; Baritz 1990: 193.
16. Harvey 1994: 52.
17. Walker 1998: 12–13; Hartmann 1982: 165; Baritz 1990: 194.
18. Anderson and Zinsser 2000: 322.
19. Anderson and Zinsser 2000: 323–324; Stortzbach 1995: 123, 125.
20. Anderson and Zinsser 2000: 405.
21. Anderson and Zinsser 2000: 407–408; Friedan 1983: 15–32; De Beauvoir 1953: xv–xxix.
22. Anderson and Zinsser 2000: 408–409.
23. Kessler-Harris 1982: 301; Anderson and Zinsser 2000: 324; Blackwelder 1997: 196.
24. Anderson and Zinsser 2000: 324.
25. Hertz 1986: 2.
26. Cherlin 1981: 18, 59, 66, 123.

27. Veroff, Douvan, and Kulka 1981: 197; May 1988: 137; Rowland 2004: 113; Anderson and Zinsser 2000: 417–419; Macura, Eggers, and Frejka 1995: 12–14.
28. Riley 1991: 156–157, 163.
29. Riley 1991: 185; Cherlin 1981: 7, 18, 59, 66.
30. Cott 2000: 206–207; Hackstaff 1999: 28–31.
31. Anderson and Zinsser 2000: 418–419; Macura, Eggers, and Frejka 1995: 16–17.
32. Veroff, Douvan, and Kulka 1981: 191.
33. Veroff, Douvan, and Kulka 1981: 147–149, 182, 191–192.
34. Cherlin 1981: 12–13; Macura, Eggers, and Frejka 1995: 16.
35. D'Emilio and Freedman 1997: 318–319, 321; Johnson 2008.
36. Gillis 1996: 231; D'Emilio and Freedman 1997: 330; Stoner 1993: 50; Macura, Eggers, and Frejka 1995: 15.
37. Kolinsky 1998: 120–121, 132–135.
38. Roberts 2006; Gillis 1996: 236–237.

Chapter 7

1. Roopmarine and Gielen 2005: 54.
2. Saraceno 2003: 238–239, 262–263.
3. Roopmarine and Gielen 2005: 44, 115, 180, 186, 376–378.
4. Saraceno 2003: 262–63; Roopmarine and Gielen 2005: 3–11, 33–45; Kertzer and Barbagli 2003: xi–xliv.
5. Abbott 1938: preface; Fass 2004, vol. 3: 988–1000; United Nations 1989.
6. Brewer 2005: 1–2.
7. Abbot 1938: 11.
8. Abbott 1938: 9–11; Brewer 2005: 261; Grossberg 1985: 196–200; Ashby 1997: 14–34; Mason 1994: 31–36; Abbott 1938: 213–234; Zipf 2005: 153–156.
9. Abbott 1938: 189–213; Illick 2002: 29; Mintz and Kellogg 1988: 33.
10. Mather 1708: 1–3, 11–12.
11. Hawes 1991: 2; Ashby 1997: 187; Mintz and Kellogg 1988: 33; Pleck 2004: 28, 48, 75–87.
12. Hawes 1991: 9.
13. Berebitsky 2000: 2.
14. Illick 2002: 3.
15. Grossberg 1985: 6; Mintz and Kellogg 1988: 43–49.
16. Zelizer 1985.
17. Grossberg 1985: 201; Castles 1993: 255.
18. Mintz and Kellogg 1988: 175.
19. King 1995: 74–80; Hoffschwelle 1998; Lindenmeyer 2005: 129–138.
20. Lindenmeyer 2005: 139–141.
21. Bremner et al., 1970: 1377–1378.
22. Lindenmeyer 2005: 111–112.
23. Chudacoff 1989: 9; Mintz and Kellogg 1988: 87–91.
24. Lindenmeyer 1997: 110–111; Graham 1987: 74; Saraceno 2003: 240–242; Kertzer and Barbagli 2003: 239.

25. Riis 1890: 134.
26. Ashby 1997: 57; Hawes 1991: 19.
27. Hawes 1991: 32–35; Platt 1977; Klapper 2007: 14–17, 108–129.
28. Lindenmeyer 1997: 9–10.
29. *Proceedings* 1909.
30. Key 1909.
31. Ladd-Taylor 1994; Lindenmeyer 1997: 24–29.
32. Bremner 1970: 811; Lindenmeyer 1997: 30–51; Meckel 1989.
33. Meckel 1989: 193; Lindenmeyer 1997: 68; Castles 1993: 252.
34. Roopmarine and Gielen 2005: 165.
35. Bryder 2003: ix.
36. Muncy 1991: 93–123; Lindenmeyer 1997: 92–107.
37. Trattner 1970: 163.
38. Hindman 2002: 84–85.
39. Kertzer and Barbagli 2003: 255; Ashby 1997: 112–117; Gordon 1994: 263–285.
40. Sealander 2003: 156–173; Reiman 1992.
41. Lindenmeyer 2005: 206–239.
42. Mintz and Kellogg 1988: 254–274; Rose 2003; Sealander 2003: 267–273.
43. Lindenmeyer 1997: 252–253.
44. Mittelstadt 2005: 169–170; Ashby 1997: 191.
45. Hawes 1991: 96–121.
46. Golden et al., 2004: 122–123.
47. Kertzer and Barbagli 2003: 265 ff.
48. Mintz and Kellogg 1988: 340; Vinovskis 1987.
49. United Nations 1989.
50. Castles 1993; Callahan and Hessle 2000; Glenn 1984; Hawes 1991; Mintz 2004: 363–364.
51. Dalley 1998; Therborn 1993.
52. Dalley and Tennant 2004.
53. Dalley 1998: 19, 41, 47.
54. National Society for the Prevention of Cruelty to Children 1972; McCullagh et al., 2002.

Chapter 8

1. Stachura 1981: 201–202.
2. Koch 1975: 2.
3. Kater 2004: 5, 14–15.
4. Quoted in Kater 2004: 10.
5. Laqueur 1962: 229.
6. Rempel 1989.
7. Bergen 1996; Kater 2004.
8. Koch 1975: 89.
9. Mosse 1990.
10. Savage 2007: 256.

11. Hamerow 1997: 152–153.
12. Kater 2004: 21.
13. Hamerow 1997: 147.
14. Kater 2004: 19, 23.
15. *Wir Mädel Singen* 1938.
16. Kater 2004: 15, 67.
17. Stachura 1981: 172.
18. "Hitler Youth" 1999.
19. Tegel 2007: 57.
20. Koch 1975: 82–83.
21. Welch 1983: 59–74.
22. Tegel 2007: 62–63.
23. *Leni Riefenstahl's Triumph of the Will* [1934] 2006: 20–38, 50.
24. *Leni Riefenstahl's Triumph of the Will* [1934] 2006: 3–55, 15.
25. Girad 1977.
26. *Nazi Primer* 1938: 78.
27. Pine 2007.
28. Pahl 1993: 172–8; Pahl 1993: 173–4.
29. Bellah 1967; Hughes 2003; Johnson 2005; Kao and Copulsky 2007.
30. Marvin and Ingle 1999.
31. Pahl 2000.
32. Lincoln and Mamiya 1990; Wimberly 2002.
33. Mamiya 1994.
34. Pahl 2000.
35. Myers 1991.
36. Pahl 2000: 82.
37. Lagerquist 1999.
38. Pahl 1993.
39. Lutheran Church—Missouri Synod 2008; Roehlkepartain and Benson 2006.
40. Borgman 1987; Gillespie 1981; Roehlkepartain and Benson 1993.
41. McNamara 1991.
42. Zotti 1991.
43. Harris 1981.
44. Greeley 1994; Riebe-Estrella 2004.
45. McAuley and Mathieson 1989; O'Brien 2000.
46. Bryk, Lee, and Holland 1993.
47. Jenkins 2003.
48. Balmer 1993.
49. Mjagkig and Spratt 1997.
50. Elfenbein 2002.
51. Carpenter 1997.
52. Senter 1992.
53. Carpenter 1985.
54. Pahl 2000.
55. Senter 1992.

56. Campolo 1989.
57. *Jesus Camp* 2006.
58. Bowman 2004; Dayton 1976.
59. Wallis 2008.
60. Friedman 2006.
61. Smith and Denton 2005.
62. Dear 2002.
63. Appleby 2000.
64. Patel and Brodeur 2006.
65. van der Bent 1986.
66. World Council of Churches 2008.
67. Cox 1995.
68. Peperkamp 2006.
69. Sikorska 1989: 90.
70. Kubik 1994.
71. Weigel 1992.
72. Sikorska 1989: 12.
73. Chidester 1987: 73, 75–79; *Kairos Document* 1986; Reidy, 1987; Setiloane 1963.
74. Carroll 2007; Gülen 2006.

Chapter 9

1. Bloom and Canning 2001: 3, 6.
2. Phelps 1908: 235.
3. Black, Morris, and Bryce 2003.
4. Wood 2003; Bakketeig Cnattingius, and Knudsen 1993; Berentsen 1987; Rainwater and Smeeding 2003; Edmondson 2005; Save the Children 2007.
5. Bryce et al., 2005; Black, Morris, and Bryce 2003; Gerlin 2006: 42.
6. Bloom and Canning 2001: 9; Gerlin 2006: 47; Pan American Health Organization, World Health Organization 2007.
7. World Health Organization 2002; Black et al., 2008; Gates 2007.
8. Bloom and Canning 2001: 8; Kremer 2002: 68.
9. World Health Organization 2005.
10. Golden, Meckel, and Prescott 2004: 3.
11. Golden, Meckel, and Prescott 2004: 14.
12. Kyvig 2002: 4; Preston and Haines 1991.
13. Golden, Meckel, and Prescott 2004: 16.
14. Golden, Meckel, and Prescott 2004: 16.
15. Golden, Meckel, and Prescott 2004: 14–18.
16. Golden, Meckel, and Prescott 2004: 21.
17. Golden, Meckel, and Prescott 2004: 78; Kamerman 1989: 372; U.S. Census Bureau 2006.
18. Markel and Golden 2005.
19. Miller 1993; Spargo 1906: 22.
20. Brosco 1999: 480.

21. Race 1933: 1.
22. Race 1933.
23. Spain 2001.
24. Brosco 1999: 480; Smith 1995: 24.
25. Herbert Hoover Presidential Library-Museum, 1999: paragraph 4 "Source Note on American Child Health Association," American Child Health Association Collection, Herbert Hoover Papers, Herbert Hoover Presidential Library, West Branch, IA. Available online: http://www.ecommcode2.com/hoover/research/hooverpapers/hoover/commerce/acha5.htm (accessed February 9, 2009).
26. Platt and Palmer 1925: 104.
27. Durham 1910; Deering 1910.
28. *Adams v. City of Milwaukee* 228 U.S. 572.
29. Platt and Palmer 1925.
30. Lindenmeyer 2004: 109; Riis 1890, quoted in Lindenmeyer 2004: 109; Markel and Golden 2005; Skocpol 1995.
31. Brosco 1999: 480–481; Stone 2008.
32. Markel and Golden 2005.
33. Lindenmeyer 2004: 107, 111.
34. Skocpol 1995; Lindenmeyer 2004: 114; Markel and Golden 2005; Phelps 1908.
35. Ladd-Taylor 1994: 174.
36. Bigelow 1921: 4.
37. Rodgers 1998; Apple 2003: 572.
38. Skocpol 1995: 494; Ladd-Taylor 1994: 170.
39. Bigelow 1920: 4, 20.
40. Martin 1920: 148.
41. Markel and Golden 2005.
42. Golden, Meckel & Prescott, 2004: 77, 78.
43. Golden, Meckel, and Prescott 2004: 77, 78.
44. Halpern 1988.
45. Lindenmeyer 2004: 121; Golden, Meckel, and Prescott 2004: 81.
46. Lindenmeyer 2004: 121; Markel and Golden 2005.
47. Hardeman 1973; Hayes 1982.
48. Golden, Meckel, and Prescott 2004: 22, 81.
49. Lindenmeyer 2004: 122.
50. Henry J. Kaiser Family Foundation 2007.
51. Dubay and Kenney 2001.
52. Centers for Disease Control 1999.
53. Golden, Meckel, and Prescott 2004: 82; Lindenmeyer 2004: 122.

Chapter 10

1. Haebich 2006; *Bringing Them Home* 1997.
2. *Rabbit-Proof Fence* 2002.
3. Stearns 2006: 133.
4. Johnston 2005: 142–175; Mortenson and Relin 2006.

5. Society for the Protection of the Rights of the Child 2003.
6. Hecht 1998: 121–123; United Nations High Commissioner for Refugees 2006.
7. Stearns 2006: 86–88; Olich 2008: 450–455; Whitney 2004: 224–226; Ginsborg 2003: 182–187.
8. Stearns 2006: 88–91; Chan 1985: 8–9.
9. Cunxin 2003.
10. Ginsborg 2003: 187; Redding 2004a: 344; Nevala-Nurmi 2007.
11. Sen 2005.
12. Mintz 2004: 304–308.
13. Grenville 1994: 786.
14. Ihimaera 1998.
15. Grenville 1994: 649–651; Heineman 2004: 907–908.
16. Austin 2004: 912–916.
17. Lamb 2003: 112.
18. Stearns 2006: 112.
19. Kanogo 2004: 9.
20. Marten 2004: 776.
21. Honwana 2008: 144–145.
22. Peterson 2004: 535; Machel 1996; Leeder 2004: 255–257.
23. Marten 2002: 1–7.
24. Mintz 2004: 269–271.
25. Scates 2002.
26. Ballantyne 1950.
27. Tuttle 1993.
28. Challinor and Lancaster 2000.
29. Janfelt 2004: 880; Judt 2007: 20–21.
30. Ericsson and Simonson 2005.
31. Machel 1996: 23–24, 39–40.
32. Holt 1992; Coldrey 2004; Moore 1990.
33. Sherington and Jeffery 1998.
34. Jablonka 2007.
35. Janfelt 2004; Starns and Parsons 2002; Te Ara 2008a.
36. Rossi 2007.
37. Theodorou and Vassiloudi 2007.
38. Machel 1996: 21; Helton 2002.
39. Leeder 2004: 92–93, 256–257; Machel 1996: 18.
40. Bhabha and Schmidt 2008.
41. Burr 2006.
42. Bartell and O'Donnell 2001.
43. Te Ara 2008b.
44. Thomas 1981.
45. Jacobsen 2004: 157–159.
46. Twum-Danso 2008: 392–399; Burr 2006: 18–19.
47. Dorsky and Stevenson 1995.
48. Bird 1995.
49. Fides 2007; Hole-in-the-Wall 2009.

BIBLIOGRAPHY

Abbott, Grace. [1938] 1968. *The child and the state*. Reprint, New York: Greenwood Press.

Abbott, Mary. 2003. *Family affairs: A history of the family in 20th century England*. London: Routledge.

Abrams, Lynn. 1998. *The orphan country: Children of Scotland's broken homes from 1885 to the present day*. Edinburgh: John Donald Publishers.

Adams, David Wallace. 1995. *Education for extinction: American Indians and the boarding school experience, 1875–1928*. Lawrence: University Press of Kansas.

Adams v. City of Milwaukee 228 U.S. 572.

Addison, Paul. 2005. "The impact of the Second World War." In *A companion to contemporary Britain, 1939–2000*, ed. Paul Addison and Harriet Jones. London: Blackwell.

Ahmad, Omar B., Alan D. Lopez, and Mie Inoue. 2000. "The decline in child mortality: A reappraisal." *Bulletin of the World Health Organization* 78: 1175–1189.

American Child Health Association. n.d. "Source note on American Child Health Association," American Child Health Association Collection, Herbert Hoover Papers, Herbert Hoover Presidential Library, West Branch, IA. Available at: http://www.ecommcode2.com/hoover/research/hooverpapers/hoover/commerce/acha5.htm. Accessed February 2009.

Anderson, Benedict. 1983. *Imagined communities: Reflections on the origins and spread of nationalism*. London: Verso.

Anderson, James D. 1988. *The education of blacks in the South, 1860–1935*. Chapel Hill: University of North Carolina Press.

Anderson, Karen. 1981. *Wartime women: Sex roles, family relations, and the status of women during World War Two*. Westport, CT: Greenwood Press.

Anderson, Bonnie S., and Judith P. Zinsser. 2000. *A history of their own: Women in Europe from prehistory to the present*. Rev. ed. Vol. 2. New York: Oxford University Press.

Anderson-Levitt, Kathryn N. 2005. "The schoolyard gate: Schooling and childhood in global perspective." *Journal of Social History* 38(4): 987–1006.

Angus, David L., and Jeffrey E. Mirel. 1999. *The failed promise of the American high school, 1890–1995*. New York: Teachers College Press.

Anonymous. 2005. *A woman in Berlin: Eight weeks in the conquered city*. Trans. Philip Boehm. New York: Henry Holt.

Apple, Rima. 2003. "Educating mothers: The Wisconsin Bureau of Maternal and Child Health." *Women's History Review* 12(4): 559–576.

Appleby, R. Scott. 2000. *The ambivalence of the sacred: Religion, violence, and reconciliation*. Lanham, CO: Rowman and Littlefield.

Archard, David. 2004. *Children, rights, and childhood*. 2nd ed. London: Routledge.

Archdeacon, Thomas J. 1983. *Becoming American: An ethnic history*. New York: The Free Press.

Armitage, Kevin C. 2007. "Bird day for kids: Progressive conservation in theory and practice." *Environmental History* 12(3): 54 pars. Available at: http://www.history cooperative.org/journals/eh/12.3/armitage.html. Accessed January 2008.

Asad, Talal. 2003. *Formations of the secular: Christianity, Islam, modernity*. Stanford, CA: Stanford University Press.

Ashby, Leroy. 1997. *Endangered children: Dependency, neglect, and abuse in American history*. New York: Twayne Publishers.

Audoin-Rouzeau, Stéphane, and Annette Becker. 2002. *14–18: Understanding the Great War*. Trans. Catherine Temerson. New York: Hill and Wang.

Austin, Joe. 2004. "Youth culture." In *Encyclopedia of children and childhood in history and society*, ed. Paula Fass, vol. 3. New York: Macmillan Reference.

Austin, Joe, and Michael Nevin Willard, eds. 1998. *Generations of youth: Youth cultures and history in twentieth-century America*. New York: New York University Press.

Babb, Sanora. 1994. *An owl on every post: A memoir*. Albuquerque: University of New Mexico Press.

Baden-Powell, Robert. 2004. *Scouting for boys: A handbook for instruction in good citizenship*. Oxford: Oxford University Press.

Bagley, William C. 1925. *Determinism in education: A series of papers on the relative influence of inherited and acquired traits in determining intelligence, achievement, and character*. Baltimore: Warwick & York.

Bagnell, Kenneth. 1980. *The little immigrants: The orphans who came to Canada*. Toronto: MacMillan.

Bailey, Beth. 1988. *From front porch to back seat: Courtship in twentieth-century America*. Baltimore, MD: Johns Hopkins University Press.

Bairoch, P. 1968. *La population active et sa structure*. Brussels: Institut de Sociologie de l'Universite Libre de Bruxelles.

Bakketeig, Leiv S., Sven Cnattingius, and Lisbeth R. Knudsen. 1993. "Socioeconomic differences in fetal and infant mortality in Scandinavia." *Journal of Public Health Policy* 14(1): 82–90.

Ballantyne, David. 1950. *The Cunninghams*. New York: Vanguard Press.

Balmer, Randall. 1993. *Mine eyes have seen the glory: A journey into the evangelical subculture in America*. New York: Oxford University Press.

Bancroft, Angus. 2005. *Roma and Gypsy-Travelers in Europe: Modernity, space and exclusion.* Aldershot, UK: Ashgate.

Baritz, Loren. 1990. *The good life: The meaning of success for the American middle class.* New York: Harper & Row.

Barnes, Annie S. 1979. "An urban black voluntary association." *Phylon* 40(3): 264–269.

Bartell, Ernest J., and, Alejandro O'Donnell, eds. 2001. *The child in Latin America: Health, development, and rights.* Notre Dame, IN: University of Notre Dame Press.

Bederman, Gail. 1995. "'Teaching our sons to do what we have been teaching the savages to avoid': G. Stanley Hall, racial recapitulation, and the neurasthenic paradox." In *Manliness and civilization: a cultural history of gender and race in the United States, 1880–1917,* ed. Gail Bederman. Chicago: University of Chicago Press.

Beito, David T. 2000. *From mutual aid to the welfare state: Fraternal societies and social services, 1890–1967.* Chapel Hill: University of North Carolina Press.

Belge, Kathy. 2008. "Where can gays legally marry?" Available at: http://lesbianlife.about.com/cs/wedding/a/wheremarriage.htm. Accessed April 2008.

Bell, James, and Nicole Lim. 2005. "Young once, Indian forever: Youth gangs in Indian country." *American Indian Quarterly* 29(3/4): 626–650.

Bellah, Robert J. 1967. "Civil religion in America." *Daedalus* 96(Winter): 1–21.

Benson, John. 1994. *The rise of consumer society in Britain, 1880–1980.* London: Longman.

Berebitsky, Julie. 2000. *Like our very own: Adoption and the changing culture of motherhood, 1851–1950.* Lawrence: University of Kansas Press.

Berentsen, William H. 1987. "German infant mortality 1960–1980." *Geographical Review* 77(2): 157–170.

Bergen, Doris L. 1996. *Twisted cross: The German Christian movement in the Third Reich.* Chapel Hill: The University of North Carolina Press.

Berlanstein, L. R. 1978–1979. "Vagrants, beggars, and thieves: Delinquent boys in mid-nineteenth century Paris." *Journal of Social History* 12: 532–533.

Bhabha. Jacqueline. 2004. "Seeking asylum alone: Treatment of separated and trafficked children in need of refugee protection." *International Migration* 42(1): 141–148.

Bhabha, Jacqueline, and Susan Schmidt. 2008. "Seeking asylum alone: Unaccompanied and separated children and refugee protection in the US." *Journal of the History of Childhood and Youth* 1(1): 127–138.

Bigelow, William Frederick. 1920. "Letter from the editor." *Good Housekeeping* 70(1): 4.

Bigelow, William Frederick. 1921. "The goblins'll git ye – If you let 'em." *Good Housekeeping* 72(3): 4, 6.

Bill & Melinda Gates Foundation. 2007. *Child health backgrounder.* Available at: http://www.gatesfoundation.org/GlobalHealth/Pri_Diseaes/ChildHealth/Child_Backgrounder.htm. Accessed April 4, 2008.

Bird, Jerine B. 1995. "Revolution for children in Saudi Arabia." In *Children in the Muslim Middle East,* ed. Elizabeth Warnock Fernea. Austin: University of Texas Press.

Black, Robert E., Lindsay H. Allen, Zulfiqar A. Bhutta, Laura E. Caulfield, Mercedes de Onisl, Majid Ezzati. 2008. "Maternal and child undernutrition: Global and regional exposures and health consequences." *The Lancet* 371(9608): 243–260.

Black, Robert E., Saul S. Morris, and Jennifer Bryce. 2003. "Where and why are 10 million children dying every year?" *The Lancet* 361(9376): 2226–2234.

Blackburn, Geoff. 1993. *The Children's Friend Society: Juvenile emigrants to Western Australia, South Africa and Canada, 1834–1842*. Northbridge, Canada: W.A. Access.

Blackwelder, Julia Kirk. 1997. *Now hiring: The feminization of work in the United States, 1900–1995*. College Station: Texas A&M University Press.

Block, Liesbeth de, and David Buckingham. 2008. *Global children, global media*. New York: Palgrave Macmillan.

Bloom, David E., and David Canning. 2001. *The health and poverty of nations: From theory to practice*. Geneva: World Health Organization.

Bock, Gisela. 1984. "Racism and sexism in Nazi Germany: Motherhood, compulsory sterilization, and the state." In *When biology became destiny: Women in Weimar and Nazi Germany*, ed. Renate Bridenthal, Atina Grossmann, and Marion Kaplan. New York: Monthly Review Press.

Bock, Gisela, and Pat Thane. 1991. *Maternity and gender policies: Women and the rise of the European welfare states, 1880s–1950s*. London: Routledge.

Bodnar, John. 1992. *Remaking America: Public memory, commemoration, and patriotism in the twentieth century*. Princeton, NJ: Princeton University Press.

Bonino, Jose Miguez. 1975. *Doing theology in a revolutionary situation*. Philadelphia: Fortress Press.

Borgman, Dean. 1987. "A history of American youth ministry." In *The complete book of youth ministry*, ed. Warren S. Benson and Mark H. Senter. Chicago: Moody.

Botsford-Fraser, Marian. 2006. *Requiem for my brother*. Vancouver: Grey Stone.

Bowman, Kate. 2004. "Body and soul. They're reading liberation theology and listening to the world's urban poor: Meet the young evangelicals of Word Made Flesh." *Sojourners* 33(July): 28–31.

Boydston, Jeanne. 1990. *Home and work: Housework, wages, and the ideology of labor in the early republic*. New York: Oxford University Press.

Bremner, Robert, John Barnard, Tamara Hareven, and Robert Mennel, eds. 1970. *Children and youth in America: A documentary history, vol. I: 1600–1865*. Cambridge, MA: Harvard University Press.

Brewer, Holly. 2005. *By birth or consent: Children, law and the Anglo-American revolution in authority*. Chapel Hill: University of North Carolina Press.

Bringing them home: The "Stolen Generation" report. 1997. Available at: http://human rights.gov.au/socialjustice/bthreport/index.html. Accessed March 1, 2008.

Brookes, Martin. 2004. *Extreme measures: The dark visions and bright ideas of Francis Galton*. New York: Bloomsbury.

Brosco, Jeffrey P. 1999. "The early history of the infant mortality rate in America: 'A reflection upon the past and a prophecy of the future.'" *Pediatrics* 103(2): 478–485.

Brown, Callum. 2006. *Religion and society in twentieth-century Britain*. New York: Longman.

Brumberg, Joan Jacobs. 1997. *The body project: An intimate history of American girls*. New York: Random House.

Bruser Maynard, Fredelle. 1964. *Raisins and almonds.* Don Mills, Canada: Paper Jacks.

Bryce, Jennifer, Cynthia Boschi-Pinto, Kenji Shibuya, Robert E. Black, and the WHO Child Health Epidemiology Reference Group. 2005. "WHO estimates of the cause of death in children." *The Lancet* 365(9465): 1147–1152.

Bryder, Linda. 2003. *A voice for mothers: The Plunket Society and infant welfare, 1907–2000.* Auckland, New Zealand: Auckland University Press.

Bryk, Anthony S., Valerie Lee, and Peter Holland. 1993. *Catholic schools and the common good.* Cambridge, MA: Harvard University Press.

Buckingham, David, and Rebecca Willet, eds. 2006. *Digital generations: Children, young people, and the new media.* London: Routledge.

Budiwski, Chris. "4-H launching partnership with Aboriginal youth." Available at: http://www.gov.mb.ca/agriculture/financial/youngfarmers/4h.html. Accessed March 15, 2010.

Burds, Jeffrey. 1998. *Peasant dreams and market politics: Labor migration and the Russian village, 1861–1905.* Pittsburgh, PA: University of Pittsburgh Press.

Burr, Rachel. 2006. *Vietnam's children in a changing world.* New Brunswick, NJ: Rutgers University Press.

Buti, Antonio. 2002. "The removal of Aboriginal children: Canada and Australia Compared." *University of Western Sydney Law Review.* Available at: http://www.austlii.edu.au/au/journals/UWSLRev/2002/2.html#Heading7. Accessed November 17, 2008.

Cable, Amanda. 2007. "Condemned to be virgins: The two million women robbed by the war." *The Daily Mail* (September 15). Available at: http://www.dailymail.co.uk/pages/live/femail/article.html?in_article_id=481882&

Callahan, Marilyn, Sven Hessle, and Susan Strega, eds. 2000. *Valuing the field: Child welfare in international context* Aldershot, UK: Ashgate.

Campolo, Tony. 1989. *The church and the American teenager: What works and what doesn't in youth ministry.* Grand Rapids, MI: Zondervan.

Canning, Kathleen. 1996. *Languages of labor and gender: Female factory work in Germany, 1850–1914.* Ann Arbor: University of Michigan Press.

Carasso, Adam, C. Eugene Steuerle, and Gillian Reynolds. 2007. *Kids' share 2007: How children fare in the federal budget.* Washington, DC: The Urban Institute.

Carpenter, Joel A. 1985. "Geared to the times, but anchored to the rock: How contemporary techniques and exuberant nationalism helped create an evangelical re-surgence." *Christianity Today* 30(November 8): 44–47.

Carpenter, Joel A. 1990. "Youth for Christ and the new evangelicals." In *Religion and the life of the nation: American recoveries,* ed. Rowland A. Sherrill. Urbana: University of Illinois Press.

Carpenter, Joel A. 1997. *Revive us again: The reawakening of American fundamentalism.* New York: Oxford University Press.

Carroll, B. Jill. 2007. *A dialogue of civilizations: Gülen's Islamic ideas and humanistic discourse.* Somerset, NJ: The Light.

Carroll, Lewis. 1906. *Through the looking glass and what Alice found there with fifty illustrations by John Tenniel.* London and New York: Macmillan.

Carter, Erica. 1997. *How German is she? Postwar West German reconstruction and the consuming woman.* Ann Arbor: University of Michigan Press.

Carter, Sarah A. 1997. *Capturing women: The manipulation of cultural imagery in Canada's prairie west.* Montreal-Kingston: McGill-Queen's University Press.

Castles, Francis, ed. 1993. *Families of nations: Patterns of public policy in Western democracies,* Aldershot, UK: Dartmouth Publishing.

Cavallo, Dominick. 1981. *Muscles and morals: Organized playgrounds and urban reform, 1880–1920.* Philadelphia: University of Pennsylvania Press.

Challinor, Deborah, and Elizabeth Lancaster. 2000. *Who'll stop the rain? Agent Orange and the children of New Zealand's Vietnam veterans.* Auckland: HarperCollins.

Chan, Anita. 1995. *Children of Mao: Personality development and political activism in the Red Guard generation.* London: Macmillan.

Chan, Shirley. 2006. "'Unidentified family, c.1910'—The girl in the picture." In *Finding memories, tracing roots—Chinese Canadian family stories,* ed. Brandy Wiên Worrall. Vancouver: Chinese Canadian Historical Society of British Columbia.

Cherlin, Andrew J. 1981. *Marriage, divorce, remarriage.* Cambridge, MA: Harvard University Press.

Chesnais, Jean-Claude. 2001. "Comment: A march toward population recession." *Population and Development Review* 27(Suppl.): 255–259.

Chidambaran, V. C., John W. McDonald, and Michael Bracher. 1985. "Infant and child mortality in the developing world: Information from the World Fertility Survey." *International Family Planning Perspectives* 11(1): 17–25.

Chidester, David. 1987. "Published by authority: Religion in the president's council report on youth." *Journal of Theology for Southern Africa* 61(December): 73, 75–79.

Child Labor Coalition. 2008. "Child labor in the US." Available at: http://www. stopchildlabor.org/USchildlabor/fact1.htm. Accessed March 2008.

Chin, Elizabeth. 2001. *Purchasing power: Black kids and American consumer culture.* Minneapolis: University of Minnesota Press.

Chudacoff, Howard. 1989. *How old are you?: Age consciousness in American culture* Princeton, NJ: Princeton University Press.

Chudacoff, Howard P. 2007. *Children at play: An American history.* New York: New York University Press.

Chupik, Jessa. 2006. "Fires burning: Advocacy, camping and children with learning disabilities in Ontario, 1950–1990." In *Exploring experiences of advocacy by people with learning disabilities,* ed. Duncan Mitchell, Rannveig Traustadottir, Rohhs Chapman, Louise Townson, Nigel Ingham, and Sue Ledger. London: Jessica Kingsley Publishers.

Chupik, Jessa, and David Wright. 2006. "Treating the 'idiot' child in early twentieth-century Ontario." *Disability & Society* 21(1): 77–90.

Clarke, Nic. 2004–2005. "Sacred daemons: Exploring British Columbian society's perceptions of 'Mentally Deficient' Children, 1870–1930." *BC Studies* 144: 61–89.

Cliché, Marie-Aimée. 2007. *Maltraiter ou punir? La violence envers les enfants dans les familles québécoises, 1850–1969.* Montréal: Boréal.

Clotfelter, Charles T. 2004. *After Brown: The rise and retreat of school desegregation.* Princeton, NJ: Princeton University Press.

Cohen, Lizabeth. 1990. *Making a new deal: Industrial workers in Chicago, 1919–1939.* New York: Cambridge University Press.

Coldrey, Barry M. 2004. "Placing Out." In *Encyclopedia of children and childhood in history and society* Paula Fass, vol. 2. New York: Macmillan Reference USA.

Comacchio, Cynthia. 1993. *"Nations are built of babies": Saving Ontario's mothers and children, 1900–1940.* Montreal: McGill-Queen's University Press.

Comacchio, Cynthia. 2006. *The dominion of youth—adolescence and the making of a modern Canada, 1920–1950.* Waterloo, Canada: Wilfrid University Press.

Cook, Daniel Thomas. 2004. *The commodification of children. The children's clothing industry and the rise of the child consumer.* Durham, NC: Duke University Press.

Coontz, Stephanie. 1992. *The way we never were: American families and the nostalgia trap.* New York: Basic Books.

Cott, Nancy F. 2000. *Public vows: A history of marriage and the nation.* Cambridge, MA: Harvard University Press.

Cottrol, Robert J., Raymond T. Diamond, and Leland B. Ware. 2003. *Brown V. Board of Education: Caste, culture, and the constitution.* Lawrence: University Press of Kansas.

Counts, George S. 1930. *The American road to culture.* New York: The John Day Company.

Cowan, Ruth Schwartz. 1983. *More work for mother: The ironies of household technology from the open hearth to the microwave.* New York: Basic Books.

Cox, Harvey. 1995. *Fire from heaven: The rise of Pentecostal spirituality and the reshaping of religion in the twenty-first century.* Reading, MA: Addison-Wesley Publishers.

Cremin, Lawrence A. 1961. *The transformation of the school: Progressivism in American education, 1876–1957.* New York: Vintage Books.

Croall, Hazel. 1998. *Crime and society in Britain.* New York: Longman.

Cross, Gary. 1997. *Kids' stuff: Toys and the changing world of American childhood.* Cambridge: Harvard University Press.

Cross, Gary. 2004. *The cute and the cool: Wondrous innocence and modern American children's culture.* New York: Oxford University Press.

Cuban, Larry. 1993. *How teachers taught: Constancy and change in American classrooms, 1880–1990.* 2nd ed. New York: Teachers College Press.

Cunningham, Hugh. 2005. *Children and childhood in Western society since 1500.* 2nd ed. London: Longman.

Cunxin, Li. 2003. *Mao's last dancer.* Camberwell, UK: Viking.

Cupers, Kenny. 2008. "Governing through nature: Camps and youth movements in interwar Germany and the United States." *Cultural Geographies* 15(2): 173–205.

Currie, Dawn. 1999. *Girl talk: Adolescent magazines and their readers.* Toronto: University of Toronto Press.

Cusick, Philip A. 1973. *Inside high school.* New York: Holt, Rinehart and Winston.

Dabis, Francois, Hoosen M. Coovadia, Anna Coutsoudis, Valériane Leroy, Marie-Louise Newell, Joanna Orne Gliemann, and Freddy Perez. 2002. *Child health research: A foundation for improving child health*. Child and Adolescent Health and Development, World Health Organization.

Dalley, Bronwyn. 1994. "Deep and dark secrets. Government responses to child abuse." In *Past judgement: Social policy in New Zealand history*, ed. B. Dalley and Margaret Tennant. Dunedin, New Zealand: University of Otago Press.

Dalley, Bronwyn. 1998. *Family matters: Child welfare in twentieth-century New Zealand*. Auckland, New Zealand: Auckland University Press.

Dalley, Bronwyn, and Margaret Tennant, eds. 2004. *Past judgement: Social policy in New Zealand history*. Dunedin, New Zealand: University of Otago Press.

Dam, H.J.W. 1894. *The shop girl*. London: Gaiety Theatre.

Davies, Margery. 1982. *A woman's place is at the typewriter: The feminization of clerical workers and changes in clerical work, 1870–1930*. Philadelphia: Temple University Press.

Davin, Anna. 1996. *Growing up poor: Home, school and street in London, 1870–1914*. London: Rivers Oram Press.

Davis, Belinda J. 2000. *Food, politics, and everyday life in World War I Berlin*. Chapel Hill: The University of North Carolina Press.

Davis, Deborah S., and Julia Sensenbrenner. 2000. "Commercializing childhood: Parental purchases for Shanghai's only child." In *The consumer revolution in urban China*, ed. Deborah S. Davis. Berkeley: University of California Press.

Dawson, Sandra. 2007. "Working class consumers and the campaign for holidays with pay." *Twentieth Century British History* 18: 56–80.

Dayton, Donald. 1976. *Discovering an evangelical heritage*. Grand Rapids, MI: Eerdmans.

Dear, John, ed. 2002. *Mohandas Gandhi: Essential writings*. New York: Orbis.

De Beauvoir, Simone. 1953. *The second sex*. Trans. H. M. Parshley. New York: Alfred A. Knopf.

Deering, Mabel Craft. 1910. "What any woman's club can do in reforming the milk supply." *Good Housekeeping* 50: 645–646.

De Grazia, Victoria. 1992. *How fascism ruled women: Italy, 1922–1945*. Berkeley: University of California Press.

De Grazia, Victoria. 1996. "Nationalizing women: The competition between fascist and commercial cultural models in Mussolini's Italy." In *The sex of things: Gender and consumption in historical perspective*, ed. Victoria de Grazia and Ellen Furlough. Berkeley: University of California Press.

D'Emilio, John, and Estelle B. Freedman. 1997. *Intimate strangers: A history of sexuality in America*. 2nd ed. Chicago: University of Chicago Press.

Dewey, John. 1938. *Experience and education*. New York: Macmillan.

Digest of educational statistics. 2001. Washington, DC: National Center for Educational Statistics.

Digital History. 2010. "Exploration: Children and the Great Depression." Available at: http://www.digitalhistory.uh.edu/learning_history/children_depression/depression_children_menu.cfm. Accessed March 15, 2010.

Dorsky, Susan, and Stevenson, Thomas B. 1995. "Childhood and education in highland north Yemen." In *Children in the Muslim Middle East*, ed. Elizabeth Warnock Fernea. Austin: University of Texas Press.

Downs, Laura Lee. 2002. *Childhood in the promised land: Working-class movements and the colonies de vacances in France, 1880–1960.* Durham, NC: Duke University Press.

Droke, Maxwell. 1945. *Good-by to G.I.: How to be a successful civilian.* New York: Abingdon-Cokesbury Press.

Dubay, L., and B. M. Kenney. 2001. "Health access and use among low-income children: Who fares best?" *Health Affairs* 20(1): 112–121.

Duis, Perry. 1996. "No time for privacy: World War II and Chicago's families." In *The war in American culture: Society and consciousness during World War II,* ed. Lewis Erenberg and Susan Hirsch. Chicago: University of Chicago Press.

Durham, Stella Walker. 1910. "The Portland pure milk war: The story of a victory won by a city's housewives." *Good Housekeeping* 50(April): 518–520.

Early, Frances H. 2001. "Staking her claim: Buffy the Vampire Slayer as transgressive woman warrior." *Journal of Popular Culture* 35(3): 11–27.

Easterlin, Richard A. 1981. "Why isn't the whole world developed?" *The Journal of Economic History* 51(1): 1–19.

Easterlin, Richard A. 2000. "The worldwide standard of living." *Journal of Economic Perspectives* 14(1): 7–26.

Edmondson, Aimee. 2005. "Infant mortality in Memphis: Memphis ranks worst in the nation for woeful rate of infant deaths." *The Commercial Appeal (Memphis),* March 6, 2005. Available at: http://www.commercialappeal.com/mca/local/article/0,2845,MCA_25340_4757 196,00.html.

Ehrenreich, Barbara. 1992. *The hearts of men: American dreams and the flight from commitment.* Garden City, NY: Anchor Press/Doubleday.

Elder, Glen. 1974. *Children of the Great Depression: Social change in life experience.* Berkeley: University of California Press.

Elfenbein, Jessica I. 2002. *The making of a modern city: Philanthropy, civic culture, and the Baltimore YMCA.* Gainesville: University Press of Florida.

Emecheta, Buchi. 1974. *Second class citizen.* New York: George Braziller.

Enfants Entraide. 2010. "Activite: Quebec, Le 8 Avrl 2010." Available at: http://www.enfantsentraide.org/ftc/source/news/2006/KRON4_apr18_06_WorldChildren Prize.pdf. Accessed March 15, 2010.

Engelstein, Laura. 1992. *The keys to happiness: Sex and the search for modernity in fin-de-siècle Russia.* Ithaca, New York: Cornell University Press.

Enssle, Manfred J. 1987. "The harsh discipline of food scarcity in postwar Stuttgart, 1945–1948." *German Studies Review* 10(3): 481–502.

Ericsson, Kjersti, and Eva Simonson, eds. 2005. *Children of World War II: The hidden enemy legacy.* Oxford: Berg.

Evangelical Lutheran Church in America. 2008. "Youth ministries." Available at: http://www.elca.org/youth.html. Accessed February 1, 2008.

Ewen, Elizabeth. 1985. *Immigrant women in the land of dollars: Life and culture on the Lower East Side, 1890–1925.* New York: Monthly Review Press.

Fass, Paula, ed. 2004. *Encyclopedia of children and childhood in history and society.* 3 vols. New York: Macmillan.

Fass, Paula. 2006. *Children of a new world: Culture, society, and globalization.* New York: New York University Press.

Fides, Jonathan. 2007. "Politics stifling $100 laptops." *BBC News*. Available at: http://news.bbc.co.uk/2technology/7094695.stm. Accessed March 11, 2008.

Finch, Janet. 1989. "Social policy, social engineering and the family in the 1990s." In *The goals of social policy*, ed. M. Bulmer J. Lewis, and D. Piachaud. London: Unwin Hyman.

Finch, Janet. 1990. "Gender, employment and responsibilities to kin." *Work Employment and Society* 4(3): 349–367.

Fink, Janet. 2005. "Welfare, Poverty, and Social Inequalities." In *A companion to contemporary Britain, 1939–2000*, ed. Paul Addison and Harriet Jones. Oxford: Blackwell.

Fletcher, Ronald. 1988. *The shaking of the foundations: Family and society.* London: Routledge.

Folbre, Nancy. 1994. "Children as public goods." *The American Economic Review* 84(2): 86–90.

Fottrell, Deidre, ed. 2000. *Revisiting children's rights: Ten years of the UN Convention on the Rights of the Child.* The Hague, the Netherlands: Kluwer Law International.

Fournier, Christophe. 2007. *International activity report 2007.* Doctors Without Borders. Available at: http://www.doctorswithoutborders.org/publications/ar/report_print.cfm?id=2906. Accessed April 15, 2008.

Fraser, Derek. 2003. *The evolution of the British welfare state: A history of social policy since the Industrial Revolution.* 3rd ed. New York: Palgrave Macmillan.

French, Katherine L., and Allyson M. Poska. 2007. *Women and gender in the Western past.* Vol. 2. Boston: Houghton and Mifflin.

Friedan, Betty. 1983. *The feminine mystique.* 20th anniversary ed. New York: Dell.

Friedman, Stan. 2006. "Poverty 101: Activism on evangelical campuses." *The Christian Century* 123(May 30): 9–10.

Gaster, Sanford. 1995. "Public places of childhood, 1915–1930." *The Oral History Review* 22(2): 1–31.

Gates, Bill. 2007. *Saving the world is within our grasp.* Bill & Melinda Gates Foundation. Available at: http://www.gatesfoundation.org/MediaCenter/Speeches/Co-ChairS. Accessed April 15, 2008.

Gerlin, Andrea. "A simple solution," *TIME Europe* 168(17): 40–47.

Giesen, Rolf. 2003. *Nazi propaganda films: A history and filmography.* Jefferson, NC: McFarland.

Giles, Judy. 2004. *The parlour and the suburb: Domestic identities, class, femininity and modernity.* Oxford: Berg.

Gillespie, Franklin B. 1981. "Youth programs of the United Presbyterian Church: An historical overview." *Journal of Presbyterian History* 59(Fall): 309–382.

Gillis, John R. 1996. *A world of their own making: Myth, ritual, and the quest for family values.* New York: Basic Books.

Gillis, John R. 1997. *A world of their own making: A history of myth and ritual in family life.* Oxford: Oxford University Press.

Ginsborg, Paul. 2003. "The family politics of the great dictators." In *The history of the European family: Volume three: Family life in the twentieth century,* edited by David I Kertzer and Marzio Barbagli. New Haven: Yale University Press.

Girard, Rene. 1977. *Violence and the sacred.* Trans. Patrick Gregory. Baltimore, MD: The Johns Hopkins University Press.

Girl Scouts of the USA. 2010. "Girl Scout timeline, 1920s." Available at: http://www.girlscouts.org. Accessed March 15, 2010.

Gleason, Mona. 1999a. "Embodied negotiations: Children's bodies and historical change in Canada, 1930–1960." *Journal of Canadian Studies* 34(1): 113–137.

Gleason, Mona. 1999b. *Normalizing the ideal: Psychology, schooling, and the family in postwar Canada.* Toronto: University of Toronto Press.

Gleason, Mona. 2001. "Disciplining the student body: Schooling and the construction of Canadian children's bodies, 1930 to 1960." *History of Education Quarterly* 41(2): 189–215.

Glenn, Myra C. 1984. *Campaigns against corporal punishment.* Albany, NY: State University of New York.

Glenn, Susan A. 1990. *Daughters of the shtetl: Life and labor in the immigrant generation.* Ithaca, NY: Cornell University Press.

Gluck, Sherna. 1987. *Rosie the riveter revisited: Women, the war, and social change.* Boston: Twayne Publishers.

Golden, Janet, Richard Meckel, and Heather Munroe Prescott. 2004. *Children and youth in sickness and in health: A historical handbook and guide.* Westport, CT: Greenwood Press.

Goldin, Claudia. 2001. "The human-capital century and American leadership: Virtues of the past." *The Journal of Economic History* 61(2): 263–292.

Goldman, Wendy. 1993. *Women, the state and revolution: Soviet family policy and social life, 1917–1936.* Cambridge, MA: Cambridge University Press.

Goldstein, Howard. 1996. *The home on Gorham Street and the voices of its children.* Tuscaloosa: University of Alabama Press.

Goode, William. 1963. *World revolution and family patterns.* New York: Free Press of Glencoe.

Goodlad, John I. 1984. *A place called school: Prospects for the future.* New York: Magraw-Hill.

Gordon, Judy. 2002. *"Four hundred brothers and sisters": Two Jewish orphanages in Montréal, Quebec 1909–1942.* Toronto: Lugus.

Gordon, Linda. 1988. *Heroes of their own lives: The politics and history of family violence.* New York: Viking.

Gordon, Linda. 1994. *Pitied but not entitled: Single mothers and the history of welfare.* New York: The Free Press.

Gordon, Linda. 2002. *The moral property of women: A history of birth control politics in America.* Urbana: University of Illinois Press.

Graff, Harvey. 1997. *Conflicting paths—growing up in America.* Cambridge: Harvard University Press.

Graham, Jeanine. 1987. "Child employment in New Zealand." *New Zealand Journal of History* 21(2): 62–78.

Graham, Jeannine. 1994. "The facts on life." Part 3 of *All in the Family* [sound recording]. Aired December 29, 1994, New Zealand National Radio.

Graham, Lawrence Otis. 1999. *Our kind of people: Inside black America's upper class.* New York: HarperCollins.

Graves, Pamela M. 1994. *Labour women: Women in British working-class politics, 1918–1939.* Cambridge, UK: Cambridge University Press.

Grayzel, Susan R. 1999. *Women's identities at war: Gender, motherhood, and politics in Britain and France during the First World War.* Chapel Hill: The University of North Carolina Press.

Greeff, Roger, Suzette Waterhouse, and Edwina Brocklesby. 1999. "Kinship fostering—research, policy and practice in England." In *Fostering kinship: An international perspective on kinship foster care,* ed. Roger Greeff. Aldershot, UK: Ashgate Arena.

Greeley, Andrew M. 1994. "The Catholics in the world and in America." In *World Religions in America: An introduction,* ed. Jacob Neusner. Louisville, KY: Westminster John Knox.

Greenspoon, David, and Stephen Heathorn. 2006. "Organizing youth for partisan politics in Britain, 1918–c. 1932." *The Historian* 68(1): 89–119.

Grenville, J.A.S. 1994. *The Collins history of the world in the twentieth century.* London: HarperCollins.

Grossberg, Michael. 1985. *Governing the hearth: Law and the family in nineteenth-century America.* Chapel Hill: University of North Carolina Press.

Grossman, Atina. 1995. *Reforming sex: The German movement for birth control and abortion reform, 1920–1950.* Oxford: Oxford University Press.

Guenther, Irene. 2004. *Nazi chic? Fashioning women in the Third Reich.* Oxford: Berg.

Gülen, M. Fethullah. 2006. *Toward a global civilization of love and tolerance.* Somerset, NJ: The Light.

Gullace, Nicoletta F. 2002. *"The blood of our sons": Men, women, and the renegotiation of British citizenship during the Great War.* New York: Palgrave Macmillan.

Habermas, Jürgen. 1975. *Legitimation crisis.* Trans. Thomas McCarthy. Boston: Beacon Press.

Hackstaff, Karla B. 1999. *Marriage in a culture of divorce.* Philadelphia: Temple University Press.

Haebich, Anna. 2000. *Broken circles: Fragmenting indigenous families, 1800–2000.* Fremantle, Australia: Fremantle Arts Centre Press.

Haig-Brown, Celia. 1988. *Resistance and renewal: Surviving the Indian residential school.* Vancouver: Arsenal Pulp Press.

Hair, P.E.H. 1982. "Children in society, 1850–1980." In *Population and society in Britain 1850–1980,* ed. Theo Barker and Michael Drake. London: Batsford.

Hall, Grenville Stanley. 1904. *Adolescence, its psychology and its relation to physiology anthropology, sociology, sex, crime, religion and education.* New York: Appleton.

Hall, Kathleen. 1995. "'There's a time to act English and a time to act Indian': The politics of identity among British-Sikh teenagers." In *Children and the politics of culture,* ed. Sharon Stephens. Princeton, NJ: Princeton University Press.

Halpern, Sydney A. 1988. *American pediatrics: The social dynamics of professionalism, 1880–1980.* Berkley: University of California Press.

Halsey, A. H. 1995. *Change in British society.* New York: Oxford University Press.

Ham, Christopher. 2004. *Health policy in Britain: The politics and organization of the National Health Service.* 5th ed. New York: Palgrave Macmillan.

Hamerow, Theodore S. 1997. *On the road to the wolf's lair: German resistance to Hitler.* Cambridge, MA: Harvard University Press.

Hardeman, Virginia M. 1973. "How to save babies for two dimes a day." *Redbook Magazine* (April): 68–75.

Hardyment, Christina. 1995. *Slice of life: The British way of eating since 1945.* London: BBC Books.

Harriman, Helga H. 1995. *Women in the Western heritage.* Guilford, CT: Dushkin Publishing Group.

Harris, Maria. 1981. *Portrait of youth ministry.* New York: Paulist.

Hartmann, Susan. 1982. *The home front and beyond: American women in the 1940s.* Boston: Twayne Publishers.

Harvey, Brett. 1994. *The fifties: A women's oral history.* New York: Harper Perennial.

Haue, Harry. 2004. "Education, Europe." In *Encyclopedia of children and childhood in history and society,* ed. Paula Fass. New York: Macmillan.

Hausen, Karin. 1987. "The German nation's obligations to the heroes' widows of World War I." In *Behind the lines: Gender and the two world wars,* ed. Margaret R. Higonnet, Jane Jenson, Sonya Michel, and Margaret Collins White. New Haven, CT: Yale University Press.

Hawes, Joseph M. 1991. *The children's rights movement: A history of advocacy and protection.* New York: Twayne.

Hawes, Joseph M. 1971. *Children in urban society.* New York: Oxford University Press.

Hawes, Joseph M., and Elizabeth I. Nybakken, eds. 2001. *Family and society in American history.* Urbana: University of Illinois Press.

Hawes, Joseph M., and N. Ray Hiner, eds. 1991. *Children in historical and comparative perspective: An international handbook and research guide.* Westport, CT: Greenwood.

Hayes, Cheryl D., ed. 1982. *Making policies for children: A study of the federal process.* Washington, DC: National Academy Press.

Hays, Samuel P. 1964. "The politics of reform in municipal government in the progressive era." *Pacific Northwest Quarterly* 55(October): 157–169.

Hecht, Tobias. 1998. *At home in the street: Street children of northeast Brazil.* Cambridge, UK: Cambridge University Press.

Hegar, Rebecca L. 1999. "The cultural roots of kinship care." In *Kinship foster care: Policy, practice and research,* ed. Rebecca L. Hegar and Maria Scannagpieco. New York: Oxford University Press.

Heidenheimer, Arnold J. 1973, "The politics of public education, health, and welfare in the USA and Western Europe: How growth and reform potentials have differed." *British Journal of Political Science* 3(3): 315–340.

Heineman, Kenneth J. 2004. "Youth activism." In ed. *Encyclopedia of children and childhood in history and society,* Paula Fass, vol. 3. New York: Macmillan Reference US.

Helton, Arthur. 2002. *The price of indifference: Refugees and humanitarian action in the new century.* Oxford: Oxford University Press.

Hendrick, Harry. 1997. *Children, childhood and English society, 1880–1990.* Cambridge: Cambridge University Press.

Hendrick, Harry. 2003. *Child welfare: Historical dimensions, contemporary debate.* London: Policy Press.

The Henry J. Kaiser Family Foundation. 2007. "United States: Health coverage and uninsured." *Kaiser State 2007 Health Facts.* Available at: http://www.statehealth facts.org/profileind.jsp?cat=3&rgn=1. Accessed December 31, 2007.

Herbert Hoover Presidential Library-Museum. 1999. *American Child Health Association—scope and content note.* Iowa City, IA: Author. Available at: http://www.ecommcode2.com/hoover/research/hooverpapers/hoover/commerce/acha5.htm. Accessed December 2008.

Hertz, Rosanna. 1986. *More equal than others: Women and men in dual-career marriages.* Berkeley: University of California Press.

Hess, Frederick M., and Chester E. Finn, Jr., eds. 2004. "Introduction." In *Leaving no child behind? Options for kids in failing schools.* New York: Palgrave Macmillan.

Heywood, Colin. 2007. *Growing up in France: From the ancien regime to the third republic.* Cambridge, UK: Cambridge University Press.

Hill, Audrey. 2000. "A First Nations experience in First Nations child welfare services." In *Valuing the field: Child welfare in an international context,* ed. Marilyn Callahan, Sven Hessle, and Susan Strega. Aldershot, UK: Ashgate.

Hilton, Matthew. 2000. *Smoking in British popular culture, 1800–2000.* Manchester: Manchester University Press.

Hindman, Hugh D. 2002. *Child labor: An American history.* New York: M. E. Sharp.

Hiner, N. Ray. 2008. "Children in American history." In *Rethinking the history of American education,* ed. William J. Reese and John L. Rury. New York: Palgrave Macmillan.

Hines, Laurie Moses. 1998. "Community and control in the development of the extracurriculum: Muncie Central High School, 1890–1930." In *Hoosier schools: Past and present,* ed. William J. Reese. Bloomington: Indiana University Press.

Historylearningsite.co.uk. 2010. "Children and World War II." Available at: http://www.historylearningsite.co.uk/children_and_world_war_two.htm. Accessed March 15, 2010.

"Hitler Youth." 1999. In *The History Place.* Available at: http://www.historyplace.com/worldwar2/hitleryouth/index.html. Accessed December 9, 2008.

Hobsbawn, E. 1995. *Age of extremes: The short twentieth century, 1914–1991.* London: Abacus.

Hochschild, Arlie Russell. 1989. *The second shift: Working parents and the revolution at home.* New York: Viking Press.

Hoffschwelle, Mary. 1998. *Rebuilding the rural Southern community: Reformers, schools, and homes in Tennessee, 1900–1930.* Knoxville: University of Tennessee Press.

Hole-in-the-Wall. 2009. Available at: http://www.hole-in-the-wall.com/. Accessed March 7, 2009.

Holt, Marilyn Irvin. 1992. *The orphan trains: Placing out in America*. Lincoln: University of Nebraska Press.

Holt, Marilyn Irvin. 2001. *Indian orphanages*. Lawrence: University of Kansas Press.

Honwana, Alcinda. 2008. "Children's involvement in war: Historical and social contexts." *Journal of the History of Childhood and Youth* 1(1): 144–145.

Howell, James. 1998. "Youth gangs: An overview." *Juvenile Justice Bulletin*. Available at: http://www.ojjdp.ncjrs.gov/jjbulletin/9808/admin.html. Accessed July 2008.

Hughes, Richard T. 2003. *Myths America lives by*. Urbana: University of Illinois Press.

Hull, Eleanor C. 1915. "The Countryside." *The Farmer's Wife* (September): 78.

"Humble start for milk fund 20 years ago." 1939. *The Memphis Press Scimitar*. May 6.

Iacovetta, Franca. 1992. *Such hardworking people: Italian immigrants in postwar Toronto*. Montreal: McGill-Queen's University Press.

Ihimaera, Witi, ed. 1998. *Growing up maori*. Auckland, New Zealand: Tandem Press.

Illick, Joseph. 2002. *American childhoods*. Philadelphia: University of Pennsylvania Press.

Iglehart, John K. 2007. "Insuring all children—the new political imperative." *The New England Journal of Medicine* 357: 70–76.

Jablonka, Ivan. 2007. "Child migration in Gaullist France (1960s–1970s)." Paper presented at the Biennial Conference of the Society for the History of Children and Youth.

Jackson, Kenneth T. 1985. *Crabgrass frontier: The suburbanization of the United States*. New York: Oxford University Press.

Jackson, Mark ed. 2002. *Infanticide: Historical perspectives on child murder and concealment, 1550–2000*. Aldershot, UK: Ashgate.

Jacobsen, Annette Faye. 2004. "Child labor in developing countries." In *Encyclopedia of children and childhood in history and society*, ed. Paula Fass, vol. 1. New York: Macmillan Reference USA.

Jacobson, Lisa. 2004. *Raising consumers: Children and the American mass market in the early twentieth century*. New York: Columbia University Press.

James, Cathy. 2001. "Reforming reform: Toronto's settlement house movement, 1900–1920." *Canadian Historical Review* 82(1): 1–20.

Janfelt, Monika. 2004. "War in the twentieth century." In *Encyclopedia of children and childhood in history and society*, ed. Paula Fass, vol. 3. New York: Macmillan Reference USA.

Jenkins, Philip. 2003. *The new anti-Catholicism: The last acceptable prejudice*. Oxford: Oxford University Press.

Jesus Camp. 2006. DVD. Produced and directed by Heidi Ewing and Rachel Grady. Los Angeles, CA: Magnolia Home Entertainment.

Jiwani, Yasmin. 2006. *Discourses of denial: Meditations of race, gender, and violence*. Vancouver: University of British Columbia Press.

Johnson, Mary Ann. ed. 1989. *The many faces of Hull-House: The photographs of Wallace Kirkland*. Urbana: University of Illinois Press.

Johnson, Paul Christopher. 2005. "Savage civil religion." *Numen* 52(3): 289–324.

Johnson, Ramon. 2008. "Where is gay marriage legal?: Gay marriage around the world." Available at: http://gaylife.about.com/od/samesexmarriage/a/legalgaymarriag.htm. Accessed June 2008.

Johnston, Alexa. 2005. *Sir Edmund Hillary: An extraordinary life*. Auckland, New Zealand: Viking.

Jones, Jacqueline. 1985. *Labor of love, labor of sorrow: Black women, work, and the family from slavery to the present*. New York: Basic Books.

Judt, Tony. 2007. *Postwar: A history of Europe since 1945*. London: Pimlico.

Kaestle, Carl F. 1983. *Pillars of the republic: Common schools and American society, 1780–1860*. New York: Hill & Wang.

The Kairos document: A challenge to the churches. A theological comment on the political crisis in South Africa. 1986. Grand Rapids, MI: Eerdmans.

Kamerman, Sheila. 1989. "Toward a child policy decade." *Child Welfare* 68(4): 371–390.

Kamerman, Sheila B., and Alfred A. Kahn, eds. 1997. *Family change and family policies in Great Britain, Canada, New Zealand, and the United States*. New York: Oxford University Press.

Kanogo, Tabitha. 2004. "Abduction in modern Africa." In *Encyclopedia of Children and Childhood in History and Society*, ed. Paula Fass, vol. 1. New York: Macmillan Reference USA.

Kao, Grace Y., and Jerome E. Copulsky. 2007. "The pledge of allegiance and the meanings and limits of civil religion." *Journal of the American Academy of Religion* 75(March): 121–149.

Kater, Michael H. 2004. *Hitler Youth*. Cambridge, MA: Harvard University Press.

Kaufmann, Franz-Xaver, Anton Kuijsten, Hans-Joachim Shultze, and Klaus Peter Strohmeier, eds. 2002. *Family life and policies in Europe: Vol. 2: Problems and issues in comparative perspective*. New York: Oxford University Press.

Keller, Robert K. 1960. "Secondary education—organization and administration." In *Encyclopedia of educational research*, ed. Chester Harris. New York: The Macmillan Company.

Kennedy, David M. 1970. *Birth control in America; the career of Margaret Sanger*. New Haven, CT: Yale University Press.

Kenyon, Chen, Megan Sandel, Michael Silverstein, Alefiya Shakir, and Barry Zuckerman. 2007. "Revisiting the social history for child health." *Pediatrics* 120(3): e734–e738.

Kertzer, David I., and Marzio Barbagli, eds. 2003. *The history of the European family: Volume three: Family life in the twentieth century*. New Haven, CT: Yale University Press.

Kessler-Harris, Alice. 1982. *Out to work: A history of wage-earning women in the United States*. New York: Oxford University Press.

Key, Ellen. 1909. *Century of the child*. New York: G. P. Putnam's Sons.

King, Charles R. 1993. *Children's health in America*. New York: Twayne Publishers.

King, Wilma. 1995. *Stolen childhood: Slave youth in nineteenth-century America*. Bloomington: Indiana University Press.

Kirschenbaum, Lisa A. 2002. "Innocent victims and heroic defenders: Children and the siege of Leningrad." In *Children and war: A historical anthology*, ed. James Marten. New York: New York University Press.

Kirst, Michael W. 1995. "Who's in charge? Federal, state, and local control." In *Learning from the past: What history teaches us about school reform*, ed. Diane Ravitch and Maris A. Vinovkis. Baltimore, MD: The Johns Hopkins University Press.

Klapper, Melissa R. 2007. *Small strangers: The experiences of immigrant children in America, 1880–1925*. Chicago: Ivan R. Dee.

Kliebard, Herbert M. 1999. *Schooled to work: Vocationalism and the American curriculum, 1876–1946*. New York: Teachers College Press.

Kliebard, Herbert M. 2004. *The struggle for the American curriculum, 1893–1958*. 3rd ed. New York: Routledge.

Koch, H. W. 1975. *The Hitler Youth: Origins and development, 1922–1945*. New York: Stein and Day.

Kolinsky, Eva. 1998. "Recasting biographies: Women and the family." In *Social transformation and the family in post-communist Germany,* ed. Eva Kolinsky. Basingstoke, UK: Macmillan Press.

Koonz, Claudia. 1987. *Mothers in the fatherland: Women, the family, and Nazi politics*. New York: St. Martin's Press.

Koos, Leonard V. 1926. *Trends in American secondary education*. Cambridge, MA: Harvard University Press.

Koslow, Jennifer. 2004. "Putting it to a vote: The provision of pure milk in progressive era Los Angeles." *Journal of the Gilded Age and Progressive Era* 3(2): 111–144.

Kotlowitz, Alex. 1992. *There are no children here: The story of two boys growing up in the other America*. New York: Anchor Books.

Kremer, Michael. 2002. "Pharmaceuticals and the developing world." *Journal of Economic Perspectives* 16(4): 67–90.

Kubik, Jan. 1994. *The power of symbols against the symbols of power: The rise of solidarity and the fall of state socialism in Poland*. University Park, PA: Penn State University Press.

Kunzel, Regina. 1993. *Fallen women, problem girls: Unmarried mothers and the professionalization of social work, 1890–1945*. New Haven, CT: Yale University.

Kwolek-Folland, Angel. 1994. *Engendering business: Men and women in the corporate office, 1870–1930*. Baltimore, MD: Johns Hopkins University Press.

Kyvig, David E. 2002. *Daily life in the United States 1920–1940: How Americans lived through the roaring twenties and the Great Depression*. Chicago: Ivan R Dee Publishers.

Ladd-Taylor, Molly. 1994. *Mother work: Women, child welfare, and the state, 1890–1930*. Urbana: University of Illinois Press.

Lagerquist, L. DeAne. 1999. *The Lutherans*. Westport, CT: Praeger Publishers.

Lamb, Christina. 2003. *The sewing circles of Herat*. London: Flamingo.

Lambert, Moira. 1990. *A suburban girl—Australia, 1918–1948*. South Melbourne, Australia: MacMillan.

Laqueur, Walter Z. 1962. *Young Germany: A history of the German youth movement*. New York: Basic Books.

Larson, Edward J. 1998. *Summer for the gods: The scopes trial and America's continuing debate over science and religion*. Cambridge, MA: Harvard University Press.

Lasch, Christopher. 1977. *Haven in a heartless world: The family besieged*: New York: Norton.

Lasch, Christopher. 1979. *The culture of narcissism: American life in an age of diminishing expectations*. New York: Norton.

Latimer, John F. 1958. *What's happened to our high schools?* Washington, DC: Public Affairs Press.

Lawrence, Mary. 1996. *My people, myself.* Prince George, British Columbia: Caitlin Press.

Lee, Ronald. 2003. "The demographic transition: Three centuries of fundamental change." *Journal of Economic Perspectives* 17(4): 167–190.

Leeder, Elaine. 2004. *The family in global perspective: A gendered journey.* London: Sage.

Leni Riefenstahl's Triumph of the Will. [1934] 2006. VHS. Synapse Films.

Levenstein, Harvey A. 1983. "'Best for babies' or 'preventable infanticide'? The controversy over artificial feeding of infants in America, 1880–1920." *Journal of American History* 70: 75–94.

Lewis, Claudia. 1970. *Indian families on the northwest coast.* Chicago: University of Chicago Press.

Lewis, Norah, ed. 1996. *"I want to join your club": Letters from rural children, 1900–1920.* Waterloo, Canada: Wilfrid Laurier University Press.

Liebenberg, Gillian. 1994. Disease and disability: Poliomyelitis, rehabilitation and social reform for disabled persons in New Brunswick, 1941–1955. MA thesis, University of New Brunswick.

Lincoln, Bruce. 1993. *Authority: Construction and corrosion.* Chicago: The University of Chicago Press.

Lincoln, Bruce. 2003. *Holy terrors: Thinking about religion after September 11.* Chicago: The University of Chicago Press.

Lincoln, C. Eric, and Lawrence H. Mamiya. 1990. *The black church in the African American experience* Durham, NC: Duke University Press.

Lindenmeyer, Kriste. 1997. *"A right to childhood": The U.S. Children's Bureau and child welfare, 1912–1946.* Urbana: University of Illinois Press.

Lindenmeyer, Kriste. 2004. "The federal government and child health." In *Children in sickness and in health: A historical handbook and guide,* ed. Janet Golden, Richard Meckel, and Heather Munroe Prescott. Westport, CT: Greenwood Press.

Lindenmeyer, Kriste. 2005. *The greatest generation grows up: American childhood in the 1930s.* Chicago: Ivan R. Dee Publisher.

Linn, Susan. 2004. *Consuming kids: The hostile takeover of childhood.* New York: The New Press.

Linton, R. 1959. "The natural history of the family." In *The family: Its functions and destiny,* ed. R. N. Anshen. New York: Harper and Brothers.

Little, Margaret J. 1998. *"No car, no radio, no liquor permit": The moral regulation of single mothers in Ontario, 1920–1997.* Toronto: Oxford University Press.

Little, Nichole. 2001. "Embracing gay, lesbian, bisexual, and transgendered youth in school-based settings." *Child and Youth Care Forum* 30(2): 99–110.

Livingston, Sonia. 2002. *Young people and the new media: Childhood and the changing media environment.* London: Sage.

Longo, Julie, and VanBurkleo, Sandra F. "Grace Abbott." *American National Biography Online.* Available at: http://www.anb.org. Accessed June 10, 2008.

Lopez, A. D., and C. D. Mathers. 2006. "Measuring the global burden of disease and epidemiological transitions: 2002–2030." *Annals of Tropical Medicine & Parasitology* 100(5–6): 481–499.

Lowe, Roy. 2005. "Education." In *A companion to contemporary Britain, 1939–2000,* ed. Paul Addison and Harriet Jones. London: Blackwell.

The Lutheran Church—Missouri Synod. 2008. "Youth ministry." Available at: http://www.lcms.org. Accessed February 1, 2008.

Lynd, Robert, and Helen Lynd. 1929. *Middletown: A study in American culture.* New York: Harcourt, Brace, and World.

Lynd, Robert, and Helen Lynd. 1937. *Middletown in transition: A study in cultural conflicts.* New York: Harcourt, Brace, and Company.

Machel, Graca. 1996. "Impact of armed conflict on children." Report submitted by the Secretary General to the General Assembly of the United Nations, August 26, 1996. A/51/50. Available at: http://www.unicef.org/graca/a51-306_en.pdf. Accessed February 9, 2008.

MacLeod, David I. 1983. *Building character in the American boy: The Boy Scouts, YMCA, and their forerunners, 1870–1920.* Madison: University of Wisconsin Press.

Macura, Miroslav, Mitchell Eggers, and Tomas Frejka. 1995. "Demographic change and public policy in Europe." In *Population, family, and welfare: A comparative survey of European attitudes,* ed. Hein Moors and Rossella Palomba, vol. 1. New York: Oxford University Press.

Mallick, Krishna, and Doris Hunter, eds. 2002. *An anthology of nonviolence: Historical and contemporary voices.* Westport, CT: Greenwood Press.

Mamiya, Lawrence H. 1994. "A social history of Bethel African Methodist Episcopal Church in Baltimore: The house of God and the struggle for freedom." In *Portraits of Twelve Religious Communities. Vol. 1: American congregations,* ed. James P. Wind and James W. Lewis. Chicago: The University of Chicago Press.

Manning, Jack. 1989. "113th campaign beginning for the Fresh Air Fund." *New York Times,* May 7, p. 46 (New York edition).

Maracle, Eva. 1995. "Eva Maracle, 1896." In *I'll sing 'til the day I die: Conversations with Tyendinaga elders,* ed. Beth Brant. Toronto: McGilligan Books.

Margo, Robert A. 1990. *Race and schooling in the South, 1880–1950: An economic history.* Chicago: University of Chicago Press.

Markel, Howard, and Janet Golden. 2005. "Successes and missed opportunities in protecting our children's health: Critical junctures in the history of children's health policy in the United States." *Pediatrics* 115(4): 1129–1133.

Marten, James, ed. 2002. *Children and war: A historical anthology.* New York: New York University Press.

Marten, James. 2004. "Soldier children: Global human rights issues." In *Encyclopedia of Children and Childhood in History and Society,* ed. Paula Fass, vol. 3. New York: Macmillan Reference USA.

Martin, Anne. 1920. "An everlasting benefit you can win in a week." *Good Housekeeping.* 70(1): 20–21, 144–148.

Marvin, Carolyn, and David W. Ingle. 1999. *Blood sacrifice and the nation: Totem rituals and the American flag.* New York: Cambridge University Press.

Mason, Mary Ann. 1994. *From father's property to children's rights: The history of child custody in the United State.* New York: Columbia University Press.

Mather, Cotton. 1708. *Corderius Americanus: An essay upon the good education of children*. Reprint, Boston: John Allen for Nicholas Boone.

May, Elaine Tyler. 1988. *Homeward bound: American families in the cold war era*. New York: Basic Books.

May, Louise. 1985. "Strathcona." In *Working Lives: Vancouver 1886–1986*, ed. The Working Lives Collective, 177. Vancouver, British Columbia: New Star Books.

May, Martha. 1982. "The historical problem of the family wage: Ford motor company and the five dollar day." *Feminist Studies* 8(Summer): 399–424.

Maynes, Mary Jo. 1985. *Schooling in Western Europe: A social history*. Albany: State University of New York Press.

McAuley, E. Nancy, and Moira Mathieson. 1989. *Faith without form: Beliefs of Catholic youth*. Kansas City, MO: Sheed and Ward.

McCullagh, John, Gail Aitken, and Donald F. Bellamy. 2002. *A legacy of caring: A history of the Children's Aid Society of Toronto:* Toronto: Dundurn Press.

McKillop, A. B. 1979. *A disciplined intelligence: Critical inquiry and Canadian thought in the Victorian era*. Montreal: McGill/Queen's University Press.

McKim, Shirley Dawn. 2002. "We had freedom galore." In *Freedom to play—we made our own fun*, ed. Norah Lewis. Waterloo, Canada: Wilfrid University Press.

McNamara, Patrick. 1991. "Catholic Youth in the modern church." In *Religion and the social order: Vatican II and U.S. Catholicism*, ed. Helen Rose Ebaugh. Greenwich, CT: JAI.

Meckel, Richard A. 1989. *Save the babies: American public health reform and the prevention of infant mortality, 1850–1929*. Baltimore, MD: Johns Hopkins University Press.

Meckel, Richard A. 2004. "Levels and trends of death and disease in childhood, 1620 to the present." In *Children in sickness and in health: A historical handbook and guide*, Janet Golden, Richard A Meckel, and Heather Munroe Prescott. Westport, CT: Greenwood Press.

Meese, Ruth Lyn. 2005. "A few new children: Postinstitutionalized children of intercountry adoption." *Journal of Special Education* 39(3): 157–167.

Mennill, Sally, and Veronica Strong-Boag. 2008. "Identifying victims: Abuse and death in Canadian families." *Canadian Bulletin of Medical History* 25(2): 311–333.

Merchants of Cool. 2001. PBS Frontline Documentary. Directed by Barak Goldman.

Mergen, Bernard. 1975. "The discovery of children's play." *American Quarterly* 27(4): 403.

Messerli, Jonathan. 1972. *Horace Mann: A biography*. New York: Alfred A. Knopf.

Miller, J. R. 1996. *Shingwauk's vision: History of native residential schools*. Toronto: University of Toronto Press.

Miller, Julie, 1993. "To stop the slaughter of the babies: Nathan Straus and the drive for pasteurized milk, 1893–1920." *New York History* 72(2): 159–184.

Miller, Susan A. 2007. *Growing girls—the natural origins of girls' organizations in America*. New Brunswick, NJ: Rutgers University Press.

Miner, Steven M. forthcoming. *Furies unleashed: Soviet peoples at war*. New York: Harper Collins.

Ministry of Information. 2007. *What Britain has done, 1939–1945: A selection of outstanding facts and figures.* London: Atlantic Books.

Minton, Henry L. 1988. *Lewis M. Terman: Pioneer in psychological testing.* New York: New York University Press.

Mintz, Steven. 2004. *Huck's raft: A history of American childhood.* Cambridge, MA: Harvard University Press.

Mintz, Steven, and Susan Kellogg. 1988. *Domestic revolutions: A social history of American family life.* New York: The Free Press.

Mittelstadt, Jennifer 2005. *From welfare to workforce: The unintended consequences of liberal reform, 1945–1965.* Chapel Hill: University of North Carolina Press.

Mjagkij, Nina, and Margaret Spratt, eds. 1997. *Men and women adrift: The YMCA and YWCA in the city.* New York: New York University Press.

Moehling, Carolyn. 2005. "'She has suddenly become powerful': Youth employment and household decision making in the early twentieth century." *Journal of Economic History* 65: 413–437.

Moeller, Robert G. 1993. *Protecting motherhood: Women and the family in the politics of postwar West Germany.* Berkeley: University of California Press.

Mohan, John. 2005. *A national health service: The restructuring of health care in Britain since 1979.* New York: St. Martin's Press.

Montgomery, Kathryn. 2007. *Generation digital: Politics, commerce, and childhood in the age of the Internet.* Cambridge, MA: MIT Press.

Moore, Allan. 1990. *Growing up with Barnardo's.* Sydney, Australia: Hale & Iremonger

Moran, Bridget. 1988. *Stoney Creek Woman. Sai'k'uz Ts'eke. The story of Mary John.* Vancouver, British Columbia: Tillacum Library.

Morantz-Sachez, Regina. 1985. *Sympathy and science: Women physicians in American medicine.* New York: Oxford University Press.

More, Charles. 2006. *Britain in the twentieth century.* New York: Longman.

Morgan, S. Philip. 2003. "Is low fertility a twenty-first-century demographic crisis?" *Demography* 40(4): 589–603.

Morgan, S. Philip, and Rosalind Berkowitz King. 2001. "Why have children in the 21st century? Biological predisposition, social coercion, rational choice." *European Journal of Population* 3: 3–20.

Mort, Frank. 1996. *Cultures of consumption: Masculinities and social space in late twentieth-century Britain.* London: Routledge.

Mortenson, Greg, and David O. Relin. 2006. *Three cups of tea: One man's mission to promote peace … one school at a time.* Camberwell, Australia: Viking.

Mosse, George L. 1990. *Fallen soldiers: Reshaping the memory of the world wars.* New York: Oxford University Press.

Muncy, Robyn. 1991. *Creating a female dominion of American reform, 1890–1935.* New York: Oxford University Press.

Muscari, Mary. 2002. "Media violence: Advice for parents." *Pediatric Nursing* 28(6): 586–591.

Myers, Tamara. 2006. *Caught—Montreal's modern girls and the law, 1869–1945.* Toronto: University of Toronto Press.

Myers, William R. 1991. *Black and white styles of youth ministry: Two congregations in America*. New York: Pilgrim.

Nasaw, David. 1985. *Children of the city: At work and at play*. Garden City, NY: Doubleday.

National Center for Educational Statistics. 2000. *Elementary and secondary education: An historical perspective*. Washington, DC: U.S. Department of Education.

National Commission on Excellence in Education. 1983. *A nation at risk: The imperative for educational reform*. Washington, DC: Government Printing Office.

National Society for the Prevention of Cruelty to Children. 1972. *A pocket history of the NSPCC*. Available at: http://www.nspcc.org.uk/whatwedo/aboutthenspcc/history ofnspcc/historyofnspcc_wda 3314 9.html. Accessed December 5, 2008.

The Nazi primer: Official handbook for schooling the Hitler Youth. 1938. Trans. Harwood L. Childs. New York: Harper and Brothers.

Nebraska Farmer, 1912–1916.

Nevali-Nurmi, Seija-Leena. 2007. "Soldier boys and lotta girls at war." Unpublished Paper presented at the Biennal Conference of the Society for the History of Children and Youth.

"New estimates of the causes of child mortality worldwide." 2005. *Child Health News,* March 28. Available at: http://www.news-edical.net/print_article.asp?id=8701. Accessed April 16, 2008.

Obama, Barack. 2004. *Dreams from my father: A story of race and inheritance*. New York: Three Rivers Press.

Oblate Sisters of Providence. n.d. *Our history*. Available at: http://www.oblatesisters. com/History.html. Accessed June 30, 2008.

O'Brien, David J. 2000. "Catholic youth: The presumed become the pursued." In *The Catholic Church in the twentieth-century: Renewing and reimaging the city of God*. New York: Paulist.

Odem, Mary. 1995. *Delinquent daughters: Protecting and policing adolescent female sexuality in the United States, 1885–1920*. Chapel Hill: University of North Carolina Press.

Olich, Jacqueline M. 2008. "The Russians love their children, too." Review of *Children's world: Growing up in Russia, 1890–91,* by Catriona Kelly. *Journal of the History of Childhood and Youth* 1(3): 445–458.

"113th campaign beginning for the Fresh Air Fund." 1989. *New York Times,* May 7, p. 46.

Otto, Henry J. 1934. *Elementary school organization and administration*. New York: D. Appleton-Century Company.

Packard, Vance. 1983. *Our endangered children: Growing up in a changing world*. Boston: Little, Brown and Company.

Pahl, Jon. 1993. *Hopes and dreams of all: The International Walther League, and Lutheran youth in American culture, 1893–1993*. Eugene, OR: Wipf and Stock.

Pahl, Jon. 2000. *Youth ministry in modern America: 1930 to the present*. Peabody, MA: Hendrickson Publishers.

Pan American Health Organization, World Health Organization. 2007. *Health in the Americas: Fact sheet 2007*. Available at: http://www.paho.org/English/DD/PUB/ HIA_2007.htm. Accessed April 16, 2008.

Panayi, Panikos. 2007. "Immigration, multiculturalism, and racism." In *20th century Britain: Economic, cultural and social change*, ed. Paul Johnson, Francesca Carnevali, and Julie Marie Strange. London: Pearson Books.

Paris, Leslie. 2001. "The adventures of Peanut and Bo: Summer camps and early twentieth-century American girlhood." *Journal of Women's History* 12(4): 47–76.

Parr, Joy. 1980. *Labouring children: British immigrant apprentices to Canada, 1869–1924*. London: Croom Helm.

Patel, Eboo, and Patrice Brodeur, eds. 2006. *Building the interfaith youth movement: Beyond dialogue to action*. Lanham, CO: Rowman and Littlefield.

Peate, Mary. 1970. *Girl in a Red River coat*. Toronto: Irwin and Company.

Peiss, Kathy. 1986. *Cheap amusements: Working women and leisure in turn-of-the-century New York*. Philadelphia: Temple University Press.

Peiss, Kathy. 1998. *Hope in a jar: The making of America's beauty culture*. New York: Henry Holt.

Peperkamp, Esther. 2006. "'There can be no vacation from God': Children's retreats, leisure and social change in Poland." *Religion, State and Society* 34(September): 271–286.

Peterson, Anna. 2004. "Wars in Central America." In *Encyclopedia of children and childhood in history and society,* ed. Paula Fass, vol. 1. New York: Macmillan Reference USA.

Phelps, Edward Bunnell. 1908. "A statistical study of infant mortality." *Publications of the American Statistical Association* 11(83): 233–235.

Pine, Lisa. 2007. *Hitler's "national community": Society and culture in Nazi Germany*. London: Hodder Arnold.

Platt, Anthony. 1977. *The child savers: The invention of delinquency*. Chicago: University of Chicago Press.

Platt, Phillip S., and George T. Palmer. 1925. "A community child health survey." *American Journal of Public Health* 15(2): 102–106.

Pleck, Elizabeth. 2004. *Domestic tyranny: The making of American social policy against domestic violence from colonial times to the present*. Urbana: University of Illinois Press.

Pomerantz, Shauna, Dawn H. Currie, and Deidre M. Kelly. 2004. "Sk8er girls: Skateboarders, girlhood and feminism in motion." *Women's Studies International Forum* 27(56): 547–557.

Preston, Samuel H., and Michael R. Haines. 1991. *Fatal years: Child mortality in late nineteenth-century America*. Princeton, NJ: Princeton University Press.

Probert, Rebecca. 2004. "Cohabitation in twentieth century England and Wales." *Law and Policy* 26(1): 1–13

Proceedings of the Conference on the Care of Dependent Children, Held at Washington, D.C., January 25, 26, 1909. 1909. Senate Document 721, 60th Cong., 2nd sess., 1909. Washington, DC: Government Printing Office.

Public Broadcasting System. 2010. "The orphan trains transcripts." Available at: http://www.pbs.org/wgbh/amex/orphan/. Accessed March 15, 2010.

Pulju, Rebecca. 2006. "Consumers for the nation: Women, politics and consumer organization in France, 1944–1965." *Journal of Women's History* 18(3): 68–90.

Pyle, Robert Michael. 1993. *The thunder tree: Lessons from an urban wildland*. Boston: Houghton Mifflin Company.

Pyle, Robert Michael. 2002. "Eden in a vacant lot: Special places, species, and kids in the neighborhood of life." In *Children and nature: Psychological, sociocultural, and evolutionary investigations*, ed. Peter H. Kahn, Jr., and Stephen R. Kellert. Cambridge: The MIT Press.

Rabbit-proof fence. 2002. Film. Directed by Phillip Noyce. Australia: Australia Film Finance Corporation—Magna Pacific.

Race, George. 1933. "Cynthia Milk Fund of the Press-Scimitar has nourished Memphis babies for 19 years." *The Memphis Press-Scimitar,* April 28, 1.

Rainwater, Lee, and Timothy M. Smeeding. 2003. *Poor kids in a rich country: America's children in comparative perspective.* New York: Russell Sage Foundation.

Rappaport, Erika Diane. 2000. *Shopping for pleasure: Women in the making of London's West End.* Princeton, NJ: Princeton University Press.

Rappaport, Erika Diane. 2002. "Art, commerce, or empire? The rebuilding of Regent Street, 1880–1927." *History Workshop Journal* 53: 95–117.

Ravitch, Diane, and Maris A. Vinovkis, eds. 1995. *Learning from the past: What history teaches us about school reform.* Baltimore, MD: The Johns Hopkins University Press.

Redding, Kimberly A. 2004a. "Fascist youth." In *Encyclopedia of children and childhood in history and society,* ed. Paula Fass, vol. 2. New York: Macmillan Reference USA.

Redding, Kimberly A. 2004b. *Growing up in Hitler's shadow: Remembering youth in post war Berlin.* Westport, CT: Praeger.

Reese, William J. 1986. *Power and the promise of school reform: Grassroots movements during the progressive era.* Boston: Routledge & Kegan Paul.

Reese, William J. 1995. *The origins of the American high school.* New Haven, CT: Yale University Press.

Reese, William J. 2001. "Education: Education in contemporary America." In *The Oxford companion to American history,* ed. Paul Boyer. New York: Oxford University Press.

Reese, William J. 2005. *America's public schools: From the common school to "No Child Left Behind."* Baltimore, MD: The Johns Hopkins University Press.

Reese, William J. 2007. *History, education, and the schools.* New York: Palgrave Macmillan.

Reidy, Miriam. 1987. "Youth are in the forefront of South Africa's struggles." *One World* 122(Jan.-Feb.): 36.

Reiman, Richard. 1992. *The New Deal and American youth: Ideas and ideals in a Depression decade.* Athens: University of Georgia Press.

Rempel, Gerhard. 1989. *Hitler's children: The Hitler Youth and the SS.* Chapel Hill: The University of North Carolina Press.

Reverby, Susan. 1987. *Ordered to care: The dilemma of American nursing, 1850–1945.* New York: Cambridge University Press.

Riebe-Estrella, Gary. 2004. "A youthful community: Theological and ministerial challenges." *Theological Studies* 65(June): 298–316.

Riis, Jacob. [1890] 1957. *How the other half lives: Studies among the tenements of New York.* Reprint, New York: Hill and Wang.

Riley, Glenda. 1991. *Divorce: An American tradition.* New York: Oxford University Press.

Riley, James C. 2001. *Rising life expectancy: A global history.* Cambridge: Cambridge University Press.

Riney-Kehrberg, Pamela. 1994. *Rooted in dust: Surviving drought and depression in southwestern Kansas.* Lawrence: University Press of Kansas.

Riney-Kehrberg, Pamela. 2005. *Childhood on the farm: Work, play and coming of age in the Midwest.* Lawrence: University Press of Kansas.

Roberts, Mary Louise. 1994. *Civilization without sexes: Reconstructing gender in postwar France, 1917–1927.* Chicago: The University of Chicago Press.

Roberts, Mary Louise. 2002. *Disruptive acts: The new woman in fin-de-siècle France.* Chicago: The University of Chicago Press.

Roberts, Sam. 2006. "It's official: To be married means to be outnumbered." *The New York Times,* October 15. Available at: http://www.nytimes.com/2006/10/15/us/15census.html. Accessed January 12, 2008.

Roehlkepartain, Eugence C., and Peter L. Benson. 1993. *Youth in Protestant churches.* Minneapolis, MN: Search Institute.

Roehlkepartain, Eugence C., and Peter L. Benson. 2006. "Loose bonds, emerging commitments: The lives and faith of Lutheran youth." *The Journal of Youth Ministry* 5(Fall): 93–113.

Roopmarine, Jaipaul L., and Uwe P. Gielen, eds. 2005. *Families in global perspective.* Boston: Pearson.

Roosevelt, Theodore. 1901. *The strenuous life.* New York: The Century Co.

Rose, Elizabeth. 2003. *A mother's job: A history of day care, 1890–1960.* New York: Oxford University Press.

Ross, Ellen. 1993. *Love and toil: Motherhood in outcast London, 1870–1918.* New York: Oxford University Press.

Rossi, Leena. 2007. "The war experiences of Karelian children during WWII: Memories of the children of Koivisto." Paper presented at the Biennial Conference of the Society for the History of Children and Youth.

Rowland, Debran. 2004. *The boundaries of her body: The troubling history of women's rights in America.* Naperville, IL: Sphinx Publishing.

Rubenstein, William. 2003. *Twentieth-century Britain: A political history.* New York: Palgrave Macmillan.

Rudolph, John L. 2002. *Scientists in the classroom: The cold war reconstruction of American science education.* New York: Palgrave.

Ryan, Mary. 1983. *Womanhood in America: From colonial times to the present.* 3rd. ed. New York: Franklin Watts.

Sanders, Lise Shapiro. 2006. *Consuming fantasies: Labor, leisure, and the London shopgirl, 1880–1920.* Columbus: Ohio State University Press.

Sandler, Lauren. 2006. *Righteous: Dispatches from the evangelical youth movement.* New York: Penguin.

Sangster, Joan. 2002. *Girl trouble: Female delinquency in English Canada.* Toronto: Between the Lines.

Saraceno, Chiara. 2003. "Social and family policy." In *The history of the European family: Volume three: Family life in the twentieth century,* ed. David I. Kertzer and Marzio Barbagli. New Haven, CT: Yale University Press.

Satterthwaite, David. 2005. *The scale of urban change worldwide 1950–2000 and its underpinnings.* London: International Institute for Environment and Development.

Saunders, Charles R. 1994. *Share and care: The story of the Nova Scotia Home for Colored Children.* Halifax, UK: Nimbus Publishing.

Savage, Jon. 2007. *Teenage: The creation of youth culture.* NY: Viking.

Save the Children. 2007. *State of the world's mothers 2007: Saving the lives of children under 5.* Available at: http://www.savethechildren.org/publications/mothers/2007/SOWM-2007-final.pdf. Accessed April 23, 2008.

Scates, Bruce C. 2002. "Imagining Anzac: Children's memories of the killing fields of the Great War." In *Children and war: A historical anthology,* ed. James Marten. New York: New York University Press.

Scharf, Lois. 1980. *To work and to wed: Female employment, feminism, and the Great Depression.* Westport, CT: Greenwood Press.

Schor, Julia. 2004. *Born to buy: The commercialized child and the new consumer culture.* New York: Scribner.

Schrum, Kelley. 1998. "'Teena means business': Teenage girls' culture and *Seventeen Magazine,* 1944–1950." In *Delinquents and debutantes: twentieth-century American girls' cultures,* ed. Sherrie Inness. New York: New York University Press.

Schwartz, Regina. 1997. *The curse of Cain: The violent legacy of monotheism.* Chicago: The University of Chicago Press.

Sealander, Judith. 2003. *The failed century of the child: Governing America's young in the twentieth century.* Cambridge: Cambridge University Press.

Seiter, Ellen. 1993. "Children's desires/mothers' dilemmas: The social contexts of consumption." In *The children's culture reader,* ed. Henry Jenkins. New York and London: New York University Press.

Sen, Satadru. 2005. *Colonial childhoods: The juvenile periphery of India, 1850–1945.* London: Anthem Press.

Senter, Mark H., III. 1992. *The coming revolution in youth ministry.* Wheaton, IL: Victor Books.

Setiloane, Gabriel. 1963. "Youth work in African churches in South Africa." *Ecumenical Review* 15(2): 144–148.

Shears, Sarah. 1971. *A village girl: Memoirs of a Kentish childhood.* New York: Simon and Schuster.

Sherington, Geoffrey, and Jeffery, Chris. 1998. *Fairbridge: Empire and child migration.* London: Woburn Press.

Sikorska, Grazyna, 1989. *Light and life: Renewal in Poland.* Grand Rapids, MI: Eerdmans.

Simonton, Deborah. 1998. *A history of European women's work: 1700 to the present.* London: Routledge.

Sizer, Theodore R. 1964. *Horace's compromise.* Boston: Houghton Mifflin Company.

Skocpol, Theda. 1995. *Protecting soldiers and mothers: The political origins of social policy in the United States.* 4th ed. Cambridge, MA: The Belknap Press of Harvard University.

Skolnick, Arlene. 1991. *Embattled paradise: The American family in an age of uncertainty.* New York: Basic Books.

Slonim, Reuben. 1983. *Grand to be an orphan*. Toronto: Clarke Irwin & Co.

Smelser, N. 1982. "The Victorian family." In *Families in Britain*, ed. R. N. Rapoport and M. Fogarty. London: Routledge and Kegan Paul.

Smith, Christian, and Melinda Lundquist Denton. 2005. *Soul searching: The religious and spiritual lives of American teenagers*. New York: Oxford University Press.

Smith, Susan Lynn. 1995. *Sick and tired of being sick and tired: Black women's health activism in America, 1890–1950*. Philadelphia: University of Pennsylvania Press.

Society for the Protection of the Rights of the Child. 2003. *The state of Pakistan's children 2002*. Islamabad, Pakistan: Oxford University Press.

Spain, Daphne. 2001. *How women saved the City*. 1st ed. Minneapolis: University of Minnesota.

Spargo, John. 1906. *The bitter cry of the children*. New York: The Macmillan Company.

Spigel, Lynn. 1998. "Seducing the innocent: Childhood and television in postwar America." In *The children's culture reader*, ed. Henry Jenkins. New York: New York University Press.

Spring, Joel H. 1976. *The sorting machine: National educational policy since 1945*. New York: David McKay.

Springhall, John. 1998. *Youth, popular culture and moral panics: Penny gaffs to gangsta-rap, 1830–1996*. New York: St. Martin's Press.

Sracic, Paul A. 2006. *San Antonio v. Rodriguez and the pursuit of equal education: The debate over discrimination and school funding*. Lawrence: University Press of Kansas.

Stachura, Peter D. 1981. *The German youth movement, 1900–1945: An interpretative and documentary history*. New York: St. Martin's Press.

Stack, Carol. 1987. "Child-keeping: 'Gimme a little sugar.'" In *Growing up in America: Historical experiences*, ed. Harvey J. Graff. Detroit, MI: Wayne State University Press.

Starns, Penny Elaine, and Martin L Parsons. 2002. "Against their will: The use and abuse of British children during the Second World War." In *Children and war: A historical anthology*, James Marten. New York: New York University Press.

Stearns, Peter. 2003. "Historical perspectives on twentieth-century American childhood." In *Beyond the century of the child: Cultural history and developmental psychology*, ed. William Koops and Michael Zuckerman. Philadelphia: University of Pennsylvania Press.

Stearns, Peter N. 2006. *Childhood in world history*. New York: Routledge.

Stone, Deborah. 2008. *The samaritan's dilemma: Should government help your neighbor?* New York: Perseus Publishing.

Stoner, Carroll. 1993. *Weddings for grownups: Everything you need to know to plan your wedding your way*. San Francisco: Chronicle Books.

Stortzbach, Bernd. 1995. "Germany: Unification in attitudes?" In *Population, family, and welfare: A comparative survey of European attitudes*, ed. Hein Moors and Rossella Palomba, vol. 1. New York: Oxford University Press.

Strong-Boag, Veronica. 1988. *The new day recalled: Lives of girls and women in English Canada, 1919–1939*. Toronto: Copp Clark Pitman.

Strong-Boag, Veronica. 2006. *Finding families, finding ourselves—English Canada encounters adoption from the nineteenth century to the 1990s*. Toronto: Oxford University Press.

Strong-Boag, Veronica. 2007. "'Children of adversity': Disabilities and child welfare in Canada from the nineteenth to the twenty-first century," *Journal of Family History* 32(4): 413–432.

Summerhayes-Cariou, Heather. 2006. *Sixty-five roses: A sister's memoir.* Toronto: McArthur & Company.

Sutherland, Neil. 1976. *Children in English Canadian society: Framing the twentieth century consensus.* Toronto: University of Toronto Press.

Sutherland, Neil. 1997. *Growing up: Childhood in English Canada from the Great War to the age of television.* Toronto: University of Toronto Press.

Swenson, Peter A. 2002. *Capitalists against markets: The making of labor markets and welfare states in the United States and Sweden.* Oxford: Oxford University Press.

Talbot, Margaret. 2001. "The new counterculture." *Atlantic Monthly,* November: 136–143.

Te Ara. 2008a. "Poles." *Online Encyclopedia of New Zealand.* Available at: http://www.teara.govt.nz/NewZealanders/NewZealandPeoples/Poles/en. Accessed February 15, 2008.

Te Ara. 2008b. "South Pacific Peoples." *Online Encyclopedia of New Zealand.* Available at: http://www.teara.govt.nz/NewZealanders/NewZealandPeoples/SouthPacificPeoples/1/en. Accessed February 15, 2008.

Tegel, Susan. 2007. *Nazis and the cinema.* New York: Hambledon Continuum.

Tennant, Margaret. 2002. "Complicating childhood: Gender, ethnicity, and 'disadvantage' within the New Zealand Children's Health Camps Movement." *Canadian Bulletin of Medical History* 19: 179–199.

Tentler, Leslie Woodcock. 1979. *Wage-earning women: Industrial work and family life in the United States, 1900–1930.* New York: Oxford University Press.

Thane, Pat. 2005. "Population and the family." In *A Companion to Contemporary Britain, 1939–2000,* ed. Paul Addison and Harriet Jones. Oxford: Blackwell.

Theodorou, Vassiliki, and Vassiliki Vassiloudi. 2007. "Childhood in displacement; different versions of experiencing separation from the family during the Greek Civil War (1946–1949)." Paper presented at the Biennial Conference of the Society for the History of Children and Youth.

Therborn, Goran. 1993. "The politics of childhood: The rights of children in modern times." In *Families of nations: Patterns of public policy in Western democracies,* ed. Francis Castles. Aldershot: Dartmouth.

Therborn, Goran. 2004. *Between sex and power: Family in the world.* London: Routledge. Toronto: MacMillan.

Thomas, Pamela, ed. 1981. *Pacific youth: Selected studies on youth and development in the South Pacific.* Suva, Fiji: Institute of Pacific Studies.

Tian-Shanskaia, Olga Semyonova. 1993. *Village life in late tsarist Russia.* Bloomington: Indiana University Press.

Tildsley, John L. 1936. *The mounting waste of the American secondary school.* Cambridge, MA: Harvard University Press.

Tillotson, Shirley. 2000. *The public at play. Gender and the politics of recreation in post-war Ontario.* Toronto: University of Toronto Press.

Tillotson, Shirley. 2002. "Time, swimming pools, and citizenship: The emergence of leisure rights in mid-twentieth century Canada." In *Contesting Canadian citizenship: Historical readings,* ed. Robert Adamoski, Dorothy Chunn, and Robert Menzies. Peterborough, UK: Broadview Press.

Tosh, John. 1999. *A man's place: Masculinity and the middle class home in Victorian England.* New Haven, CT: Yale.

Townsend, Peter. 1979. *Poverty in the United Kingdom: A survey of household resources and standards of living.* Harmondsworth, UK: Penguin.

Trattner, Walter I. 1970. *Crusade for the children: The National Child Labor Committee and child labor reform in America.* Chicago: Quadrangle Books.

Tuttle, William M., Jr. 1993. *"Daddy's gone to war": The Second World War in the lives of America's children.* New York: Oxford.

Twum-Danso, Afua, 2008. "The construction of childhood and the socialization of children in Ghana." Paper presented at the Biennial Conference of the Society for the History of Children and Youth.

Twum-Danso, Afua. 2008. "A cultural bridge, not an imposition: Legitimizing children's rights in the eyes of local communities." *Journal of the History of Childhood and Youth* 1(3): 391–413.

Tyack, David B. 1974. *The one best system: A history of American urban education.* Cambridge, MA: Harvard University Press.

United Nations. 1989. *Convention on the rights of the child.* New York: UNICEF.

United Nations. 1999. *The state of the world's children 1999.* New York: UNICEF.

United Nations. 2000a. *The progress of nations.* New York: UNICEF.

United Nations. 2000b. *The state of the world's children 2000.* New York: UNICEF.

United Nations. 2002. *The state of the world's children 2002.* New York: UNICEF.

United Nations. 2005. *The state of the world's children 2005.* New York: UNICEF.

United Nations Development Fund. 2001. *Human development report 2001: Making new technologies work for human development.* New York: Oxford.

United Nations Development Program. 2000. *Human development report 2000.* New York: Oxford University Press.

United Nations High Commissioner for Refugees. 2006. *The state of the world's refugees 2006: Human displacement in the new millennium.* Available at: http://www.unhcr.org/static/publ/sowr2006/toceng.htm. Accessed February 29, 2008.

United Nations International Children's Emergency Fund. 2008. "What we have learned: A century of evolving health systems and practices." *State of the world's children 2008—child survival.* Available at: http://www.unicef.org/sowc08/profiles/child_health.php. Accessed April 23, 2008.

U.S. Bureau of the Census. 1943. *Statistical abstracts of the United States: 1942.* Washington, DC: Government Printing Office.

U.S. Census Bureau. 2006. "Table B01001. Sex by Age," *American factfinder.* Available at: http://factfinder.census.gov. Accessed March 15, 2010.

U.S. Department of Agriculture. 2010. "About 4-H: The 4-H pledge." Available at: http://4-h.org/4hstory.html. Accessed March 15, 2010.

Usherwood, Barbara. 2000. "'Mrs. housewife and her grocer': The advent of self-service food shopping in Britain." In *All the world and her husband: Women in twentieth-*

century consumer culture, ed. Maggie Andrews and Mary Talbott. London: Cassell.

U.S. Supreme Court. 2007. *Morse et. al. v. Frederick.* No. 06-278. Available at: http://www.supremecourtus.gov/opinions/06pdf/06-278.pdf. Accessed September 7, 2008.

Van der Bent, Ans J. 1986. *From generation to generation: The story of youth in the world council of churches.* Geneva: WCC.

Van Krieken, Robert. 1991. *Children and the state: Social control and the formation of Australian child welfare.* North Sydney, Australia: Allen & Unwin.

Van Slyck, Abigail A. 2006. *A manufactured wilderness: Summer camps and the shaping of American youth, 1890–1960.* Minneapolis: University of Minnesota Press.

Verhellen, Eugeen. 2000. *Convention on the rights of the child: Background, motivation, strategies, main themes.* 3rd ed. Ghent, Belgium: Ghent University Children's Rights Centre.

Vernon, James. 2007. *Hunger: A modern history.* Cambridge, MA: Harvard University Press.

Veroff, Joseph, Elizabeth Douvan, and Richard Kulka. 1981. *The inner American: A self-portrait from 1957 to 1976.* New York: Basic Books.

Vicinus, Martha. 1985. *Independent women: Work and community for single women, 1850–1920.* Chicago: University of Chicago Press.

Vinovskis, Maris. 1987. *An "epidemic of teenage pregnancy?": Some historical and policy considerations.* New York: Oxford University Press.

von Feilitzen, Celia, and Ulla Carlsson, eds. 2002. *Children, young people and media globalisation.* Goteborg, Sweden: UNESCO International Clearinghouse on Children, Youth, and Media.

Walker, Lawrence D. 1970. *Hitler Youth and Catholic youth, 1933–1926: A study in totalitarian conquest.* Washington, DC: Catholic University of America Press.

Walker, Nancy A. 1998. "Introduction: Women's magazines and women's roles." in *Women's magazines 1940–1960: Gender roles and the popular press,* ed. Nancy A. Walker. Boston: Bedford/St. Martins.

Wall, Sharon. 2005. "Totem poles, teepees, and token traditions: 'Playing Indian' at Ontario summer camps, 1920–1955." *Canadian Historical Review* 86(3): 513–544.

Wallis, Jim. 2008. *The great awakening: Reviving faith and politics in a post-religious right America.* New York: HarperOne.

Wandersee, Winifred. 1981. *Women's work and family values, 1920–1920.* Cambridge, MA: Harvard University Press.

Wandersee, Winifred. 1991. "Families face the Great Depression." In *American families: A research guide and historical handbook,* ed. Joseph Hawes and Elizabeth Nybakken. New York: Greenwood Press.

Ward, Florence E. 1920. *The farm woman's problems.* Washington, DC: Government Printing Office.

Wassong, Stephan. 2008. "The German influence on the development of the US playground movement." *Sport in History* 28(2): 313–328.

Watson, Katherine. 2007. "Education and opportunity." In *20th century Britain: Economic, cultural and social change,* ed. Francesca Carnevali, Julie-Marie Strange, and Paul Johnson. London: Pearson Books.

Webster, Windy. 2005. "Immigration and racism." In *A companion to contemporary Britain, 1939–2000*, ed. Paul Addison and Harriet Jones. Oxford: Blackwell.

Wegs, J. Robert. 1989. *Growing up working class: Continuity and change among Viennese youth, 1890–1938*. University Park: Pennsylvania State University Press.

Weigel, George. 1992. *The final revolution: The resistance church and the collapse of communism*. New York: Oxford University Press.

Weiner, Susan. 2001. *Enfants terribles: Youth and femininity in the mass media in France, 1945–1968*. Baltimore, MD: Johns Hopkins University Press.

Welch, David. 1983. *Propaganda and the German cinema, 1933–1945*. Oxford: Clarendon Press.

Welshman, John. 2005. "Health." In *A companion to contemporary Britain, 1939–2000*, ed. Paul Addison and Harriet Jones. Oxford: Blackwell.

West, Elliott. 1989. *Growing up with the country: Childhood on the far western frontier*. Albuquerque: University of New Mexico Press.

West, Elliott. 1996. *Growing up in twentieth-century America: A history and reference guide*. Westport, CT: Greenwood Press.

Westbrook, Robert. 1993. "Fighting for the American family: Private interests and political obligation in World War II." In *The power of culture: Critical essays in American history*, ed. Richard Wightman Fox and T. J. Jackson Lears. Chicago: University of Chicago Press.

Westermarck, Edward Alexander. 1901. *History of human marriage*. 3rd ed. London: Macmillan.

Whitney, Susan. 2004. "Communist Youth." In *Encyclopedia of children and childhood in history and society*, ed. Paula Fass, vol. 1. New York: Macmillan Reference USA.

Wiebe, Robert H. 1967. *The Search for Order, 1877–1920*. New York: Hill & Wang.

Wilson, Chris. 2001. "On the scale of demographic convergence 1950–2000." *Population and Development Review* 27(1): 155–171.

Wilson, Dolly Smith. 2005. "Gender: Change and continuity." In *A companion to contemporary Britain, 1939–2000*, ed. Paul Addison and Harriet Jones. Oxford: Blackwell.

Wimberly, Anne Streaty. 2002. "The violence of racism, the strategy of empowerment: Relational hope and co-action with black youth." *Black Theology* 1(November): 53–66.

Wintermute, Robert, and Mads Andanaes, eds. 2001. *Legal recognition of same-sex partnership*. Oxford: Hart Publishing.

Wir Mädel Singen: Liederbuch des Deutscher Mädel. 1938. Available at: http://bdmhistory.fotki.com/digitized/songbooks/we-girls-sing/. Accessed January 28, 2008.

Wolffe, John. 2007. "Religion and secularization." In *20th century Britain: Economic, cultural and social change*, ed. Francesca Carnevali, Julie-Marie Strange, and Paul Johnson. London: Pearson Books.

Wood, David. 2003. "Effect of child and family poverty on child health in the U.S." *Pediatrics*, 112: 707–711.

Woollacott, Angela. 2001. *To try her fortune in London: Australian women, colonialism, and modernity*. Oxford: Oxford University Press.

World ORT. n.d. *Music and the Holocaust*. Available at: http://holocaustmusic.ort.org. Accessed December 4, 2008.

World Council of Churches. 2008. "Public witness: Addressing power, affirming peace." Available at: http://www.oikoumene.org/en/programmes/public-witness-addressing-power-affirming-peace.html. Accessed February 1, 2008.

World Health Organization. 2002. *Child health research: A foundation for improving child health*. Geneva: Author. Available at: http://www.who.int/child-adolescent-health.

World Health Organization. 2005. *The European health report 2005*. Available at: http://www.euro.who.int/ehr2005. Accessed April 16, 2008.

World Health Organization. 2006. *Public health action for healthier children and populations*. Available at: http://www.euro.who.int/ehr2006. Accessed April 16, 2008.

Yans-MacLaughlin, Virginia. 1977. *Family and community: Italian immigrants in Buffalo, 1880–1930*. Ithaca, NY: Cornell University Press.

Zelizer, Viviana. 1985. *Pricing the priceless child: The changing social value of children*. New York: Basic Books.

Zilversmith, Arthur. 1993. *Changing schools: Progressive education theory and practice*. Chicago: University of Chicago Press.

Zipf, Karen L. 2005. *Labors of innocents: Forced apprenticeship in North Carolina, 1715–1919*. Baton Rogue: Louisiana State University Press.

Zotti, Mary Irene. 1991. *A time of awakening: The young Christian worker story In the United States, 1938 to 1970*. Chicago: Loyola University Press.

CONTRIBUTORS

David Barrett is professor of applied social studies and dean at the University of Bedfordshire. He has researched and published on the subject of children who are abused through prostitution, and associated social policy, for a number of years. He is responsible for a number of books and articles on these subjects and is an internationally recognized authority on child trafficking. He is currently working on material relating to the trading of children under five, including babies.

Mona Gleason is an associate professor in the Department of Educational Studies at the University of British Columbia. She is the author of *Normalizing the Ideal: Psychology, Schooling, and the Family in Postwar Canada* (University of Toronto Press, 1999), and coeditor (with Adele Perry) of *Rethinking Canada: The Promise of Women's History,* 4th edition, and (with Jean Barman) of *Children, Teachers, and Schools in the History of British Columbia.* Her pending manuscript is titled *Embodying Difference: Children in Sickness and Health in English Canada, 1900–1960.*

Jeanine Graham retired recently from teaching history at the University of Waikato (New Zealand). Examples of her publications on aspects of New Zealand childhood history can be found in *Children and War: A Historical Anthology,* edited by James Marten (2002); the *Encyclopedia of Children and Childhood in History and Society,* edited by Paula Fass (2004); the April 2006 issue of the *New Zealand Journal of History* (vol. 40, no. 1); and *Paedagogica Historica* (vol. 44, no. 4, August 2008).

Joseph M. Hawes is professor emeritus at the University of Memphis. He is a past president of the Society for the History of Children and Youth. He is coeditor, with N. Ray Hiner, of *Growing Up in America: Children in Historical Perspective* (1985), *American Childhood: A Research Guide and Historical Handbook* (1985), and *Children in Historical and Comparative Perspective: An International Handbook and Research Guide* (1991). His most recent works include *Family and Society in American History* (2001), edited with Elizabeth Nybakken, and *Family in American, an Encyclopedia* (2001), with the assistance of Elizabeth Shores.

N. Ray Hiner is professor emeritus of history and education at the University of Kansas. He has been president of the History of Education Society and the Society for the History of Children and Youth. He is coeditor with Joseph M. Hawes of *Growing Up in America: Children in Historical Perspective* (1985), *American Childhood: A Research Guide and Historical Handbook* (1985), and *Children in Historical and Comparative Perspective: An International Handbook and Research Guide* (1991).

Doug Imig is professor of political science at the University of Memphis and a director at the Urban Child Institute in Memphis, Tennessee. His work is on social movements and the well-being of children, with an emphasis on the twentieth century in the United States.

Lisa Jacobson is an associate professor of history at the University of California, Santa Barbara, and the author of *Raising Consumers: Children and the American Mass Market in the Early Twentieth Century* (2004) and the editor of *Children and Consumer Culture in American Society* (2008), a collection of essays and primary source documents. She is now working on a history of alcohol promotion and consumption in the United States after the repeal of Prohibition.

Katherine Jellison is professor of history at Ohio University, where she teaches courses in U.S. women's history. She is the author of *Entitled to Power: Farm Women and Technology, 1913–1963* (1991) and *It's Our Day: America's Love Affair with the White Wedding, 1945–2005* (2008).

Maria Kukhareva is a research and development officer at the University of Bedfordshire. In her job, Maria combines research and designing aspiration-raising activities for young people. Maria is currently undertaking a professional doctorate in youth justice at the University of Bedfordshire's Vauxhall School of

Crime. Her research portfolio includes women and child trafficking, experiences of ethnic minority groups, and access to higher education.

Kriste Lindenmeyer is professor and chair of the Department of History at the University of Maryland, Baltimore County. She is past president of the Society for the History of Children and Youth and author of several books, including *The Greatest Generation Grows Up: American Childhood in the 1930s* and *A Right to Childhood: The U.S. Children's Bureau and Child Welfare, 1912–1946*.

Jon Pahl is professor of the history of Christianity in North America at the Lutheran Theological Seminary at Philadelphia and has been a visiting professor in the Religion Departments at Temple University and at Princeton University. He is the author of *Youth Ministry in Modern America, 1930–the Present* and the forthcoming *Empire of Sacrifice: The Religious Origins of American Violence* (New York University Press, 2010).

Erika Rappaport teaches European gender and modern British history at the University of California, Santa Barbara. She is the author of *Shopping for Pleasure: Women in the Making of London's West End* (Princeton, 2001) and of several essays and articles on consumerism and gender in Britain and its empire. She is currently working on a book on globalization and consumer culture that is tentatively titled *Tea Parties: Britishness, Imperial Legacies, and Global Consumer Cultures*.

William J. Reese is the Carl F. Kaestle WARF Professor of Educational Policy Studies and History at the University of Wisconsin–Madison. Former president of the History of Education Society, he is also the author of several recent books, including *The Origins of the American High School* (1995, Yale) and *American Public Schools: From the Common School to "No Child Left Behind"* (Johns Hopkins, 2005). He recently coedited, with John Rury, *Rethinking the History of American Education* (Palgrave Macmillan, 2008).

Pamela Riney-Kehrberg is professor of history and director of the Agricultural History and Rural Studies Program at Iowa State University. She is the author of *Rooted in Dust: Surviving Drought and Depression in Southwestern Kansas* (1995) and *Childhood on the Farm: Work, Play and Coming of Age in the Midwest* (2005), and she is the editor of *Waiting on the Bounty: The Dust Bowl Diary of Mary Knackstedt Dyck* (1999).

Veronica Strong-Boag has written extensively on Canadian women and children, including *The New Day Recalled: Lives of Girls and Women in English Canada, 1919–1939* and *Finding Families, Finding Ourselves: English Canada Encounters Adoption from the 19th Century to the 1990s*. She is a former president of the Canadian Historical Association, a fellow of the Royal Society of Canada, and a professor of women's studies and educational studies at the University of British Columbia.

Frances Wright, BA, MA, is currently a student in the PhD program in history at the University of Memphis, where she is a research assistant focusing on women's and gender history. She was employed by the Center for Urban Child Policy (CUCP) at the Urban Child Institute from 2006 through 2009. During her time at the CUCP, she worked on multiple projects including a century-long longitudinal study of social movements for children and policy briefs on education, poverty, and family structures as they affect early childhood development.

INDEX